MAKING GOOD NEIGHBORS

MAKING GOOD NEIGHBORS

Civil Rights, Liberalism, and Integration in Postwar Philadelphia

ABIGAIL PERKISS

CORNELL UNIVERSITY PRESS
ITHACA AND LONDON

First published 2014 by Cornell University Press

Printed in the United States of America

Library of Congress Cataloging-in-Publication Data

Perkiss, Abigail, 1981– author.
  Making good neighbors : civil rights, liberalism, and integration in
postwar Philadelphia / by Abigail Perkiss.
     pages cm
  Includes bibliographical references and index.
  ISBN 978-0-8014-5228-4 (cloth : alk. paper)
  1. Philadelphia (Pa.)—Race relations.
  2. Civil rights—Pennsylvania—Philadelphia—History—20th century.
  3. Liberalism—Pennsylvania—Philadelphia—History—20th century.
  4. Mount Airy (Philadelphia, Pa.) I. Title.

  F158.68.M68P47 2014
  305.8009748'11—dc23
                                                      2013032843

Cornell University Press strives to use environmentally responsible
suppliers and materials to the fullest extent possible in the publishing of
its books. Such materials include vegetable-based, low-VOC inks and
acid-free papers that are recycled, totally chlorine-free, or partly composed
of nonwood fibers. For further information, visit our website at
www.cornellpress.cornell.edu.

Cloth printing   10 9 8 7 6 5 4 3 2 1

For my family

CONTENTS

ACKNOWLEDGMENTS

In August of 1986, a local news crew came to Kiley Guyton's fifth birthday party to film a story about the child of a white mother and a black father. Karen and Odell Guyton had chosen to raise their family in West Mount Airy, a nationally acclaimed model of an integrated community. Kiley and I had met as toddlers at a Mount Airy daycare center, housed at the Summit Presbyterian Church. Our class was a rough reflection of the demographics of the neighborhood itself. Three years later, many of us attended that birthday party. That was the day I learned that race matters.

I lived in West Mount Airy until I was nine years old. The white child of two progressive Jews, I grew up with an emerging consciousness that my daily life experience could and should serve as a reflection of my own ideas and values. Growing up, I took part in community events, participated in neighborhood activities, and through second grade, attended local schools. But I was also a product of Philadelphia in the 1980s, and as the city experienced the effects of widespread deindustrialization and waning federal and state resources, local institutions suffered, crime rates increased, and houses went up for sale. My parents—like the parents of many of my classmates and friends—pulled me from the neighborhood elementary school and then, a year later, relocated to Elkins Park, an inner-ring suburb just across the city border in Montgomery County.

In 2005, I returned to West Mount Airy. As a twenty four-year-old graduate student, I chose the community for the same reasons my parents had more than two decades earlier: the legacy of tolerance and activism and the intentionality with which many residents continue to negotiate the world. But as I settled into life there as an adult, I began to move past my own romanticized vision of the neighborhood I had left as a child. Through the lens of my doctoral studies in history, I listened to homeowners discuss (and dance around) contemporary questions of racial politics and residential cohesion, and I found myself compelled to explore the complicated roots of the integration project that had emerged and evolved in the wake of the Second World War, as communities around the country worked to contend with rapidly changing demographics and shifting notions of race and urban space.

Writing about the neighborhood in which I grew up and currently live has presented an interesting challenge, but it has also provided remarkable opportunities. Thank you to the current and former residents of West Mount Airy, for sharing your stories with me, for offering insights while waiting in line at the co-op, sitting in local coffeeshops, or running alongside me at the gym. Thank you to my neighbors and friends, for letting me think critically about our community, and for allowing me to complicate and challenge the historical ideal of integration that has led so many to this space.

Over the course of the development of this book I have had the opportunity to work with and learn from a diverse group of scholars and teachers, all of whom have shaped this project in profound ways. Thank you to David Farber, who challenged me daily and supported me when it mattered most, who let me figure out my own process, while holding me accountable to his high standards. You pushed me to slow down and think about the big questions; you have taught me how to be a historian. To Beth Bailey, who reminded me to pay attention to contingency, and to always think about what's at stake. To Bryant Simon, for forcing me to see what wasn't yet there. To Kevin Kruse, whose own work showed me that the study of space could be a vehicle for so much more. To Richard Immerman and Marylouise Esten, for helping me to navigate the bureaucratic waters of two large university programs with (relative) ease. To Susan DeJarnatt, David Hoffman, Nancy

Knauer, and Kathy Stanchi, for pushing me to think about the legal construction of the social world and the social construction of the legal system. And to Bruce Lenthall, who nurtured my curiosity and showed me what it meant to do history. You helped me understand why the past matters.

To my colleagues and friends, who made writing this book an engaging and exciting and even fun process. You have offered someone who gains energy from the people around her an intellectual and social community in what otherwise could have been a very isolating experience. Thanks, in particular, to Jeff Barg, Polly Bennell, Christina Cooke, Terry Farish, Donna Galluzzo, Paul Hendrickson, Brendan Hughes, Mira Ptacin, Teya Sepinuck, Kate Walker, and the rest of my collaborators at Penn's Kelly Writers House and the Salt Institute for Documentary Studies, for turning me on to the art of a good story, and to Ben Brandenberg, Tim Cole, Lindsay Helfman, Zach Lechner, Michele Louro, Roberta Meek, Steve Nepa, Dan Royles, and Kelly Shannon, for challenging me to think about why this story matters. To my colleagues in the Kean University History Department, who have shown me the true model of a teacher-scholar. And a special note of gratitude to Kate Scott for our many caffeine-fueled collaborative writing sessions, and to Matt Johnson and Sarah Johnson (no relation) for reading multiple drafts of sections of the manuscript and pushing me toward a more precise analysis of postwar race relations.

Over the course of this project, I have also had the opportunity to learn from and trade ideas with a generous and supportive community of scholars— at conferences, through e-mail, and in quiet corners of coffeeshops. Thanks to Alan Braddock, Lila Corwin Berman, Matthew Countryman, Natanya Duncan, David Grazian, Cheryl Greenberg, Brenna Greer, Leonard Heumann, Amy Hillier, Lauren Kientz Anderson, Stephanie Kohlberg, Amy Phillips, Amy Scott, Tom Sugrue, Heather Thompson, and James Wolfinger. Thanks to the members of the Urban History Association, the Association for the Study of African American Life and History, the Organization of American Historians, the Oral History Association, and the Oral History Association in the Mid-Atlantic Region. Thanks to the external reviewers and the editorial and faculty boards at Cornell University Press, who offered both encouragement and constructive feedback on two versions of this manuscript. And many, many thanks to Michael McGandy and the editorial team at Cornell for their patience, attentiveness, and care in guiding me through the editing process.

Portions of chapters 1 and 2 were previously published in "Northwest Philadelphia," *Encyclopedia of Greater Philadelphia* (http://philadelphiaency clopedia.org/archive/northwest-philadelphia/); portions of chapters 1, 2, 3, and 6 were previously published in "Managed Diversity: Contested Meanings of Integration in Post-WWII Philadelphia," *Journal of Urban History* 38, no. 3 (2012): 410–49, doi: 10.1177/0096144212445451.

This work also benefited immensely from the support of the archivists and librarians around Philadelphia and throughout the country, who have helped me piece together and contextualize the story of the Mount Airy integration efforts. Thanks to the Special Collections Research Center at Temple University, the Germantown Historical Association Archives, the Philadelphia City Archives, the American Friends Service Committee Archives, the Philadelphia Jewish Archives (now under the auspices of Temple's Special Collections Research Center), the Fairmount Park Commission Archives, the Amistad Archives at Tulane University, the Library of Congress, and the archival collections at the Weavers Way Co-op and the University of Pennsylvania. As well, thanks to Temple University and Kean University, for their generous support of the project, and to all the local coffeeshops where I "rented space" over the past four years as this manuscript was taking shape: High Point Cafe, Chestnut Hill Coffee Company, Mugshots Coffeehouse, and in particular Infusion Coffee and Tea, with its bottomless mugs and ample workspace.

Finally, to my family and friends outside of the academic world: thank you for your guidance and support, for the coffee and brunch dates, the long runs and longer races, and the cross-time-zone phone calls and marathon movie sessions. Thank you for helping me to get outside my own head. To my parents, Steve and Cindy Perkiss, who have shown me the value of boundless energy, who each, in their own way, has an uncanny ability to make the big picture clearer, and who both have instilled in me a deep pull to make sense of the world around me. To Marta Perkiss, for allowing me to see that world through a different set of eyes. And to Brent Freedland, who came into my life just as this project was taking shape and with whom I've built a new community in Mount Airy. My world is far better with you in it.

Joan Didion once said "we tell ourselves stories in order to live." Thank you all for teaching me to tell stories.

Abbreviations

CCRC	Church Community Relations Council
CORE	Congress of Racial Equality
EMAN	East Mount Airy Neighbors
FHA	Federal Housing Administration
GJC	Germantown Jewish Centre
HHSA	Henry Home and School Association
JDL	Jewish Defense League
NAACP	National Association for the Advancement of Colored People
RRC	Reconstructionist Rabbinical College
WMAA	West Mount Airy Action
WMAN	West Mount Airy Neighbors Association

MAKING GOOD NEIGHBORS

INTRODUCTION

Civil Rights' Stepchild

On June 20, 1975, at the sixth annual meeting of National Neighbors, an initiative bringing together racially integrated communities from across the country, Eleanor Holmes Norton took the podium as the keynote speaker. In front of a crowded ballroom filled with representatives from dozens of interracial community organizations, the New York commissioner of human rights spoke on the state of racial justice in the United States. "There is a special urgency attached to housing discrimination in America today," said Norton, "more special than continuing discrimination in unemployment and, despite the harangue and failure of busing in some cities, more special than school desegregation. For housing is the stepchild of civil rights progress in America."[1]

Norton's plea for open housing came on the heels of decades of work to bring neighborhood integration onto the national civil rights agenda. This struggle over residential space lay at the center of America's fight for racial justice in the latter half of the twentieth century. While activists made great strides in effecting change in the arenas of politics and business, swift demographic changes in the years following World War II remade neighborhoods into tense battlegrounds. Middle-class African Americans, capitalizing on new economic opportunities and legal reforms, had for the first time in large numbers fled the overcrowding of the inner cities and tried to make their homes in previously all-white areas. In some of these transitioning neighborhoods, residents responded with campaigns to "protect" their homes from black infiltration, transforming their blocks into sites of hostility and violence. In other neighborhoods, integration became defined as the period between the first black family moving into a community and the last white family moving out. To many, this racial transition in northern cities appeared to have exposed the limits of postwar civil rights progress. Patterns of resistance and flight fostered a new sense of instability that set off still more resistance and flight. It seemed an unbreakable cycle. Deep-seated hostilities were breaking America's neighborhoods apart.[2]

Some communities, though, took a different approach. Around the country, small groups of homeowners opted not to give in to the belief that racial transition necessarily brought about neighborhood decline. Instead of meeting would-be black buyers with antagonism or acquiescing to the efforts of blockbusting realtors, these residents, largely white and middle class, decided to welcome their new neighbors. Community leaders attempted to create and manage integration in the face of the same tensions that existed in cities across the country. In the midst of deeply entrenched cultural racism and formal legal and governmental policies that promoted segregated housing, these innovative homeowners came together to save their neighborhoods with a coordinated drive toward residential integration.[3]

This is the story of northwest Philadelphia's West Mount Airy, one of the first neighborhoods in the nation to embrace this integrationist mission. Though Philadelphia is home to the neighborhoods of both East Mount Airy and West Mount Airy, for the purposes of this book, *Mount Airy* and *West Mount Airy* are used interchangeably, as community leaders, residents, and journalists are quoted as using them as such. Here, organizers worked to understand and put into practice the ideals of an integrated society. Beginning with a coordinated pledge in the mid-1950s, homeowners in Mount Airy waged a community-wide battle toward intentional integration. Through innovative real-estate efforts, creative marketing techniques, religious activism, and institutional partnerships, residents worked to preserve the viability of their community. By replacing residential segregation with residential integration, they sought to disrupt a system of separation and infuse their day-to-day lives with the experience of interracial living.[4]

Accounts of postwar neighborhood racial struggles are not new. Historians, sociologists, and urban planners have written at length about the contentious relationship between race and urban space in the middle of the twentieth century. When taken together, these scholars have established a dominant narrative in which the movement of African American home buyers into previously all-white enclaves prompted aggressive clashes over the historical primacy of private property and individual freedom, the threat of instability and criminality, and the quest for racial equality. The long-standing focus on structural racism, economic volatility, community antagonism, and white flight has offered important challenges to the historical assumptions about the relationship between racial justice, black power, and urban space. Segregation and racial inequity in American cities, these works have ably revealed, were not the inevitable outcome of postwar race relations, nor were they a reaction against 1960s radical racial power movements. The racial composition of neighborhoods in the latter half of the twentieth century was the result of intentional political, legal, and economic initiatives that fostered residential separation.[5]

But just as neighborhood segregation was not inevitable, neither was it the only possible consequence of these deliberate legal and governmental reforms. West Mount Airy's integration efforts offer insight into the decisions that individual homeowners had to make as they negotiated the racial landscape of postwar American cities. When community members came together to change the patterns of transition that they were witnessing all around them, integration was not a foregone conclusion. Here, people who loved their neighborhood worked to examine what many believed to be diametric polarities—racial transition and economic stability—in the hope of finding a way to preserve the integrity of their community. In this book I reveal that complicated process of residential racial integration in the decades following World War II. The book works to, in the words of sociologist Mario Luis Small, open the "black box" of interracial living.[6]

This is the story of a community wrestling with questions of social capital and identity politics, of liberalism and individual choice, of urban sustainability and racial justice; it is a story of a small group of committed homeowners stuck in a moment of deep political and cultural change, and it is a story of how they negotiated that change. From the early 1950s onward, residents of West Mount Airy encountered and were forced to contend with questions of what it meant to live in an interracial community. Homeowners fought economic practices that incentivized moves to the suburbs and city- and statewide policies that redrew school district catchment areas and withdrew resources from neighborhood schools. They struggled to adapt to changing notions of racial justice and shifting political agendas throughout the city and across the nation. African American and white residents conflicted over racial representation within the community, and black homeowners withstood charges of racial betrayal from Philadelphia's larger black population. Ultimately, these conflicts and contours of interracial living gave way to a compromise turn toward diversity, as the neighborhood—and the nation—negotiated new notions of racial justice and race relations in the waning decades of the twentieth century. As historian Thomas Sugrue wrote in his 2008 book, *Sweet Land of Liberty: The Forgotten Struggle for Civil Rights in the North*, "all the trends that have reshaped the experiences of blacks and whites in the north are visible in microcosm in West Mount Airy."[7] Taken together, what residents and civic leaders experienced here mirrored the struggles that neighborhoods were facing in cities across the country, amid rapidly transitioning demographics and widespread cultural transformation.

These Mount Airy integrationists, well educated and historically minded, believed that their work was reshaping the experience of race relations in the United States. As such, involved individuals and the organizations they created retained extensive records detailing their efforts as they unfolded. This book was born out of the vast archival collections that have preserved the story of the Mount Airy integration project, the widespread journalistic and scholarly accounts that have chronicled, assessed, and critiqued these efforts toward interracial living, and the lived memory of integration in the community.[8] Over the course of this project, I collected interviews from close to fifty current and former residents of West Mount Airy and the surrounding neighborhoods. Through the process of snowball sampling, I began with a small group of subjects and followed the names that emerged from those conversations to create a temporal and spatial map of the Mount Airy integration experience. Local institutions, specifically the West Mount Airy Neighbors Association (WMAN) and the Germantown Jewish Centre (GJC), offered their support for the project. GJC hosted an evening of guided conversation on the historical and contemporary experience of integration in the community; more than twenty people attended and shared their stories. In each instance, I interrogated these oral history narratives as artifacts of historical memory, evaluating them with a critical eye toward the time, place, and context in which each interview was conducted. Though by no means comprehensive, these interviews, evaluated in tandem with a collection of oral histories housed at the Germantown Historical Society of several of the neighborhood's earliest integrationists, served to flesh out the archive-based narrative of West Mount Airy that emerged and add both nuance and texture to the institutional history of the neighborhood's integration project.

On one level, the story of West Mount Airy is highly particularized; this liberal middle-class community in northwestern Philadelphia was born out of a specific set of physical, economic, religious, and ideological circumstances. Integration in Mount Airy was possible because a unique group of people with a distinctive set of resources came together with a new vision of what a community could be. More broadly, though, Mount Airy's integration project reveals a carefully calibrated formula for community development in postwar America. In an era of Cold War liberalism, which privileged rights-based politics over economic transformation, the implementation and maintenance of integration in the neighborhood was successful because community organizers adopted a practice of leadership predicated on a balance between local control and government support.[9] Leaders of the Mount Airy integration project developed a model for organizing that blended individual responsibility and persuasion with structural accountability: a system of grassroots moral liberalism. When these two forces worked in tandem, Mount Airy functioned as a vibrant, economically stable, racially integrated neighborhood. When internal pressures or external influences altered that balance, the community experienced waves of tension and volatility. In this way, the *process* of integration—the strategies and tactics that neighborhood leaders employed—situate the story of West Mount Airy within broader national conversations about community organizing and activism in the latter half of the twentieth century.

Over the next seven chapters, I will show how integration happened, at board meetings and in classrooms, in living rooms and during religious services, on street corners and across fences. I will describe the individual decisions and deliberate actions taken by community leaders and the intended and unintended consequences that reverberated throughout the neighborhood. This book, organized both thematically and chronologically, offers a broad assessment of the movement toward intentional residential integration: the motivations and tactics, the goals and effects, the accomplishments and the challenges.

Chapter 1, "'A Home of One's Own': The Battle over Residential Space in Twentieth-Century America," traces the historical relationship between race and property in American cities, culminating in a profound clash, in the middle of the twentieth century, as the movement of upwardly mobile black families into previously all-white communities prompted a racialized struggle over space. Here, while many white homeowners throughout northeastern and midwestern cities responded with either hostility and violence or widespread flight, in a small corner of northwest Philadelphia residents came to believe that the secret to preserving their homes and their quality of life lay in welcoming their new neighbors into the community.

Chapter 2, "Finding Capital in Diversity: The Creation of Racially Integrated Space," chronicles the on-the-ground efforts in West Mount Airy to create a racially integrated, economically stable community. Whereas at first integrationists grounded their efforts in the belief that individual moral suasion would be sufficient to successfully preserve the viability of the neighborhood, by the end of the 1950s community leaders had shifted their tactics toward a concerted interventionist push to effect concrete legal and social change. Through this fusion of emotional appeal and structural reform, Mount Airy residents created a system of grassroots moral liberalism, working to stabilize the community in the face of rapid transition and to position themselves as a model of racial justice in the urban North.

Chapter 3, "Marketing Integration: Interracial Living in the White Imagination," steps back from this historical account of the integrating process to examine how middle-class white liberals interpreted the meaning of integration. For many of Mount Airy's white residents, living in an integrated community served to legitimate their identities as liberal, urban Americans. At the same time, though, this white conception of integration was grounded in a sense of de facto economic exclusivity attached to middle-class notions of postwar liberalism. In 1962, community leaders embarked on a widespread publicity campaign, presenting this white-centric image of integration to a regional, national, and even international audience and claiming a place for the neighborhood at the forefront of the fight for racial integration.

Chapter 4, "Integration, Separation, and the Fight for Black Identity," explores the varying meanings of integration for Philadelphia's black residents. For African American homeowners in Mount Airy, the prospect of integration brought with it a set of very material conditions—more secure investments, better schools, safer streets, more reliable municipal services—and a window into a professional culture with which they were trying to engage. Although the neighborhood's black residents certainly believed in the democratic ideal of an integrated community, their interest in living among whites often stemmed as much from these tangible opportunities as it did from an abstract sense of justice. At the same time, around the city, other black voices emerged condemning the integrationist African Americans of Mount Airy for having abandoned the "true" black community. By the mid-1960s, Cecil Moore, president of the local branch of the NAACP (National Association for the Advancement of Colored People), had painted the neighborhood's black homeowners as symbols of the cultural and spatial abandonment of black America by African American elites.

Chapter 5, "'Well-Trained Citizens and Good Neighbors': Educating an Integrated America," assesses how the fight for integrated education fits into the larger integration project in West Mount Airy. In many ways, the early movement toward residential and social integration in the neighborhood was successful in spite of larger economic pressures and formal policy directives aimed at segregation on a systemic level. Integrationists had embarked on a grassroots campaign designed to overcome what many viewed as the natural tendency toward separation in the private sphere. When West Mount Airy leaders expanded their scope beyond residential integration to work toward educational integration, residents were forced to contend with conflicting ideas over the value of education and city, state, and national policies that often undermined local efforts.

Chapter 6, "Confrontations in Black and White: The Crisis of Integration," reveals rising tensions within Mount Airy as an ethos of black cultural empowerment spread through the neighborhood's African American community. Amid a backdrop of urban deindustrialization and within the context of changing conceptions of racial justice in the United States, white and black residents of West Mount Airy found themselves at odds over the problem of rising crime rates in the region. White community leaders, still committed to integration as a visible representation of liberal politics, criticized city policies that sought to stanch criminal activity by targeting black youth. For African American residents, however, recently infused with a sense of cultural nationalism and self-help but still seeking to protect the material advantages that came with interracial living, this crisis over crime became the terrain on which the battle over local control and racial representation was fought in West Mount Airy.

Chapter 7, "The Choice to Live Differently: Reimagining Integration at Century's End," explores the causes and consequences of Mount Airy's shifting reputation, from *integration* to *diversity*. For local homeowners, the need to come together and rebuild after the conflict of the mid-1970s prompted an institutional push to bring residents together in ways that transcended racial identity and racial politics. Through these efforts, WMAN worked to shift the focus of both rhetoric and action away from the historical paradigm of black-white interracialism and toward a more generalized liberal ethos of tolerance and diversity. This movement coincided with demographic and cultural shifts that crafted Mount Airy as a haven for a countercultural coming of age. By the mid-1980s, the neighborhood was home to an emerging cohort of lesbian families, progressive Jewish scholars and activists, and, ultimately, young professionals. Although these new residents invigorated the community, their arrival also inevitably replaced, and displaced, prior residents, resulting in a loss of local memory surrounding the early years of conscious organizing. When national and regional economic volatility threatened the economic stability of the neighborhood, WMAN embarked on a comprehensive oral history project to document and present the stories of some of the area's earliest integrationists. In facilitating these public remembrances of the history of Mount Airy, neighborhood leaders worked to create a new collective consciousness about the past, through which they worked to negotiate the present, and shape the future, of the community.

Finally, the epilogue, "West Mount Airy and the Legacy of Integration," assesses the state of the neighborhood at the turn of the twenty-first century. In the early years of the new millennium, stories of the acclaimed community continued to filter through the local, regional, and national imagination, even as the goals of integration had become increasingly outmoded in contemporary American society. This final section is a meditation on the significance of Mount Airy's integration project and on the varied experiences of intentional residential integration and the values, costs, and consequences of growing up in a community steeped in an activist ethos toward interracial living.

This book is not meant to serve as a blueprint for interracial living, nor is it a predictor of success or failure. It will not describe a utopian version of integration, nor offer a polemical critique of an idealized conception of American liberal democracy. Rather, readers will encounter the process by which a group of committed homeowners set out to break the seemingly inevitable cycle of antagonism, hostility, and flight in their own postwar American city. Here, a community in transition came together to find an alternative to racial separation, without knowing what they would create in its place.

Chapter 1

"A Home of One's Own"

The Battle over Residential Space in Twentieth-Century America

In 1945, the 4600 block of Labadie Avenue was a quiet street in a residential St. Louis neighborhood. In the thirty-nine homes between Taylor Avenue and Cora Avenue, there lived thirty-nine white families.[1] Though houses turned over, as houses do, the community remained relatively cohesive with stable demographics and little outside pressure and no national attention. And residents liked it that way.

In September of that year, though, everything changed. Louis and Fern Kraemer decided it was time for a move, and they put their Labadie Avenue home on the market. The duplex, selling for $5,700, attracted a fair number of potential buyers, including J. D. and Ethel Shelley, a black couple who had moved from Mississippi to Missouri a few years earlier. J. D. worked for a small-arms ammunition plant during the war, and Ethel had a job in childcare. Week after week, they put part of their paychecks aside and, though he wanted to purchase a new car, Ethel convinced J. D. that they should move out of their North Ninth Street rental and look for a home of their own. They spoke to Elder Robert Bishop, their pastor at the Church of God in

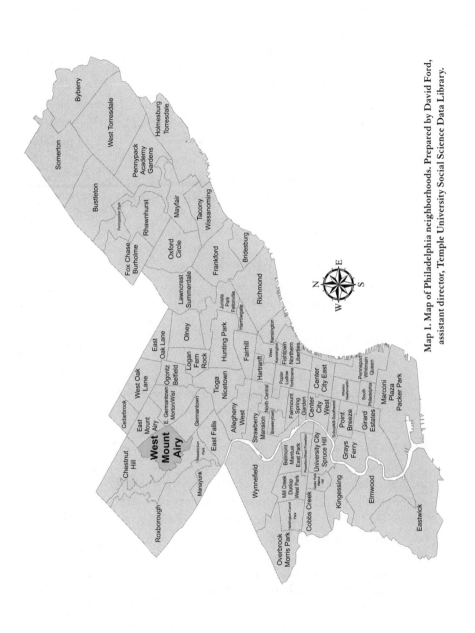

Map 1. Map of Philadelphia neighborhoods. Prepared by David Ford, assistant director, Temple University Social Science Data Library.

Christ, and learned that he also worked in real estate. Bishop showed the couple the Kraemer's Labadie Avenue property. They made an offer, and it was accepted. The pastor secured the home on behalf of the Shelleys, placing it in the name of his wife, Josephine Fitzgerald Bishop.[2]

Unknown to both the Shelleys and the Kraemers, the home was subject to a restrictive covenant dating back to 1911 that precluded the use of the property by "any person not of the Caucasian race."[3] According to the deed, "people of the Negro or Mongolian race" were forbidden from using or occupying the property, or contracting to purchase the property, for a period of fifty years after the original covenant had gone into effect.[4]

Although neither party wanted to rescind the agreement, the Marcus Avenue Improvement Association, a local homeowners' group, filed suit in municipal court demanding that the contract for sale be terminated. George Vaughan, attorney for the Shelleys, succeeded in convincing the trial court that the restrictive term in the deed was unenforceable. On appeal, though, the Missouri Supreme Court reversed the decision and ordered the couple to vacate the premises. In 1947, the U.S. Supreme Court agreed to review the case, consolidating the Shelleys' dispute with three others that raised questions about the constitutionality of restrictive covenants.[5] The court sought to determine the scope of an individual's right to control his or her private property.

Shelley v. Kraemer, the 1948 Supreme Court case that arose out of the Labadie Avenue dispute, took its place in a long line of political and legal decisions that set the standard for how communities could use racial identity in managing the residential landscape of the United States. Private property had been central to American law and life since the nation's founding, built in to its legal and political structure.[6] Beginning with the early constitutional debates, Americans have wrestled with the relationship between race and property, most strikingly regarding the institution of slavery. With emancipation in 1865, white Americans began to reinvent racialized property laws. Throughout the first half of the twentieth century, politicians, policymakers, and businessmen worked to create a system of residential separation predicated on the belief that black infiltration of white space would pollute neighborhoods and depreciate property values. These practices had the effect of markedly restricting African Americans' access to private property and, consequently, constraining their residential mobility.

By the middle of the twentieth century, after two hundred years of un-
even progress in the realm of race relations, the United States had reached a
crossroads. A heightened sense of the need for racial justice in the wake of
the Second World War and an international imperative directed by the nation's burgeoning Cold War agenda brought to fruition the modern civil
rights struggle, where the abstract ideal of equality gave way to a concrete
movement toward genuine racial integration.[7] But this push toward civil
rights in public spaces clashed almost immediately with these racialized notions of private property, situating America's neighborhoods at the center of
the struggle for racial justice in the latter half of the twentieth century.[8]

In the wake of the Civil War, the United States experienced a residential
crisis. As newly emancipated African Americans began the long migration
from southern towns to northern cities, white homeowners struggled with
how to manage these changes.[9] Between 1860 and 1900, the percentage of
the nation's African Americans residing in urban centers swelled from 4.2
percent to nearly 20 percent.[10] Deeply rooted racial prejudices, combined
with the realities of a growing population of poor and often illiterate black
residents, prompted whites to create restrictions to limit access to their neighborhoods. In Philadelphia, for instance, the first major wave of black mi-
grants came in the years surrounding World War I. From 1910 to 1930, more
than 140,000 African Americans arrived in the city. Philadelphia had the
third largest black community in the nation among industrial centers, behind only New York and Chicago.[11] Though the area had long been home
to an established black elite, most of these new arrivals were still working to
overcome the devastating conditions they had experienced in the rural
South.[12] Housing opportunities for these new residents were scarce. Most
had little choice but to settle along the banks of the Delaware River in South
Philadelphia or to push their way into the already overcrowded tenements a
few miles north of City Hall.[13]

This same demographic concentration was taking place throughout the
urban North. At first, some cities attempted to pass formal legislation restricting the access of these new black immigrants to private property. In
1910, Baltimore, Maryland's city council enacted a residential segregation
ordinance designed to cluster the black poor into the city's most desolate
regions. Like Philadelphia, the region had seen a sharp rise in its African

American population during the Great Migration; between 1880 and 1900, the city's black community grew from fifty-four thousand to seventy-nine thousand, an increase of 47 percent.[14] Most of these new residents had gathered in the cheapest housing in southwest Baltimore, prompting the area's small but established black middle class to relocate to the city's northwestern neighborhoods. A group of Progressive Era leaders, backed by a Social Darwinist agenda that espoused the belief that African Americans were a source of contamination for the larger population, set about to isolate the black population in slum conditions, in order to safeguard against disease and social unrest throughout the rest of the city. The law, first proposed by petition, called for "measures to restrain the colored people locating in the white community, and proscribe a limit beyond which it shall be unlawful for them to go."[15] Reformers believed that by separating people according to race, the ordinance would prevent conflict and unrest between the region's white and black residents and "promot[e] the general welfare of the city."[16] There is no evidence that the law achieved these aims; instead, it had the effect of restricting the mobility of African American residents across the city and increasing rates of crime and violence in the poorest communities in the southwest.

Baltimore's segregation ordinance was short-lived. In 1913, local pressure from realtors and white property owners living in middle-class mixed-race neighborhoods forced extensive revisions to the law. That year, the city passed a second bill confining the scope of the legislation to already segregated areas.[17] Four years later, the U.S. Supreme Court took up the issue of legalized residential segregation in the case of *Buchanan v. Warley*, where a unanimous bench held that such ordinances are unconstitutional under the Fourteenth Amendment.[18] Still, the Baltimore controversy evidenced a fundamental belief in intrinsic racial difference. During the early years of the twentieth century, white Americans overwhelmingly subscribed to the idea that their black counterparts were inherently inferior, and as such could not occupy the same geographic space.[19] When this legal segregation in northern cities failed to create physical separation between blacks and whites, policymakers, businessmen, and property owners worked to construct new mechanisms for managing and restricting black access to residential neighborhoods.

In some areas, public-private partnerships in housing reform became an obvious solution to the problems of racial mixing. Though public housing

had originally grown out of a Progressive Era impulse that highlighted bureaucratic responses to social and economic problems, by the early 1930s
many policymakers saw low-income housing as a means to geographically
constrain black workers. In Philadelphia, by 1930 the African American
population had risen to 219,599, a 63.5 percent increase over 1920.[20] Black
Americans now made up more than 11 percent of the total population of
the city.[21] Most of these new residents, relatively poor and uneducated, were
consigned to the least desirable housing in the region. As European immigrant groups relocated to the neighborhoods along the outer reaches of the
city and in the expanding inner-ring suburbs, African Americans crowded
into the abandoned areas. Philadelphia officials worked hard to maintain
these boundaries. In 1935, Walter Thomas of the City Planning Commission argued that containing the region's black population would serve to
uplift the rest of the city. The area east of Broad Street near Girard Avenue,
wrote Thomas, was "heavily negro, and should remain so."[22] Philadelphia,
he said, should develop "a negro area having a physical outlet into Fairmount
Avenue and Girard Avenue, and Broad Street, and Girard Avenue business
area. Such a defined negro area [would] contribute to the stabilization of the
area [and would] have a wholesome effect on the values of Girard Avenue
west of Broad Street."[23] A year later, more than one-third of the residents of
these North Philadelphia neighborhoods designated by Thomas were African American.[24]

Even though low-income-housing policies in Philadelphia worked well
to confine the city's black poor, property owners had to find new strategies
to contend with the region's established and growing middle-income and
elite black communities. By the early years of the twentieth century, the city
had long been home to a small group of well-to-do African Americans, those
whom scholar and activist Sadie Tanner Mossell called in 1921 "Negroes of
culture, education, and some financial means."[25] With the Great Migration
and the gradual expansion of employment opportunities, though, the population of financially stable blacks grew steadily, and more upwardly mobile
black families began to look beyond the confines of the low-income pockets
that Thomas's City Planning Commission had developed.[26]

In order to restrain this movement and to preserve the established white
culture of their residential communities, developers and homeowners throughout northern cities crafted contractually mandated restrictions on property.
At first designed to control how land was used, by the 1920s these provisions

served to constrain who could use or occupy the land as well.[27] Fearful that the influx of black residents into all-white communities would prompt a decline in property values, developers and realtors attached these provisions to deeds in order to achieve through private agreement what they could not through legal manipulation. Through such contractual stipulations as defeasible fees, negative easements, equitable servitudes, and restrictive covenants, contracting parties were able to prevent African Americans from purchasing or renting homes in their neighborhoods, protecting the whiteness of their communities.[28] Most of these provisions were conveyed with sale, so the restrictions carried over from one homeowner to the next. Nearly every housing development constructed from the 1920s through the 1940s included these restrictive provisions in their deeds.[29]

Throughout the first half of the twentieth century, policymakers developed an awkward marriage between a conception of private property as a right of exclusion and the common understanding of inherent black inferiority in order to craft a firm system of residential separation. As realtors ascribed contractual limitations to deeds, municipal governments utilized exclusionary zoning tactics to exercise control over the use of land and property. Such policies, ostensibly predicated on notions of self-protection from the perceived problems associated with urbanization, were initially affirmed by the U.S. Supreme Court. In 1926, in *Village of Euclid v. Ambler Realty Company*, the court held that zoning—the practice of allowing city governments to designate areas for particular uses—was a valid exercise of municipal police power.[30] Even though the Court declared race-based zoning unconstitutional two years later in *Nectow v. City of Cambridge*, such practices continued to persist in less official capacities for the next half century.[31] The so-called neutral zoning policies of the post-*Nectow* era utilized seemingly race-blind variables such as property status and land use restrictions to model how a community could be organized. These practices often had the desired effect of maintaining the regional status quo, where wealthy white enclaves attracted wealthy white families, and urban blight produced further economic devastation. It was not until 1977, in *Moore v. City of East Cleveland*, that the U.S. Supreme Court began to step in to restrict these apparently neutral zoning practices.[32]

At the federal level, in 1934 President Franklin Roosevelt called on Congress to create the Federal Housing Administration (FHA), a New Deal era institution that, among its many other functions, served to provide racial assessments for mortgages.[33] The FHA and the Home Owners' Loan Corporation, established a year earlier, developed a system of redlining, which categorized neighborhoods based on such factors as residents' occupation, income status, and ethnicity, in an effort to eliminate subjectivity in home appraisals. The policy ranked loan candidates from A through D, "most favorable" to "least favorable," and used race as a primary indicator for determining the validity of a loan request. Whereas blocks populated with middle-class white residents received an A rating, neighborhoods made up largely of recent immigrants and racial and ethnic minorities earned a C or a D.[34] In 1940, for instance, the Home Owners' Loan Corporation assigned one St. Louis suburb an A ranking based, in part, on the absence of "foreigner[s] or Negro[s]" in the community.[35] Housing conditions and relative congestion did serve as an indicator for FHA ratings in some neighborhoods, particularly in communities composed largely of poor whites or immigrants from southern and eastern Europe. However, predominantly African American and mixed-race neighborhoods overwhelmingly earned a D ranking, regardless of economic status or physical conditions.[36]

These ratings had the effect of markedly constricting black mobility. As the FHA's *Underwriting Manual* mandated, if an African American homebuyer sought entry into a white neighborhood, absent extenuating circumstances "the valuator must not hesitate to make a reject ranking."[37] If a community was to maintain a stable environment, the manual stated, "[it was] necessary that properties . . . continue to be occupied by the same social and racial classes." According to Leslie S. Perry of the NAACP, the FHA "[did] more than any other single instrumentality to force nonwhite citizens into substandard houses and neighborhoods."[38]

These policies and practices by local, state, and federal governments came together to effectively create a system of residential separation in the United States, with far-reaching repercussions. But in the middle of the twentieth century, such efforts to preserve restrictions on private property were coming up against a growing liberalization of public space. In 1941, U.S. entry into World War II prompted a fundamental reimagination of race relations. The battle against fascism abroad forced many in the United States to confront the nation's own legacy of racial discrimination.[39] Around the country, Americans started to question the long-standing belief in the fundamental differences between blacks and whites. Rather than conceiving of racial categories as a system of hierarchy, some communities began to consider the possibility that black and white Americans could work together toward the creation of an interracial nation.

In 1944, Swedish economist Gunnar Myrdal published *An American Dilemma*, a meditation on race relations in the United States that brought into focus this growing consciousness about racial discrimination and offered liberal Americans a new language for addressing issues of race throughout the country. Laid out in 1,024 pages of text and 258 pages of citations, Myrdal's work called on Americans to redeem the character of the country by repairing the disconnect between the American Dream and the reality of race relations. According to Myrdal, this break between the historical ideals of the nation and the reality of racial prejudice was creating a pervasive moral angst in American society. Although much of the study was directed toward racial injustice in the South, the scholar noted that the absence of legal barriers to equality sheltered northern whites from the realities of racial inequity in U.S. cities. According to Myrdal, herein lay the hope for a national reconciliation of race relations. Once white liberals understood the problem of discrimination, he believed, they would work to reshape the hearts and minds of the American public. The solution to race relations in the United States, said the economist, lay not in a dramatic reconfiguration of the nation's political and economic systems, but in a small but persistent group of whites promoting individual change grounded in the historic ideals of American democracy.[40] In the years to follow, housing activists relied on Myrdal's rhetoric of moral persuasion in developing their integrationist agenda.

Myrdal's ideas and the call for racial equality gained further traction with the emergence of the Cold War, as the status of American race relations became a critical question in the international battle between communism and democracy. If the nation was to maintain its image as a bastion of tolerance and equality, the president and State Department officials believed, the country needed to solve its race problem. As Acting Secretary of State Dean Acheson wrote to the chairman of the Fair Employment Practices Commission in 1947:

> The existence of discrimination against minority groups in this country has an adverse effect upon our relations with other countries. We are reminded over and over by some foreign newspapers and spokesmen, that our treatment of various minorities leaves much to be desired. . . . An atmosphere of

suspicion and resentment in a country over the way a minority is being treated in the United States is a formidable obstacle to the development of mutual understanding and trust between the two countries. We will have better international relations when these reasons for suspicion and resentment have been removed.[41]

In the years following the Second World War, the United States employed the language of civil rights reform in order to bolster its reputation in the global fight against communism.[42]

This notion of liberal race reform quickly began to spread to all corners of public life, from popular culture and law enforcement to politics and academia. Reformers saw the opportunity in the postwar years to instruct the American people on changing race relations. Hundreds of interracial agencies were founded in the late 1940s. Police departments hired race specialists to educate officers on prejudice and discrimination. Within the business world, corporate elites commissioned focus groups to reconsider racist hiring practices and reeducate their workers on intergroup relations. In colleges and universities, students employed social science methodologies to understand the dynamics of race and human interaction.[43]

The federal government, too, brought its strategic policies of liberal racial reform into its public message on race relations during the 1950s and 1960s. In 1946, President Harry Truman created the first-ever biracial committee to study the role of the government in American race relations. The following year, the committee published its landmark report, *To Secure These Rights*. The group called for an executive and legislative push toward the creation of permanent government initiatives designed to safeguard the fundamental rights of American citizens. The report evidenced a growing sense of optimism concerning the power of education, reform, and government intervention to combat discrimination and prejudice.[44] This agenda created an institutional mandate for racial integration and privileged change backed by social science rigor. And as community organizations, the business world, and government agencies heeded this call, it did not take long for efforts to reach into the legal sector.

In 1948, the conflict surrounding the Kraemer property on Labadie Avenue in Saint Louis reached the U.S. Supreme Court. At oral argument, NAACP attorneys led by Thurgood Marshall launched a two-pronged legal and policy attack. First, they argued that by enforcing the restrictive covenants, the lower courts were in breach of the due process clause of the Fifth and Fourteenth Amendments of the U.S. Constitution. Though the covenant was part of a private agreement for sale, by upholding or enforcing it, the NAACP argued, the courts were intervening and thereby creating a situation where the state action doctrine would apply.[45] Second, Marshall and cocounsel Charles Hamilton Houston asserted that it was critical to present a racially just democratic nation to the rest of the world. Playing on the sensibilities of Cold War era culture and politics, they insisted that restrictive covenants were an example of the failure of the United States to live up to its own promise of equality under the law. These discriminatory stipulations, the attorneys maintained, were both morally wrong and strategically dangerous in a time when projecting an image of a unified, democratic nation was crucial to furthering the country's anti-Soviet agenda.[46]

As a marker of just how pervasive restrictive covenants had become, three justices were forced to recuse themselves when they learned that their own deeds included such a provision. On January 16, 1948, though, the remaining six justices issued a unanimous opinion vindicating the Shelleys' struggles.[47]

When news of the *Shelley* opinion reached the streets, African Americans rejoiced in the victory. "The ruling by the courts gives thousands of prospective home buyers throughout the United States new courage and hope in the American form of government," Thurgood Marshall exclaimed in an NAACP press release.[48] "Live Anywhere," proclaimed the *Pittsburgh Courier*, one of the nation's premier black newspapers.[49] Civil rights advocates saw the decision as a green light toward a race-blind, reform-minded agenda, where racial integration could become the practical manifestation of the abstract idea of the American creed.

Shelley v. Kraemer was the first case in American legal history to formally begin to undo the generations of legally prescribed residential segregation in the United States. The decision evidenced a tangible shift in the culture of race relations in the United States, and it laid the groundwork for a legal strategy toward desegregation at the federal level that both activists and courts came to employ throughout the latter half of the twentieth century.[50]

In the years to follow, cities across the United States ushered in new municipal governments asserting platforms of equality of opportunity and interracial collaboration. These reform-minded administrations saw the expansion of African Americans' rights as a state imperative. In the realm of employment, local, state, and the federal administrations created a widely accepted mandate for integration of the workplace. Such a protocol could be implemented relatively seamlessly from a policy level, by revamping hiring practices and wage and benefit structures. In the public domain, the nation saw great strides in legislative civil rights reform and grassroots efforts to break down the structural barriers toward integrated space.[51]

In Philadelphia, after decades of Republican control and several years of pervasive governmental corruption, residents elected Democratic candidate Joseph Clark, running on a platform of broad liberal reform, to the office of mayor in 1951. A year earlier, Philadelphians had passed a new city charter, which included a widespread ban on discriminatory practices based on race and religion in public employment.[52] The legislation evidenced a fundamental change in the power structure of a city with a deep history of racist and anti-Semitic practices and policies.

Philadelphia had been home to a permanent population of Jews since before the American Revolution. In 1848, there were roughly four thousand Jews in the city, and by the middle of the nineteenth century an established Jewish community had been largely integrated into the power structure of Philadelphia's elite institutions and organizations. With mass Jewish immigration beginning in the 1880s, the city saw its Jewish population expand precipitously. By 1904, there were 75,000 Jews in Philadelphia. By 1915, there were 200,000 Jews across the city; twenty years later, the number had risen to 250,000. Most were recent immigrants from eastern Europe, settling in small clusters in North and South Philadelphia, even as the existing small elite population of Jewish industrialists and lawyers maintained an active presence in city business and political life through the 1920s.[53]

With the rise of anti-Jewish fervor throughout Europe in the 1930s, however, Philadelphia saw a marked increase in religious discrimination. The city had long been home to a sizeable German American population with deep roots in Germanic culture and heritage, and it became one of the central hubs for German propaganda in the United States. The city saw a strong and visible presence of the German Bund, an American Nazi organization led locally by Gerhardt Wilhelm Kunze. Kunze published acerbic condemnations of American Jews in the *Philadelphia Weckrug and Beobachter*, the city's bilingual German–English newspaper, and WDAS, one of the region's preeminent radio stations, aired the sermons of Father Charles Coughlin, a Detroit-based Catholic priest whose vitriolic attacks on American Jews were

broadcast across the nation. By the end of the decade, sociologist Digby Balt-
zell observed that the city that had once opened up to American Jewish elites
had become divided into a rigid parallel social hierarchy, where Jews were
systemically locked out of the city's power structure.[54]

Just as the Second World War had brought into focus the deep racial inequity in American society, so, too, did it underscore the rising tide of anti-
Semitism in the United States. The fight against Nazism abroad prompted
many to question discriminatory practices across the nation. Though intolerance persisted, reforms at all levels of government served to ameliorate formal anti-Semitic directives and integrate Jews into contemporary American
public life. Philadelphia mayor Joseph Clark's new charter was one of the
first such documents to recast the status of Jews across the city. The new legislation also established the Philadelphia Human Relations Commission.
With this provision, Philadelphia became the first city in the country to provide for a human relations agency in its charter. Taking over from the city's
Fair Employment Practices Commission, established in 1948, the new organization expanded both the capacity and the power of the previous commission. It had a larger budget and more employees; it provided for additional
commissioners and sought to assert a comprehensive overhaul of current
practices.[55]

Clark wasted little time in implementing policies that he believed would
result in a new culture of race relations. In his first year in office, he recruited
analysts and policymakers from around the nation to join his administration and put into practice those liberal reforms on which he ran. In 1953, he
wooed George Schermer away from his post as director of the Detroit Mayor's
Interracial Committee to lead the burgeoning Philadelphia Commission on
Human Relations. Schermer had gone to Detroit twelve years earlier to
serve as the assistant director for management of the Detroit Housing Commission, and after several years of combating unfriendly mayoral administrations, he was relieved to come in as one of Clark's "carpetbaggers."[56]

Schermer and Clark created a new culture of liberal racial reform in Philadelphia. Through comprehensive education campaigns and policy initiatives,
the new administration set out to reorient the city's long-standing reputation
for racial antagonism, once so pervasive that it had caused W. E. B. Dubois in
1927 to remark that "[Philadelphia is] the best place to discuss race relations
because there is more race prejudice here than any other city in the United
States."[57] Clark believed that continued racial segregation threatened to

undermine the city's urban industrial development, and his reformers worked to pave the way for a more racially inclusive society.[58]

As Philadelphia and other northern cities moved toward an ethos of racial equality in public life, however, the push for racial inclusion in the residential sphere was met with increasing ferocity.[59] Though the movement toward racial reform was shifting American conceptions of equality, the historic primacy of private property held strong. As the dynamics of race relations in government and employment liberalized and the legal restrictions of residential exclusion lifted, these conflicting ideals and the tangible results they produced brought the issue of housing into the center of the struggle for racial justice in northern cities.

Critical to this postwar residential crisis was the simultaneous expansion of the black middle class throughout the urban North and the wartime creation of a pronounced housing shortage. Spurred by New Deal and wartime economic opportunities, blacks once again flocked to America's cities, in what has been called the Second Great Migration. In Philadelphia, nearly fifty thousand African Americans moved to the city between 1941 and 1943. Even after the war ended, black families continued to arrive. Philadelphia's black population swelled, from nearly 251,000 in 1940 to more than 376,000 in 1950. Because the number of whites remained relatively stagnant at 1.7 million, the percentage of African Americans rose from 13 percent of the city's overall population to 18 percent.[60]

At first, most of these newcomers concentrated in North Philadelphia. But this influx of people, combined with a wartime reallocation of resources that halted residential construction, quickly created an acute housing shortage. At the same time that these fifty thousand new black residents settled into the city in the early 1940s, property developers built only twenty-four thousand new homes, public and private alike.[61] Once production restarted after the war, the housing market was unable to keep up with increased demand. By 1946, 17 percent of the city's residential units were in deteriorating condition, with sixty-five thousand families living communally in units meant for single-family occupancy. The vacancy rate in the city was near nonexistent, hovering between 0.5 percent and 1 percent.[62] Old city neighborhoods were ready to burst.

Furthermore, with expanded job opportunity and those postwar legal reforms, a new black middle class began to emerge. These upwardly mobile African Americans began to push outward, seeking to escape the overcrowded pockets of North Philadelphia. The swift demographic changes created intense anxieties within neighborhoods, where white homeowners believed that both their property values and their ways of life were being jeopardized by the influx of black residents.[63]

Across the nation's urban centers, the prospect of black families moving into previously all-white enclaves created intense hostility. The situation seemed dire, particularly for economically stable working-class homeowners, those who could not afford to buy new homes when their current property values diminished but who were not so poor as to be lifelong renters who could abandon their units in search of new communities. Desperate to uphold their single most valuable investment—their homes—these blue-collar families came together to wage often-violent campaigns against new black families seeking to purchase homes.[64]

Prospective African American homebuyers often found themselves met with harassment and threats when they tried to move into such a community. When Luther and Juanita Green moved onto North Philadelphia's North Thirteenth Street in the 1940s, white homeowners on the block mounted an unyielding attack. Longtime resident William Seymour grabbed Mrs. Green as she walked down the street, threatening that he would make her life miserable so long as she remained in the neighborhood. Later, as the Greens sat in their new dining room with friends, white residents threw full paint cans through the front window and fired shots at the home. Even those white neighbors who might have befriended the Green family, or at least tolerated them, maintained their distance and their silence in order to preserve their own safety and security.[65]

For many such white residents, the underlying rationale for this aggressive defense of their neighborhoods related directly to the historic importance of private property. Homeowners believed that protecting their blocks against the influx of black buyers was not only a means to preserve the value of their neighborhoods; it was fundamentally about their rights to make choices about their own lives. Property ownership meant independence and autonomy, a sense of freedom from government intervention in their private space. In this way, these homeowners developed a new political rhetoric, a model of resistance that pitted their right to control their property against the right of African Americans to choose where to live.[66]

In contrast to this active resistance emblematic of the experience of white blue-collar property owners, middle-class white urban homeowners often responded to these demographic shifts by fleeing their transitioning neighborhoods for the expanding all-white suburbs. Once viewed as second-class entities, home to the poor and dispossessed, by the 1940s and 1950s these suburban areas began to gain esteem as alternative spaces to build communities.[67] After more than a decade of Depression era want and wartime sacrifice, an emerging American middle class was eager to buy.[68] In the five years after the Second World War, consumer spending rose 60 percent, with the dollar total spent on household products and consumer goods climbing 240 percent.[69] The postwar housing shortage in the nation's cities, combined with this burgeoning consumer-driven culture that could draw on significant household savings, provided new opportunities for land developers.

Beginning in the late 1940s, communities along the city borders saw their underdeveloped green spaces quickly fill with new housing stock. Inner-ring suburban development proliferated as well. Residents were on the move, from neighborhood to neighborhood, from city to suburb. The rate of transition was overwhelming. In Philadelphia, between 1950 and 1960, 700,000 white homebuyers moved from the city into the surrounding suburbs.[70] These suburbs became, for many, a spatial manifestation of the American Dream. They came to represent a sense of safety, stability, modernity, and autonomy; in a sense, they became the fulfillment of that consumer-oriented postwar culture.[71] But these new suburban communities represented something insidious as well: a new incarnation of residential exclusion. With race-based legal ordinances unconstitutional and contractually mandated racial restrictions unenforceable, the suburbs became the postwar embodiment of managed racial separation.

Real estate agents were quick to capitalize on white fears of instability. When a black family attempted to purchase a house in a previously all-white area, "blockbusting" realtors worked to instill a sense of panic in the community by warning homeowners of the risk of property depreciation and violence. These techniques had the effect of encouraging massive white flight, as entire neighborhoods sold their homes to incoming black families. Corrupt real estate agents profited from the transition by undervaluing the original sales and then marking up prices for the prospective black homebuyers. Often, these areas tipped from exclusively white to predominantly black in a period of just a few years.[72] These extreme racial and residential shifts in the postwar years were threatening the very livelihood of some of the nation's oldest and most established urban centers. Cities throughout the Northeast and Midwest were experiencing the early warning signs of crisis. The future of the American city was in jeopardy, and, for many, resegregation seemed inevitable.

Some communities around the country, though, began to think about alternate ways to respond to the rising influx of African Americans to their neighborhoods. In such communities as Oak Park, in Chicago; West Mount Airy, in Philadelphia; and Shaker Heights, outside of Cleveland, residents saw the growing instability around them and decided to try something different.[73] Instead of meeting would-be black homebuyers with antagonism or flight, these small pockets of middle-class white liberals resolved to welcome their new neighbors. Rather than face the prospect of relocation with declining property values, these innovative homeowners worked to save their neighborhoods by making interracial living a marketable commodity, by creating capital in integrated spaces.

Philadelphia's West Mount Airy was one of the first in the nation to embrace this integrationist agenda. Beginning with a moral pledge in the mid-1950s, neighborhood residents waged a community-wide campaign for intentional integration. The historically wealthy enclave in the city's northwest reaches was uniquely positioned to spearhead this integrationist crusade. Founded in 1683 by a community of Dutch Mennonite immigrants, southeast Pennsylvania's Germantown region had gained its identity as a wealthy white enclave by the early eighteenth century. The area's relatively high elevation (at 336 feet) offered scenic views and lazy breezes, making it a desirable respite from the frenzy of the city for Philadelphia's elite.[74] In 1750, William Allen, who went on to become chief justice of the Supreme Court of Pennsylvania, built a country estate at what is now Germantown Avenue and Allens Lane, and called the home Mount Airy.[75]

This Germantown Borough remained a quiet retreat for well-to-do Philadelphians until 1854, when the city passed the Consolidation Act, dissolving the townships, boroughs, and districts surrounding it and incorporating the entirety of Philadelphia County under the authority of the Philadelphia municipal government. As this legislative action brought the region under the auspices of city institutions and services, the expansion of the railways made the region more accessible to the city center. The earliest trains had arrived in Germantown in 1832, and the community soon developed into one of the nation's first railroad suburbs. Two decades later, steam rail service came to the region, carrying multipassenger vehicles along the iron rails. In Chestnut Hill, the wealthy enclave occupying the northernmost section of Germantown, local commuters raised funds for a permanent railroad connecting the southern and northern ends of the region. The new terminal opened at Chestnut Hill and Bethlehem Pike on July 3, 1854. By 1859, more than forty trains were making commuter stops along the Germantown lines.[76]

With these political and technological changes, the population growth expanded rapidly. By the 1870s, the once-isolated enclave was experiencing high-percentage growth.[77] The arrival of city residents prompted new housing development throughout northwest Philadelphia, but residents held strongly to the community's wealthy, independent roots even as the population surged. Throughout the first half of the twentieth century, property developers and realtors attached restrictive covenants to deeds, seeking to maintain control over incoming homebuyers. Within a few decades, as members of the city's black elite began to slowly migrate to the area, these contractual mandates gave way to a sense of a de facto exclusivity by class.[78] The high cost of living meant that only the most financially stable buyers were able to purchase homes in Mount Airy. The neighborhood promised to provide the ideal escape for wealthy black families from the crowded inner-city neighborhoods, just as it had for generations of wealthy whites. By the 1940s, these early black settlers had gradually opened northwest Philadelphia to upwardly mobile African American families, who were just as invested as the existing white community in maintaining the economic and social status of the neighborhood.[79]

At first, many of the area's white homeowners articulated concerns over the oncoming transition. In 1950, West Mount Airy was home to 18,462 residents.[80] Outside of the neighborhood's Sharpnack section, an industrial village that had sprung up in the eighteenth century as a home for domestic workers and was, by the 1890s, known for its densely populated blocks of narrow two-story stucco homes, 98.6 percent of the community's residents were white.[81] As in urban neighborhoods throughout the northern United States, West Mount Airy residents experienced deep racial anxieties and worked hard to preserve what they saw as the integrity of their community. With the sudden influx of African American buyers, they worried that their property values would diminish, that the instability would breed volatility and crime, and that their neighborhood institutions would fall apart. Enterprising realtors quickly stepped in, spreading rumors of mass home sales and projecting intense instability and a pronounced decline in housing values.[82]

But many residents of West Mount Airy saw the possibility of something different. Well versed in the postwar liberalism that had prompted reform in governance and employment, and not wanting to give in to the belief that racial transition necessarily brought about neighborhood decline, white homeowners set out to maintain their place in the community, while welcoming the new African American families seeking to move in.

In the years following the Second World War, Mount Airy's unique physical, economic, and cultural character ideally positioned the neighborhood for interracial living. Key to the effectiveness of the neighborhood's integration project was the area's spatial layout; over the course of the region's history, West Mount Airy had experienced five distinct periods of residential development, resulting in marked diversity of the built environment. In the early 1950s, housing stock in the neighborhood ranged from historically prestigious pre–Revolutionary War farmhouses to nineteenth-century summer estates, from elegant early twentieth-century row houses and twins to privately commissioned modern homes constructed before and during World War II. Among its owner-occupied homes, the neighborhood was made up of 29 percent row houses, 41 percent twins, and 30 percent single-detached houses.[83] This rich variety of housing stock attracted a wide range of people to the community and made many residents resistant to flight, as the region's distinctiveness was difficult to replicate in other areas of the city and surrounding suburbs.

Contributing further to the unique physical landscape of the neighborhood was the region's proximity to Philadelphia's Fairmount Park and the Wissahickon Gorge. In 1824, Germantown-born merchant George W. Carpenter began construction of an estate, ultimately totaling 350 acres, in the area that would become West Mount Airy. Utilizing the Wissahickon, once a critical outpost during the Revolutionary War, Carpenter created expansive parks with creeks meandering through, laying the rudiments of the geographic landscape of Mount Airy in the mid-twentieth century. By the time the neighborhood experienced its first hints of postwar racial transition, the area was surrounded on two sides by Fairmount Park and bisected by Carpenter's Woods, one of the lasting remnants of the original Carpenter estate. Though some white residents had chosen to leave the historic neighborhood in favor of the modern split-level homes in the expanding suburbs, many more saw value in the traditional housing styles and ubiquitous green space.[84]

Those white residents who remained embraced the neighborhood's growing reputation as a socially liberal community. Although the region's roots as

Figure 1. Families sled and ice skate on Wissahickon Creek in Fairmount Park's Wissahickon Gorge, *Philadelphia Bulletin*, 1955. Used with permission from Special Collections Research Center, Temple University Libraries, Philadelphia.

a well-to-do retreat from the rush of city life remained, Mount Airy residents in the middle of the twentieth century professed a sense of cultural liberalness that lent itself to the possibility of open-minded acceptance. In the years following the Second World War, the neighborhood was home to a broad community of high-achieving white residents. They were well educated, politically oriented, and liberally minded. They were physicians and judges, lawyers and business owners, race relations specialists and longtime activists, acclaimed jazz musicians and established members of the Philadelphia orchestra. Educator and ornithologist Joe Cadbury, of the famed Cadbury Chocolate family, lived on the 100 block of West Hortter Street.[85] Charles Darrow, one of the developers of the game Monopoly and the first board-game millionaire, lived on the unit block of Westview Street.[86] George

Schermer, director of the Philadelphia Human Relations Commission, moved to the 6700 block of McCallum Street in 1953.[87] Dress manufacturer Lester Sacks lived at 506 W. Springer Street, where, on November 7, 1951, Frank Sinatra married Ava Gardner in a secret ceremony.[88] As Shirley Melvin, who moved to the neighborhood with her family as a teenager in 1942, later reflected, many Mount Airy residents had experienced working and engaging with African Americans through their professional and social networks.[89] They had grown accustomed to interracial interaction in their public lives and were perhaps more open to the prospect of such friendly relations in their residential community as well.

These cultural and political leaders were members of a well-established professional class in Philadelphia. Though Mount Airy residents spanned the spectrum of middle-class status, most were relatively fiscally stable; unlike the blue-collar homeowners of many of the rapidly transitioning communities who resisted racial transition, in part out of a fear of the property devaluation that so often came with neighborhood volatility. The residents of West Mount Airy were generally more economically secure, and as such were risking less during the unpredictable period of transition.[90]

This unique combination of circumstances, individuals, and social and material conditions created possibilities for residential integration in the neighborhood. In the early 1950s, community leaders in West Mount Airy became part of a small but important national movement that conceived of alternative ways to think about race and residential space.[91] Sometimes in conversation with one another and more often working as independent entities, reform-minded middle-class neighborhood organizations in northern and midwestern cities drew lessons from public integration efforts, working to reclaim control over their blocks from panic sellers and create a system for interracial residential stability. They waged community-wide campaigns toward intentional integration; by replacing residential segregation with residential integration, they sought to disrupt a system predicated on separation and infuse their day-to-day lives with the experience of interracial living.

Chapter 2

Finding Capital in Diversity

The Creation of Racially Integrated Space

In May 1967, George Schermer came to Philadelphia to participate in a panel discussion on the future of racial integration. The trip took the Washington, DC-based consultant back to the place he had called home for more than ten years. Schermer had moved to West Mount Airy in 1953, just as the integration efforts were gaining steam, and he became one of the most influential forces in the creation of an economically stable, racially integrated community. Reflecting on the success of that integration project that they had embarked on nearly fifteen years earlier, he spoke of the way his community elected to allocate financial resources and residential muscle. "The amount of busing it would take would be beyond belief," Schermer said of the prospect of integration. "Instead, we did it with moving vans."[1]

When African American buyers began to make their way to West Mount Airy, Schermer and his neighbors organized grassroots efforts to welcome them into the community. Throughout the 1950s, integrationist leaders guided residents through the complicated process of developing an experiment in interracial living in northwest Philadelphia. At first, the community relied on a Myrdalian vision of postwar racial justice, grounding their efforts in the belief that with individual moral suasion, organizers could successfully coax their neighbors into working toward integration.[2] As they moved forward, though, activists worked to bridge their emotional pleas with the growing governmental push toward racial liberalism in public and professional worlds. By the end of the decade, through this fusion of moral appeal with a concerted interventionist effort toward concrete legal and economic change, Mount Airy residents created a reform movement predicated on a strategy of grassroots moral liberalism that relied upon both individual persuasion and structural accountability. Schermer's 1967 invocation of moving vans, then, implied a rather simplified tale of intentional integration. Most glaringly, his association of vans with school buses conflated residential and educational integration, two distinct processes that—despite, at times, West Mount Airy residents' efforts to the contrary—required markedly different tactics for implementation and maintenance.[3] But more fundamentally, Schermer's celebration of moving vans belied the significance of this innovative two-tiered approach through which residents worked to stabilize their community in the face of rapid transition and, in the process, created a model of neighborhood organizing and social change.

In early 1953, a group of white residents in West Mount Airy came together to discuss their growing concerns over the changing face of their community. Two years earlier, upwardly mobile black families had begun to move into the homes along the neighborhood's Lincoln Drive corridor.[4] The large thoroughfare—the only north-south thruway without shopping districts or trolley tracks to connect Center City (the central business-residential district in Philadelphia) with northwest Philadelphia and the suburbs beyond——was by the postwar years cluttered with traffic, as automobiles encroached on the residential character of Lincoln Drive. At the same time, some homeowners were beginning to see the large turn-of-the-century single and twin houses lining the street as architecturally passé. As those white families left for the modern homes of the contiguous suburbs, black home buyers began to move in. The neighborhood's Pelham section, just east of Lincoln and south of Greene Street, experienced the change particularly acutely.[5]

Realtors saw their chance. In a familiar pattern that played out in communities across the country, agents steered prospective black buyers to the Pelham pocket and solicited sales from the area's white residents, seeking to capitalize on the growing demographic and economic instability.[6] The white homeowners that remained were becoming nervous about the very real possibility that, spurred by these unseemly real estate practices, the projections of swift demographic turnover would become a reality. They did not want to leave Mount Airy, with its old stone houses, its sidewalk-lined streets and vast network of parks and trails, its well-regarded elementary schools and well-established religious institutions. But they had to find a way to ensure that the neighborhood would remain a stable and, indeed, vibrant urban community. All around them they saw evidence of transition, of resistance and flight giving way to turnover and decline. They knew they needed a new approach.[7]

That spring, a group of Mount Airy homeowners, led by clergy from four area religious institutions—the Germantown Jewish Centre, the Epiphany Episcopal Church, the Unitarian Church of Germantown, and Summit Presbyterian Church—set out to learn all they could about local and national trends in housing and race relations. For months, they studied census data, city charters, religious texts, sociological studies, real estate appraisals, state, federal, and international constitutions, and human relations literature. By the end of the summer, they were convinced: their research, the group maintained, provided ample evidence to support the idea that a racially mixed neighborhood was both sustainable and, just maybe, desirable.[8]

Clergy members and lay leaders from each institution approved the report that October and presented the findings to focus groups from their congregations. These groups, too, lauded the results and decided to bring the material to the larger communities, giving congregants an opportunity to adopt, reject, or revise a proposal for a coordinated effort toward effecting interracial stability in the neighborhood.[9] Still uncertain of the planned objectives, the membership of Summit Presbyterian Church voted by a slim majority to withdraw from the burgeoning organization. The Jewish, Unitarian, and Episcopal congregations all passed the proposal. Under the plan, the institutions appointed a steering committee composed of the head clergy member and three parishioners from each congregation. On February 18, 1954, the group, adopting the name Church Community Relations Council of Pelham (CCRC), held its first meeting.[10]

Following the stalled campaign at Summit, a number of parishioners came together to voice concern over the church's unwillingness to join the local efforts. Though they remained unsure of the focus of the budding

CCRC, congregants saw the need for a community group to take on the unseemly realtors that were invading the neighborhood.[11] If they were unable to coordinate through the religious organization, they decided, they would create a secular space to address the growing unease over potential block-busting and redlining efforts. During the fall of 1953, the Summit Church group gathered several Mount Airy residents to carry on the research that the Council had collected that summer. Meeting in the home of Summit congregant Alan Mann, George Schermer of the Philadelphia Human Relations Commission, Jane Reinheimer of the American Friends Service Committee, and Kay Briner and William Cannaday of the Germantown Human Relations Committee continued to scrutinize the literature on race relations, seeking to understand how to create an integrated community. On February 3, 1954, weeks before the first meeting of the CCRC, the group issued its findings to an audience of forty-seven homeowners at the Unitarian Church.[12] A month later, following the selection of officers and the appointment of a steering committee, the West Mount Airy Neighbors Association (WMAN) was born. The new organization concentrated on building like-minded coalitions on individual blocks in an attempt to stave off rapid transition, with particular emphasis on the small area bounded by Lincoln Drive, Ellet Street, Wayne Avenue, and the Pennsylvania Railroad.[13]

Though the West Mount Airy Neighbors Association was originally founded as an alternative to the church-based organizing of the CCRC, board members quite consciously invoked a religious ethic in their publications and communications.[14] In the middle of the 1950s, in the early years of the Cold War and the domestic Red Scare, many Americans pitted a sense of pious democracy against godless Communism.[15] The fear of being branded a Communist was powerful. At the very first meeting of WMAN, members of the temporary steering committee expressed concerns over residents' willingness to join a left-leaning organization operating without the backing of religious authority. "People might hesitate to commit themselves," one board member warned, "because . . . of present fears regarding involvement in organizations. . . . [They] might be suspicious."[16] Without the institutional support that benefited the Church Community Relations Council, WMAN was careful in its literature to establish itself as a liberal prodemocracy organization. Before long, the West Mount Airy Neighbors Association and the CCRC realized that they were working toward similar goals. The two groups held joint meetings and organized collaborative interracial committees.[17]

In its statement of principles, "This We Believe About Our Neighborhood," the Church Community Relations Council set the tone for Mount Airy's integration efforts for decades to come: we want to remain in our community, and we'll welcome others in. "Gradually, Negro families of means are buying homes in the better neighborhoods," the statement said:

> Those that are moving into our neighborhood show every evidence of being good neighbors and of keeping their property up to standard. However, because of the myths and legends of race, the history of segregation and some of the traditional practices of the real estate market, a spirit of fear and panic often seeps into the hearts and minds of many people, causing them to list their houses for sale and run away. This running away is detrimental to the community. It forces too many sales in too short a time. It sometimes depreciates market values and disrupts patterns of community leadership and neighborhood acquaintance. People who love good homes, gracious living, a cultural atmosphere, should be encouraged to stay. People who appreciate and can contribute to such an environment should be encouraged to buy or rent in the neighborhood.[18]

Not wanting to give in to the idea that the American Dream had been relocated to newly forming suburbs, the CCRC presented a message of an elite liberal cosmopolitan identity; it was out of this desire to maintain their urban liberalness that community leaders created an affirmative civil rights duty.

Their comments played on the economic sensibilities of the northwest Philadelphia community. The CCRC evoked a dignified middle-class character not as something that West Mount Airy homeowners should seek to attain but rather as a truism. "The residents of the neighborhood are known to be people of refinement and culture," the statement of principles said. "Philadelphia, and Germantown in particular, has traditionally been a community in which democracy, human dignity, and respect for all people have been held in high esteem. The citizens of Germantown are known for their mature, unhurried exercise of good judgment in meeting social issues."[19] In linking the historic commitment to democratic ideals with the contemporary residential self-interest of maintaining the viability of the neighborhood, the CCRC sought to convince Mount Airy homeowners of the social and cultural value of an integrated community. The Council's vision of interracial living was, in a sense, performative, an outward manifestation of both economic status and liberal politics.[20] Whereas middle-class families across the nation were seeking refuge in newly constructed homogeneous suburbs, the CCRC attempted to convince its constituents that it was their very financial and social stature that made such a commitment to integration their providence.

At the same time, the CCRC aligned this middle-class economic sensibility with the country's Cold War agenda, outlining an international responsibility to uphold the principles of democracy, racial equality, and human dignity. "Today," it said, "from all over the world comes a challenge. 'Show us that democracy in America means dignity and respect for every person regardless of his color, his ancestry, or the manner of his worship. Show us that under your system, people . . . can live together in peace and mutual respect without boundary lines that segregate them by race, color, or religious creed.'"[21] The integrationists of the CCRC, well educated and well versed in contemporary political and social ideologies, justified their actions by grounding them in a policy-driven imperative to herald racial justice domestically in order to bolster the image of American democracy around the globe. As community leaders spoke of a democratic impulse and a drive toward the fulfillment of the American Dream, they employed this Cold War-infused language to attract the attention of mainstream white homeowners. According to the Council, residential integration lay at the core of American democracy. By working toward that ideal, they implied, Mount Airy residents were not only preserving their community; they were becoming better Americans.

The CCRC also worked to place local efforts within the larger movement toward residential integration across the United States. "The challenge is being met by many people of good will in neighborhoods throughout the country," the statement continued. "From San Francisco, Chicago, Detroit, Connecticut, and New York come stories of people who do not want to resist and run away when people of a different group become their neighbors."[22] Mount Airy's religious leaders sought to show their congregants that they were not alone in their integrationist approach to racial transition, that they were a part of a network of liberal Americans, all working toward creating genuine interracial communities.

By the middle of the 1950s, across the nation, city planners and community organizations were embarking on experimental projects to recast residential integration as both financially viable and morally compelling.[23] In Shaker Heights, Ohio, community leaders responded to the influx of black neighbors by working to redefine the character of their neighborhood from one advocating racial homogeneity to one that promoted class-based exclusivity. The suburban Shaker Heights had been founded in the first decades of the twentieth century as a retreat from the perceived harsh streets of Cleveland. The community was able to maintain that identity in the late 1950s and beyond by invoking a liberal agenda toward equality and marketing itself as a haven for the middle and upper classes regardless of race.[24]

City planner Morris Milgram saw the greatest potential for integration in the construction of entirely new neighborhoods. Beginning in the early 1950s, Milgram, who was born and raised on Manhattan's Lower East Side, built planned communities in urban and suburban spaces around the country. A pioneer of the open housing movement, the innovative businessman conceived of whole neighborhoods with controlled demographics. Between 1945 and 1960, the United States saw the construction of approximately fifty such private interracial housing developments, nearly eight thousand units in total. Roughly 40 percent of them were located in the mid-Atlantic region.[25] Although Milgram was reportedly ideologically opposed to racial quotas in his communities, he adopted the system to avoid the creation of all-black neighborhoods.[26] He mandated that his properties reflect the racial demographics of the region. In one of his northeast Philadelphia developments, Milgram sought an 80–20 percent, white-to-black ratio. Though he confronted challenges in securing funding and enticing white families to purchase homes, in total he developed integrated housing for more than twenty thousand people in Pennsylvania, New Jersey, New York, Virginia, Maryland, Illinois, California, Texas, and Washington, DC. Milgram went on to become the first recipient of the National Human Rights Award of the Federal Department of Housing and Urban Development in 1968.[27]

In West Mount Airy, following the CCRC's summer of research and the subsequent formation of WMAN, neighborhood integrationists saw promise in a different model of integration, one that stalled transition by highlighting mutual benefit and community involvement. George Schermer, who knew Milgram through his work in race relations, was one of the most vocal advocates for such an approach. When Schermer and his wife, Bernice, first began exploring neighborhoods in Philadelphia, Milgram tried to convince them to purchase a home in Greenbelt Knoll, one of his earliest planned communities, constructed in the far northeast reaches of the city. Milgram, himself, lived there for much of his adult life. But Schermer was not persuaded that the future of integration lay in new development. Instead, he said, the hope for creating racially integrated space rested in the areas experiencing demographic shifts; he believed that there was potential "in the process of a racially changing neighborhood, to slow down [that] process of transition."[28] Schermer moved his family to West Mount Airy because he believed that residential integration was the pathway to better race relations. He and his wife made their home in the neighborhood at the same time that residents of Mount Airy were trying to reconstitute their community to create a stable integrated neighborhood. He did not introduce the idea of intentional integration to local homeowners, but he quickly became integral to the success of the movement.

Born in Wright County, Minnesota, in 1910, Schermer found his way to race relations activism through local New Deal initiatives in Chicago in the 1930s. After graduating from high school in 1927, he spent eleven years working his way through various colleges around the Midwest. He briefly attended the University of Minnesota before enrolling in 1931 at North Central College in Naperville, Illinois. The following year, he transferred to George Williams College in Chicago, and ultimately graduated from the University of Chicago in 1937.[29] To earn money for school, Schermer took odd jobs, first working for a local 4-H organization, then with the Service for Unattached Men, developing group activities for men living in shelters. Eventually, he found himself at the Abraham Lincoln Center, a settlement house specializing in interracial programming. He was hired as the activities director and quickly became immersed in the divisive racial climate of Chicago's South Side. "That's where I received my initial orientation toward race relations," Schermer later reflected. The center was located on Cottage Avenue, the dividing line between a white and a black community. Hostilities were intense, Schermer recalled; they had "minor race riots" every few weeks.[30]

Working at the center offered him a staging ground for his early activism. A few nights each week, guests would come for dinner, political and civic and academic elites from around the nation who brought with them new and innovative ideas about the future of race relations in the United States. One of the greatest thrills of Schermer's young life was the night that A. Philip Randolph, acclaimed civil rights and labor activist and president of the Brotherhood of Sleeping Car Porters, arrived as a guest at the Settlement House: "I remember him talking about his hopes that someday he would stage a march on Washington. This was in the 1930s. He had great faith in the basic decency of the American people . . . and believed that by staging such a march, the plight of the American Negro would be brought to the attention of the American people and that good things would happen." Randolph later helped to organize the 1963 March on Washington for Jobs and Freedom, which brought more than two hundred thousand people to the Washington Mall to hear Martin Luther King, Jr. deliver his "I Have a Dream" speech. Schermer sat quietly during the meal, watching, listening, and learning all he could from the civil rights leader.[31]

In 1938, Schermer moved on from the Abraham Lincoln Center. He worked for two years in tenant services with the Chicago Housing Authority and then headed to Detroit to serve as the assistant director for management of the Detroit Housing Commission. He spent the next twelve years there, with the city's Housing Commission, the Federal Public Housing Authority, and, finally, the Mayor's Interracial Committee. Even as he struggled to combat unfriendly mayoral administrations and city officials, he worked hard to put into practice the abstract ideas that he had been mulling over ever since those settlement house dinners.[32] When Mayor Clark wooed him to Philadelphia in the early 1950s, Schermer brought with him the expertise that came from close to twenty years of working in the realm of race relations.

Schermer believed that if a community could come together with an intentional mandate toward integration, it could stave off the economic downturn traditionally associated with racial change. He and his wife, Bernice, moved to Philadelphia with their three children, intent on finding such a neighborhood. His work at city hall connected him with tight-knit communities around the city, bastions of liberalism that were intent on putting the interracial ideologies of Clark's reform government into practice. Schermer's colleagues immediately guided him to West Mount Airy, and upon visiting the neighborhood and talking to local residents and community leaders, he came away with the conviction that if any place could be intentionally integrated, it was this one. The Schermers moved to the 6700 block of McCallum Street and quickly settled in.[33] Though Schermer's professional life was dictated by the demands of his new position, in the evenings and on weekends he offered his time and expertise to the Mount Airy community.

Schermer's plans for reform—both in West Mount Airy and across the city—were clearly informed by the recent postwar turn in the philosophy of government liberalism. Whereas, during the 1930s, President Roosevelt's New Deal administration offered a widespread critique of unfettered capitalism and pursued an agenda of redistributive economic policies, by the World War II era the federal government had moved away from such class-oriented initiatives.[34] Postwar liberal reformers turned from economic transformation to rights-based politics, placing race relations and equality of opportunity at the center of the national agenda. Schermer considered his middle-class reform mandate a plausible goal for the city as a whole and for his own community of Mount Airy.[35]

As Schermer pursued an agenda grounded in reform-minded government liberalism, other community leaders in Mount Airy continued to focus their energy on faith-based organizing. In 1954, the Church Community Relations Council crafted a comprehensive approach for putting the integration project into action. The organization articulated a clear plan to educate residents and build understanding across racial lines, so as to counterbalance fear and panic.[36] Through the early years of stabilization, this ethos of individual change held strong. The CCRC initiative implored current homeowners to remain active members of the community and called on them to participate in "sell your neighborhood" campaigns, encouraging prospective buyers of "high standard" to purchase homes in the area.[37] Through public sermons, focus groups, and informal gatherings, the Council promoted a positive attitude about the racial change that was occurring in the neighborhood. These religious leaders, capitalizing on their esteem in the community, crafted a series of guidelines for how Mount Airy residents should react to their incoming black neighbors.

Mount Airy's religious organizing took place amid national conversations among faith-based communities over how best to respond to racial transition. Catholic neighborhoods often saw antagonism mount as white residents waged aggressive campaigns against African Americans moving onto their blocks. Many Jewish enclaves, where rabbis preached accommodation over resistance, experienced profound flight as congregations moved en masse from city neighborhoods to suburbs.[38] Jewish homeowners in West Mount Airy watched fellow Jews across Philadelphia rush to flee as African Americans began to move into their communities. To prevent a similar mass exodus, clergy members pushed hard to maintain an active and vibrant Jewish presence in the neighborhood.

Though small pockets of Jews had been living in historic Germantown since the colonial era, in the early twentieth century upwardly mobile Jewish immigrants began purchasing homes in the area, in search of a change from their North Philadelphia ethnic neighborhoods.[39] This demographic shift provided the impetus for an increasing Jewish cultural presence in the area and a growing desire for a formalized Jewish community. By the early 1930s, more than five hundred Jewish families were scattered throughout northwest Philadelphia, yet there were still no synagogues in the region and, as such, no cohesive Jewish identity. Some families joined congregations in other parts of the city and the surrounding suburbs, and many remained unaffiliated. As the Jewish population grew, though, and younger families began to move into the neighborhood, the community experienced a marked shift. Suddenly, Jewish residents in Germantown and Mount Airy articulated a pressing need for a Jewish space for their children. It was not that these American-born Jews necessarily wanted a religious presence in their lives; rather, they sought the social and cultural connectedness that a synagogue could provide. In 1934, Beth Israel, a Strawberry Mansion congregation, supervised Hebrew school programming for Jewish youth in the Germantown area. Two years later, the Germantown Jewish Centre began to take shape.[40]

During the summer of 1936, Philadelphia Jewish leaders held public and private meetings throughout the region, garnering support for the new institution. By early fall, nearly one hundred families had signed on. On September 28, at a dinner at the Benjamin Franklin Hotel in downtown Philadelphia, the burgeoning congregation elected its board of directors. One of the first orders of business was to determine the name of the new institution. After much deliberation, the board settled on the Germantown Jewish Centre, asserting that the Anglicized spelling would imply a secular connotation. Their decision was part of a larger recognition that the institution would serve as more than a synagogue; it would be a communal gathering space, grounded as much in ethnic identity as in religious adherence. It was the first step toward the formation of a cohesive Jewish community center in West Mount Airy, made up of a diverse group of families, many of whom were unfamiliar with traditional Jewish practices, customs, and observances.[41]

Two weeks later, the group signed a lease to rent the Georgian Hall Annex of the Pelham Club for $200 a month. On November 11, the congregants, under the leadership of interim rabbi Solomon Grayzel, formally dedicated their new institution.[42] The Germantown Jewish Centre had become a reality. By June 1942, when Elias Charry of Indianapolis took over as head rabbi, the congregation was home to more than three hundred families. They held services and lectures several times each week, and two hundred children were enrolled in religious school. The community was overflowing the small space it occupied at the corner of Emlen and Carpenter. It was time to look for a new home. After an exhaustive search of the region, GJC settled on a large tract of land at the corner of Lincoln Drive and Ellet Street in West Mount Airy. Contractors broke ground on June 8, 1946. Fifteen months later, the expanded Hebrew school was completed; on May 21, 1954, the community finally gathered to dedicate their new synagogue.[43]

Though the land had cost a mere $10,500, over the course of construction the building budget ballooned to nearly $1 million.[44] As the numbers continued to climb, Rabbi Charry noted hints of the changing composition of the neighborhood. Having worked closely with civic and governmental organizations throughout the Midwest, he was well aware of the national trends toward Jewish flight.[45] The rabbi realized that he would have to take quick, affirmative steps to convince Mount Airy Jews to remain in the neighborhood, and to entice new Jewish families to move in. Having made the fiscal investment in the community, Charry's commitment to the integration efforts of the Church Community Relations Council came as much out of economic necessity as it did out of liberal ideological fervor.

In the early 1950s, with Charry at the helm, GJC began a proactive campaign to retain and expand its membership base. The rabbi and the board of directors contacted new Jewish residents in the neighborhood, welcoming them to the community and inviting them to attend events and services at the synagogue. At times, they called upon the rhetoric of other religious practices to drive their message home. In a 1954 set of letters that went out to new homeowners, Charry wrote, "Since you have moved into our neighborhood, let me extend to you a warm welcome to the Germantown community. We consider Germantown, Mount Airy, and Chestnut Hill our 'parish.'"[46] Familiar with the trends against dislocation among Catholic neighborhoods in the United States, in evoking the imagery of the neighborhood parish Charry may well have been highlighting the geographic parameters that bound Catholic homeowners to their local churches, in the hopes that his constituents would make the same connection.

Charry and the board sent dozens of these letters each month, adhering to a detailed protocol designed to personalize the mailings as much as the mass appeal would allow. Handwritten revisions to an early draft mandated

Figure 2. Rabbi Elias Charry and Cantor Soloman Winter lead procession at Germantown Jewish Centre dedication, May 1954. Used with permission from Germantown Jewish Centre, Philadelphia.

that all further letters be typed, not mimeographed, and that each be hand-signed by the rabbi himself—stamped signatures were not acceptable—and addressed to an individual family.[47] Charry relied on established members of the congregation to be the eyes and ears of the neighborhood, alerting him of Jewish families moving into Mount Airy. On August 28, 1951, he received a letter from long-standing GJC member Leo Dushoff. "Mr. Benjamin Zieve, one of the founders of the Diamond Paper Box Company . . . decided to move to the new Presidential Apartments," the letter read. "He is a man of means, interested in synagogues, and would be a welcome addition to our membership."[48] Charry promptly followed up on Dushoff's referral, writing a personal letter to Mr. Zieve, inviting him to visit the congregation. "It would delight us greatly," he wrote, "if, after you have moved in, you would come to the Centre for religious services. . . . I have heard many nice things about you from Mr. Dushoff and would personally deem it an honor to greet you."[49] The GJC rabbi sought to build personal connections with his constituents in order to foster a sense of commitment both to the synagogue and to the larger neighborhood. By developing these relationships, he created a sense of accountability among his parishioners to support the viability of the community.

As Charry reached out to new residents in the Germantown area, he also worked to restructure the curriculum of the school and reorient religious services to liberalize congregational practices, in an effort to draw in a more diverse Jewish clientele. He hosted movie nights to attract younger, newly married couples to the Centre, in hopes that they would make a long-term commitment to the neighborhood and the congregation.[50] He spoke to senior groups, men's clubs, and women's organizations, doing all he could to spread the word about the benefits not only of *a* Jewish community but of *this* Jewish community. Rarely mentioning racial transition, he offered sermons that spoke to the liberal ideals of justice and liberty.[51] Throughout the 1950s and early 1960s, working as much within his own community as with the larger religious council in the neighborhood, Charry provided the key link, maintaining a Jewish institutional presence in northwest Philadelphia and expanding the Jewish (and consequently white) population in Mount Airy.

While religious institutions laid the foundation for residential integration in West Mount Airy, other organizers came together independently to try to foster a sense of social integration. Though many of these residents had worked for years in race relations in Philadelphia's political, educational, and business worlds, their efforts in the mid-1950s centered on bringing community members together in ways that, in a sense, transcended race. In this early period of integration in the neighborhood, activists built their campaigns on a platform of individual choice.[52]

The Allens Lane Arts Center, founded in 1953, was one of the most prolific organizations to emerge from this initial wave of reform. That year, the Henry Home and School Association (HHSA)—the parent-teacher organization at C. W. Henry School, the public elementary school at the geographic center of the neighborhood's integration efforts—joined together with a group of committed neighborhood residents to create a community space that would use the arts as a vehicle through which like-minded people of different races and creeds could come together.[53]

Marjorie Kopeland, who presided over the HHSA and spearheaded the project, came to neighborhood organizing by way of her work with the Fellowship Commission. Founded in 1941 as the Young People's Interracial Fellowship of Philadelphia, the Commission would become the nation's oldest private human rights organization. Though it originated as a series of disparate groups responding to the institutionalized anti-Semitism in the city, by the middle of the decade the association had expanded its agenda to include race-based discrimination. Bringing together such groups as the local NAACP chapter, the International Institute, the National Conference of Christians and Jews, the Society of Friends, and, ultimately, the American Civil Liberties Union, the Commission worked both to educate the public on issues of tolerance and to implement initiatives to combat concrete racial discrimination.[54] "My roots were really in Fellowship House," Kopeland later reflected. "That is where I got my orientation about group relations."[55] She worked on the organization's "Units for Unity" campaign, teaming up individuals of different faiths and races to lead intergroup dialogues throughout the city.

Kopeland joined the HHSA when her children entered elementary school, and in 1952, when her oldest daughter was getting set to graduate, she became the organization's president. At the beginning of the fall semester that year, the new leader brought together more than a dozen fathers from the neighborhood to discuss how to put Henry School's annual theme, Living Together in the Community, into practice. "I invited men to that meeting instead of mothers," Kopeland later said, "[because] I was aware that we as mothers were very active during the day at the HHSA, and I was very interested in involving more fathers in their children's activities." Sitting in Kopeland's Mount Pleasant Avenue living room that evening were two members of the Philadelphia Orchestra, as well as several accomplished artists and well-connected art supporters. By the end of that night, the group had conceived of a community center that would bring people together around a common interest in the arts.[56]

Though community energy was critical to the formation of the new arts center, the group quickly saw the need for external support to create a sustainable presence in the neighborhood. The new organization solicited the financial support of the Ford Foundation's "Living Together through the Arts" fund. Founded in 1936 with the mandate to offer support "for scientific, educational, and charitable purposes, all for the public welfare," the Ford Foundation emerged in the years following World War II as a national resource for domestic and global nonprofit organizations working toward community betterment.[57] As part of the early Cold War rights-based agenda, the foundation provided support to local institutions that were advancing the goals of postwar liberalism.

According to a public report disseminated in 1950, the Ford Foundation, evoking familiar Cold War era democratic principles, was working to support organizations that would contribute to global peace and justice. Their mission statement employed the rhetoric of freedom and equality in highlighting the need for technological, educational, and cultural innovation in order to "increase knowledge of factors that influence or determine human conduct, and extend such conduct for the maximum benefit of individuals and society."[58] The Ford Foundation provided key resources for fostering both individual commitment and organizational capacity at the local level, and the founders of the Allens Lane Arts Center, by positioning their integration efforts within this larger movement toward fulfilling American ideals on a global scale, found the institutional support they needed to develop long-term infrastructure and programming. With the backing of Ford, Kopeland and her associates successfully petitioned the Fairmount Park Commission to lease them public parklands at the corner of McCallum Street and Allens Lane for one dollar annually.[59] On June 29, 1953, the Allens Lane Arts Center was officially incorporated as a nonprofit organization.[60]

As they waited for the Park Commission to refurbish the small guard station on the property, the group held its first classes at Henry School and Summit Church. And though it was the fathers who Kopeland initially called together to craft a plan for the organization, it was the mothers who went on to run the board and coordinate staff and volunteers.[61] At its inception, Kopeland was elected the center's first president. Shirley Melvin, who went on to cofound one of the first all-female real estate agencies in the city, joined the executive committee, and Bernice Schermer, wife of the ever-present Human Relations Commission director, signed on as vice president.[62]

When the Schermers first moved into the neighborhood, George had thrown himself into his work with the Commission and Bernice joined in neighborhood activities. She quickly formed a network of friends, a combination of members of the Unitarian Church, which the couple joined as soon as they arrived to the area; the wives of George's colleagues in the city government; and the mothers of their children's classmates. As she familiarized herself with the neighborhood efforts, she involved herself in community organizing.[63] "There were a number of us," Bernice later recalled, "who were willing to work at making life richer. [We were] willing to roll up our sleeves and really work at making this happens. We wanted to be integrated. We formed committees, within the school, within the church, within the synagogue. Everyone seemed to pitch in . . . there was a groundswell of activity."[64] Their early meetings lasted long into the night. Often, the women would plan and organize and corral support until two and three o'clock in the morning.[65] "Everybody is nervous . . . when you start something as big [and] brand new as that," Shirley Melvin remembered, "and it was a huge amount of work."[66]

Though artistic expression was central to the art center's mandate on paper, it was clear that the organization sought to use the arts as a vehicle through which to unite Mount Airy residents of all races, ages, and religions. The center offered ballroom dance lessons and watercolor classes. It housed spaces for music and ceramics and drama. And neighbors flocked to its doors.[67] "I wish I could say . . . we had some high, lofty aesthetic reasons for wanting to bring people to the arts," Kopeland later reflected, "but we felt we could bring people together through the arts."[68] One of the center's early initiatives was a community nursery school. For some of the women on the board, it served as an alternative to the religious institutions around the neighborhood. "Lots of people were going to the synagogues and the churches," Shirley Melvin later recalled, "but most of my friends wanted their kids to have an art background rather than a religious background."[69]

Figure 3. Children dance at Allens Lane Arts Center, *Philadelphia Bulletin*, 1957.
Used with permission from Special Collections Research Center, Temple University
Libraries, Philadelphia.

The nursery school, Melvin believed, could offer neighborhood families an
art-oriented early childhood experience instead. Shortly after its founding,
the program expanded to include one of the city's first integrated summer
day camps as well.[70]

The arts center offered a shared experience to disparate groups of individuals. The goal of social integration required organizers to bring people together under a set of common interests, breaking down identity barriers. In
that way, Allens Lane became an outlet for neighbors to foster relationships
that went beyond race. These communal gathering grounds—the religious
institutions, the HHSA, and the arts center—served the neighborhood
well. The everyday interactions that grew out of them bolstered the emotional
appeals toward morality that organizations such as the Church Community
Relations Council and the West Mount Airy Neighbors Association espoused
at meetings, giving residents the space to put their integrationist philosophies
into action.

The neighborhood began to see concrete results from community efforts within the first few years of transition. By 1955, West Mount Airy's black population had expanded to 6.4 percent, distributed over 45 percent of the area's geographic reach. Though 50 percent of the black families that had moved to the area in the first years of integration settled along the Lincoln-Pelham corridor, by the middle of the decade new African American transplants were living on eighteen of the neighborhood's forty-one residential blocks.[71] These blocks made up the physical and organizational center of the integration efforts, bound by Johnson Street, Germantown Avenue, Wissahickon Avenue, and Allens Lane. Even as the densely populated Sharpnack area remained overwhelming black, African American families were buying homes across the community, and while some white homeowners were leaving, the overall transition left little cause for concern; West Mount Airy saw turnover through the decade settle at 8 percent to 10 percent annually, in line with estimates for the normal rate of turnover, defined by the American Institute of Planners as 8 percent to 12 percent.[72]

Still, the stability that neighborhood activists created was precarious. In 1953, housing prices in this integrated center began to decline.[73] Further, community leaders believed that realtors were continuing to direct most prospective black home buyers to the region's south-central Pelham section, the same area where black families first began to congregate at the beginning of the decade. White families in Pelham started to panic at the new cries of instability.[74] Though these early efforts had the effect of slowing down the rate of change, by the late 1950s George Schermer and other Mount Airy leaders had come to believe that in order to create long-term stability and, indeed, social capital in integrated space, community initiatives would have to be consolidated.

These discrete organizations, said Schermer, were able to effect change in localized regions around the community. They brought people together and encouraged one-on-one interactions that started to break down some of the racial barriers that were so deeply entrenched in the larger American society. But, he said, such ad hoc, singularly focused groups could only go so far in creating long-term stabilization. Schermer had learned from his work in Detroit that the only way to create sustainable change was to develop a larger infrastructure, bridging individual responsibility with institutional authority.[75]

By the late 1950s, under Schermer's leadership, the West Mount Airy Neighbors Association was beginning to position itself as both neighborhood clearinghouse and voice of the community. The group worked to serve as a filter, gathering and disseminating information and facilitating communication between city and state government officials and Mount Airy residents. Schermer believed that the group could function as a localized version of an urban renewal corporation, a civic organization designed to rehabilitate the neighborhood and offer a sense of stability in an era of social, residential, and cultural transformation.[76]

With the reconstitution of West Mount Airy Neighbors as this larger umbrella institution, Schermer believed that his vision could become a reality. In 1958, he issued a call to a cadre of the Mount Airy citizenry, those he thought had both the means and the influence to serve as the building blocks for such an organization. Several residents heeded Schermer's call. After a series of planning meetings, they founded the Neighbors League of West Mount Airy. Their statement of intent, issued on November 18, 1958, described the group as a collaboration of more than fifty Mount Airy families seeking to create a formal organization, incorporated as a nonprofit civic group, with the goal of maintaining and improving the quality of life in Mount Airy. Specifically, the Neighbors' League perceived itself as an organization to unite all those who lived in or had an interest in the neighborhood. While never mentioning race or racial transition, the statement of intent called for a solution to problems with an eye toward the greatest mutual benefit, including real estate and zoning initiatives, schools and education, public relations and information, membership, and finance.[77] With careful scripting, the League was speaking to the quiet majority of West Mount Airy residents, those who simply wanted to go about their day-to-day lives and feel assured that their community would remain stable. In addressing these mutual benefits and highlighting the services and institutions that attracted families to the area, Schermer's group worked to allay the concerns of many in the neighborhood who did not consider themselves to be integrationists, not the few who were actively pushing for integrated living.

Two months later, the organization renamed itself West Mount Airy Neighbors (WMAN), but the objectives remained the same. On January 13, 1959, the new community group held its first public meeting at the recently constructed Lingelbach Elementary School. More than three hundred Mount Airy residents attended.[78] The flyers advertising the event, distributed by the Germantown Jewish Centre, the Unitarian Church, and local Boy Scout troops 187 and 188, called on local residents to take a proactive role in shaping the identity of the community. "Protect your property and its surroundings through community organizing," the call read.[79] Like the original Neighbors' League platform, the WMAN advertisements did not mention the movement of African Americans into the community; they simply invited residents to discuss what makes—and how to achieve—a "good community."[80] By not calling attention to race or integrated living, organizers hoped to avoid the residential panic that so often characterized periods of racial transition.

In an early WMAN brochure, disseminated to more than seven hundred households in the neighborhood, the organization described the changes taking place in the community. "Americans are the moving-est people," it said. "We move an average of once every five years. So all kinds of Americans are moving out of our neighborhood and all kinds of Americans are moving in."[81] The brochure went on to explain that West Mount Airy Neighbors would provide a venue for residents to think and talk about these changes. It said that the organization was dedicated to "seeking solutions to our neighborhood problems and encouraging changes that [would] lead to an even better place to live."[82] The group promised to ensure that the school would meet the educational needs of local children; that they would hold accountable real estate brokers who were pushing for panic selling; that they would provide services for the neighborhood youth; and that they would foster communication to relieve the inevitable misunderstandings that arise when five thousand families live in close proximity to one another. Finally, it called on residents to actively involve themselves in the community.[83]

Quickly, the organization gained momentum. In March 1959, WMAN had 180 members, with a hundred more new membership forms to process. By December of that year, membership had grown to 335, and six months later, 500 residents had signed on.[84] Many of the group's earliest members were clustered along the neighborhood's northwestern borders. These blocks were generally home to wealthier white families, many of whom would not see their first black neighbors until the late 1960s. With much invested in the stability and status of the neighborhood, these residents likely joined West Mount Airy Neighbors not out of a commitment to interracial living but out of a desire to preserve the economic, social, and cultural viability of the community.[85]

From WMAN's inception, though, both the membership and the leadership of the group were interracial. Although the organization never set a formal mandate for racial quotas, believing that it was antithetical to its egalitarian mission, the demographics of the group quickly stabilized to mirror the racial composition of the neighborhood—by the late 1950s, roughly 15 percent of West Mount Airy residents were African American, as were 15 percent of the WMAN membership and leadership. By 1965, the neighborhood was 36 percent black and 64 percent white, and by 1970 the breakdown stabilized at 42 percent black and 58 percent white.[86] As part of its central mission, West Mount Airy Neighbors, in fact, insisted on inter-racial participation and collaboration. Although such an objective made initial meetings a bit awkward, leaders believed that it was essential to the organization's desire to offer a model for genuine interracial living. Just two years after its founding, in 1961, WMAN elected its first black president, Matthew J. Bullock.[87]

At the organization's first official meeting on February 19, 1959, the Real Estate Practices Committee laid out a plan for dismantling local steering, redlining, and blockbusting efforts. Like the Church Community Relations Council before it, WMAN's early efforts focused on eliminating these un-savory real estate practices that were still beleaguering the neighborhood.[88] But unlike the CCRC, the 1959 incarnation of WMAN sought to effect structural change, to move beyond the notion of individual moral suasion and challenge the deeply enmeshed political and economic practices that perpetuated residential segregation. The group wanted to attack racism at an institutional level. First, the WMAN board worked to establish relation-ships with local realtors, demanding that both black and white potential buyers be shown houses on every block. They called on local brokers to sign on to their newly passed Real Estate Code of Ethics. They sought to mini-mize the presence of sale-related notices by calling for the abolition of "For Sale" signs throughout the community.[89] To provide incentives for compli-ance, WMAN directed prospective sellers and buyers to conforming brokers. The organization worked with local newspapers, including the city's paper of record at that time, the *Philadelphia Bulletin*, to publish the names of ethical realtors in the neighborhood.[90] They sent out brochures to residents with lists of the region's principled agents and urged them to consider using their services if they were considering a move. At the same time, the organi-zation collected information about offending realtors. With each blockbust-ing effort, WMAN contacted the soliciting broker and threatened him with loss of business. Later, WMAN took its mission a step further, issuing a plan to bar realtors from the neighborhood who had induced panic selling in other areas of the city.[91]

Month after month, the committee addressed residents' complaints about real estate practices. Board members would speak to offending agents, asking them to reconsider their efforts and sign on to the neighborhood's code. In January 1962, the committee reviewed the case of realtor Thomas J. McCarthy, who had left in place a "Sold" sign on the 600 block of West Hortter Street. The secretary of WMAN called McCarthy personally and alerted him to the new real estate ethics campaign. After reading the materials sent to him, McCarthy signed on to the statement and removed the "Sold" sign from in front of the house. McCarthy became the twenty-third realtor in the area to meet the organization's requirements.[92]

WMAN employed similar techniques to curtail the practice of redlining. The board solicited local banks and lending institutions to offer favorable mortgages to all financially secure prospective buyers, regardless of race.[93] Board members met individually with bank managers and representatives for the city's Mortgage Bankers Association to explain their neighborhood efforts. They believed that "if mortgage lenders [knew] how many people [were] working actively to maintain and improve [the] area, they [would] feel secure in their loans to the community."[94] In the early 1960s, some area banks also joined the effort to highlight the neighborhood as a stable, integrated community. Following WMAN's 1962 marketing campaign, the local branch of Hamilton Savings and Loan Association displayed brochures in its lobby for interested clients.[95] At the same time, the group worked to ensure long-term stability, by petitioning the city council and the local and state planning commissions to create and enforce fair housing laws.[96]

Gradually, these efforts began to pay off. The neighborhood saw rates of unwanted solicitations drop dramatically and housing turnover begin to slow. Even in the most affected sections of the neighborhood along the Lincoln Drive corridor, where annual rates of change had reached 14.3 percent in the first years of transition, by the early 1960s turnover had stabilized to a 5.65 percent annual average.[97] A 1959 report by the Church Community Relations Council noted that in a 1,000-home section of the neighborhood, only 80 properties had changed hands in the previous twelve months; 52 to white home buyers, 26 to African Americans, one to a Chinese American, and one to someone of "undetermined race." "Nearly all new buyers are business and professional people," noted the report, and "the physical appearance of the neighborhood has maintained at the same high standard."[98]

Of course, the process of integrating was not without disruption. Throughout this first decade of community efforts, the neighborhood did see isolated instances of racial discrimination, hostility, and outright ignorance. A white woman on Washington Lane had all of her windows changed because she believed that her black neighbors were listening through the metallic putty on her well-worn panes. There was the black man on Walnut Lane who was resting in his backyard after surgery. His neighbor, a white woman, jumped over the fence and hit the man in the leg with one of his own crutches. And there was the time that an African American man, angered by the remarks of his white neighbor, put a garden hose through the neighbor's mail slot and turned on the water.[99]

Ernestine Thornton, who moved to Mount Airy in 1957, felt unwelcomed by the community at the outset. "I have lived on Sedgwick Street two days," she said at a September meeting of the Sedgwick Neighbors Association. "I don't like my neighbors and I'm thinking seriously about moving again." Thornton, who the *Philadelphia Tribune* described as a well-dressed, attractive Negro woman, implied that she had experienced racially motivated antagonism after moving to Mount Airy. "My children attend a private interracial school and although they know the differences in the color, they have never felt that difference to be shameful," she said. "I have never been made to feel that I was a problem, and I don't want to be a problem."[100] African American resident Don Black, who moved to Mount Airy with his family in 1955, experienced occasional instances of racialized aggression toward his children. One afternoon, Black's son, Donald Jr., came home from school distraught, wondering why his last name was Black. "The kids at school were kidding him," the elder Black later recalled.[101] In 1958, when stones shattered the windows of a neighbor's home, Black's children were blamed. As Black later recounted, the neighbor received an anonymous postcard, suggesting that his two children were responsible, though the kids were too small even to throw the stones that far. The events followed on the heels of the brutal gang murder of In-Ho Oh, a Korean graduate student at the University of Pennsylvania.[102] Soon after the windows were broken, Black remembered, his family received a threatening postcard of their own. "If you don't watch your children and stop them from throwing stones," he recalled it saying, "they're going to end up like In-Ho Oh."[103]

Still, by the end of the decade West Mount Airy seemed to be beginning to resemble Schermer's vision of an intentionally integrated residential community. The Allens Lane Arts Center was thriving. WMAN's membership rolls were growing weekly. Blockbusting realtors were abandoning their efforts and house prices were beginning to stabilize.[104] Organizers believed that they had successfully stemmed the movement of white residents out of the community and laid the groundwork for a stable integrated neighborhood. In the early 1960s, West Mount Airy Neighbors began to look outward. Recognizing that sustainable interracial living would require both ongoing vigilance and a widespread creative marketing campaign, community leaders sought to bring their message to a wider audience, proclaiming racial integration as the new American Dream.

Chapter 3

MARKETING INTEGRATION

Interracial Living in the White Imagination

On May 13, 1962, two hundred individuals from thirty-one United Nations member countries came to West Mount Airy to, as WMAN described it, see how Americans lived. As the *Philadelphia Evening Bulletin* reported, "They [saw] Americans from a grass roots level: eating typical meals, enjoying a get-together, watching TV, seeing historical sites—finding out what [made] the average family tick."[1] West Mount Airy Neighbors had organized the event to "[sell] the neighborhood through creative marketing."[2] Seeking to offer an example of a thriving interracial community, residents invited UN delegates and employees to stay in their homes and live with their families, and they compelled local and national media outlets to report on it. With these efforts, leaders in the fight for residential integration encouraged the rest of the world to witness their conception of democracy in action.

The United Nations Delegates Weekend marked a critical moment in the life of West Mount Airy Neighbors. The event was part of the organization's first widespread publicity campaign; through a comprehensive regional and national media push, neighborhood leaders set out to sell the Mount

Airy integration project. Capitalizing on the success of early efforts to drive out blockbusting realtors and stem the flight of white families from the neighborhood, the WMAN board saw an opportunity to take their message beyond the confines of the area to try to attract new prospective home buyers and to spread the virtues of integration across the nation. In presenting West Mount Airy as a model postwar American neighborhood, leaders worked to craft a vision of a new urban ideal: an economically stable, liberally minded, racially integrated space.

This innovative marketing came to play a vital role in the organization's long-term goals of preserving the neighborhood as a vibrant, open community through the remainder of the twentieth century. But even as the efforts had the effect of maintaining interracial living, it also highlighted the limitations of the neighborhood's collaborative vision. WMAN's 1962 campaign was fundamentally grounded in the meaning of integration as it lived in the white imagination. For the white homeowners of West Mount Airy, the integrated community functioned because of a careful balance between economic preservation and democratic ideal. The WMAN integration project at once allowed residents to protect their homes and their quality of life in the Philadelphia neighborhood and to live out their vision of manifested racial justice.[3] In the postwar conception of liberalism, where economic welfare had given way to a rights-based agenda and middle-class identity had become the focal point of race-based reform, integration in Mount Airy, for the area's white homeowners, was grounded in notions of middle-class access and equality of opportunity.[4] Even as this conception of integration complemented the motivations of many black families moving into the area—as the class-based exclusivity critical for white residents allowed for the economic security that so many black home buyers sought—the West Mount Airy Neighbors publicity campaign of the early 1960s revealed a profound disconnect in the meaning of integration. The experience of interracial living in northwest Philadelphia had become bound by racial identity.[5]

By the early 1960s, West Mount Airy Neighbors had begun to experience a degree of success in their efforts to drive out blockbusting realtors and stem the flight of white families from the community. Though the organization continued to serve as a watchdog group, involving itself in situations that required institutional attention, WMAN shifted its focus toward the larger goal of maintaining and fostering integration. To manage the character of the neighborhood, organizers saw the need to expand localized networks, to bring the story of integration into broader conversations about racial justice and the viability of postwar American cities. In order to sustain their newfound residential integration, community leaders believed, they had to craft an image of the neighborhood as an ideal blend of racial liberalism, cosmopolitan urbanity, and middle-class respectability.[6]

A decade earlier, in the wake of the Second World War and amid growing Cold War tensions, the United States saw the emergence of a new middle-class orientation that heralded home ownership, the primacy of the nuclear family, and a rising consumer culture. For many, this new American ideal existed in the modern housing stock of the recently forming homogeneous suburbs. These homes offered a postwar baby-boom generation more room for their expanding families and more space for their new consumer goods, as wartime restrictions on production lifted and the economy expanded rapidly.[7] The federal government incentivized suburban relocation, with subsidized loans through the Federal Housing Administration and new road construction under the Federal Highway Act, which made travel around urban centers easier than ever before. By 1960, more than 40 percent of Americans were living in suburban communities; the rates had doubled in twenty years.[8]

In addition to new construction, these developing neighborhoods offered families larger plots of land and manicured green spaces. For many Americans, cities came to be seen as overcrowded, industrial landscapes; they believed that the suburbs could offer them more room, bigger yards, and tree-lined streets. According to sociologist Herbert Gans in his 1967 study of Levittown (one of the first postwar suburban developments), 34 percent of individuals moving to the planned community in suburban Philadelphia cited lack of playgrounds and "urban dirt, noise, and traffic" as key reasons for leaving the city.[9] Neighborhoods such as Levittown were carefully constructed to offer the feeling of a garden community. Architects of the planned suburb included fruit trees and evergreens on each plot of land, working to integrate a park-like atmosphere into the residential landscape.[10] These managed green spaces were meant to highlight those amenities that older, industrialized cities could not offer.

With such emphasis on the merits of suburban development, in northwest Philadelphia integrationist leaders recognized that to retain current residents and attract new buyers, they needed to craft an image of the neighborhood that at once capitalized on the physical values of the suburban ideal and extolled the virtues of city living. In the early 1960s, organizers worked to reorient the contemporary American Dream away from newly erected communities, and instead position it within West Mount Airy. By creating a nexus between race, class, and respectability, they sought to challenge the suburban ideal by depicting interracial communities as both models of consumer-oriented middle-class culture and havens for liberal race relations.[11]

In 1962, WMAN published its first brochure to be disseminated to a city-wide audience. Titled *West Mount Airy: Green Country Town in Philadelphia Welcomes You,* the advertisement touted the neighborhood as "a beautiful green community in northwest Philadelphia [that] has in abundance the serene, satisfying atmosphere that many families want." Offering all of the city's advantages, the publication said, "West Mount Airy proves that you need not move to the suburbs to enjoy the peaceful, relaxed tempo of living with nature. Here, twenty minutes from City Hall, is a truly green country town in Philadelphia."[12] WMAN's allusion to the region as a "green country town" referenced one of William Penn's early descriptions of Philadelphia. On September 30, 1681, Penn relayed to his commissioners his vision for the city: "Let every house be placed, if the person pleases, in the middle of its plat, as to the breadthway of it, so that there may be ground on each side for gardens or orchards, or fields, that it may be greene country towne, which will never be burnt and always wholesome."[13] By evoking green space as a hallmark of Mount Airy, organizers sought at once to link the neighborhood to the city's historic heritage and to challenge the apparent conflict between urban space and the natural world, to bridge the desire for trees and parks with the liberal ethos of urbanity. Residents did not need to leave the city, WMAN implied; they could find in the northwest Philadelphia neighborhood a lush physical landscape and a cosmopolitan culture. In a sense, the organization was offering a model for an alternative urbanism. In an era when the American ideal was quickly becoming synonymous with a suburban utopia, WMAN set out to sell the integrated community by recasting urbanity as a beacon for middle-class liberalism. Although crime and disinvestment still existed in the slums of North Philadelphia, in West Mount Airy, neighborhood activists maintained, residents could attain an identity of urbane refinement that combined middle-class propriety with social liberalism.

At the same time, integrationists in Mount Airy worked to redefine the meaning of modernity within the context of their integrationist ideal. Because the neighborhood could not compete with suburban communities for new housing stock and amenities, leaders tried to separate the material conditions of the region from the ideological.[14] In selling the physical landscape of the area, they relied on the language of refinement over trend-setting, of a natural ideal over a suburban homogeneity. Even the title of the 1962 brochure, referencing Penn's 1681 vision of Philadelphia as a "greene country town," highlighted the historic roots of the city, focusing on celebrated tradition over contemporary style. In casting the *character* of the community, however, organizers showcased notions of progress, of worldliness, of advancement. Working against powerful cultural trends, WMAN sought to reshape the image of the "modern" from material to philosophical.

Journalist Kenneth Gehret, special contributor to the *Christian Science Monitor*, offered such a description in assessing the viability of Mount Airy as a stable integrated community in postwar America. "Can a neighborhood maintain its attractiveness as a place to live," wondered Gehret, "as its houses and other structures age and its population changes?" The writer equated the outdated stone architecture with the community's push back against the realtor-driven panic and suburban flight in the early 1950s. But, Gehret went on, this stasis was not simply a reaction against progress. "The purpose was not to stand pat on tradition or in some contrived way to 'control' the influx of Negroes," he wrote. "Traditions, [the community] said, are only the foundation for the future. WMAN was formed not only to maintain but also to improve the community as a place to live."[15] Gehret made clear that the organization strived not just to preserve the neighborhood as it existed in the years following World War II but to serve as a model for a liberal, urban space in the latter half of the twentieth century.

This image of integration that West Mount Airy Neighbors put forth in its early publicity efforts focused primarily on the would-be white residents of the neighborhood, and tended to minimize the experience of the African American families moving in.[16] Those working on the marketing campaign were largely white and middle class, and they were selling integration to a decidedly white middle-class audience. They painted a picture of natural traditionalism, economic stability, social liberalism, cultural vibrancy, and ideological modernism; this, the predominantly white leadership of WMAN claimed in 1962, was what integration could provide.

This integrationist model that West Mount Airy Neighbors asserted was a part of a developing national movement aimed at celebrating the economic and cultural virtues of interracial living. In 1957, for instance, filmmaker Lee Bobker directed *All the Way Home*, a thirty-seven-minute fictional account of a black family moving into a white neighborhood. Bobker's work took on a definitively documentary style in promoting the trends toward residential integration. Though the project was commissioned by the NAACP, Bobker, by telling the story of open housing from the perspective of white middle-class suburbanites, allowed white viewers to see the world from the fictional residents' perspective. They expressed fears over threats to safety and economic instability. They worried that their property values would fall, that their daughters would fall victim to racially motivated crimes, that the quality of their schools would decline.[17] Bobker's film gave voice to the very same fears expressed by white residents of transitioning neighborhoods around the country, both in heated community conversations and in the privacy of their own homes.

But Bobker did not stop there. Rather, the filmmaker responded to these concerns with images and voice-over commentary of the well-dressed, well-behaved black family moving in. The African Americans seeking to gain entry into the neighborhood are just like the whites who already live there, Bobker seemed to be saying. "A man is a desirable neighbor if he's alright financially and he doesn't throw beer cans all over his front lawn," one resident in the film proclaimed.[18] It was not skin color that created community cohesion; it was common values, similar goals, and comparable bank accounts. Films like Bobker's made their way to Mount Airy for Rabbi Charry's popular Movie Nights at the Germantown Jewish Centre.[19]

Two years later, the *Saturday Evening Post* published a seven-page spread titled "When a Negro Moves Next Door." The 1959 piece chronicled the experience of a Baltimore neighborhood as the first African American family moved into the community. According to Ellsworth Rosen, Ashburton, Maryland, resident and the author of the article, "the color of my neighbor's skin does not bother me at all. His income and behavior are just about the same as mine." Rosen went on to decry the unsavory real estate tactics designed to drive out white homeowners.[20] Throughout the article, his message was clear: integrated neighborhoods are not only inevitable but also beneficial to the larger society when those working toward integration possess a common conception of community. These depictions of residential integration in the national media evidenced the way in which many white liberals conceived of integrated space. Underlying the necessary political orientation toward race relations was the notion that for interracial living to work, all residents had to subscribe to the ideals of middle-class respectability.[21]

Such a conception of common values was fundamental to the success of integration in West Mount Airy. Long-time residents articulated a clear focus on the economic standing of black residents moving into the community during the early years of transition. "The people I knew . . . , their values were so stable," Marjorie Kopeland, cofounder of the Allens Lane Arts Center, remembered. "They were values that I reflected, that I found in my own family. [The Black families moving in placed an] emphasis upon family, an emphasis upon education."[22] "The people who came in were just as professional as the people who were leaving . . . , as the white people who lived there," Doris Polsky, who moved to the neighborhood as a teenager in 1942, recalled.[23] It was this economic equilibrium that allowed for the initial sense of stability on the blocks and in the homes; for these white homeowners, the professional status of incoming African American buyers was paramount to the success of peaceful, stable integration. It was a necessary precursor to the liberal politics that residents came to stress in their public pronouncements of the neighborhood.

When West Mount Airy Neighbors began to plan the 1962 United Nations Delegates Weekend, community leaders highlighted this white-centric vision of integration to the two hundred representatives from thirty-one U.N. member countries coming to visit. They welcomed their guests to the neighborhood and drew their attention to virtues of interracial living. But even as the event focused on the international visitors, Mount Airy activists, through a carefully coordinated media campaign, used the weekend to showcase for the nation their vision of a reconceived American ideal, manifested in the form of an economically stable, racially integrated city neighborhood.[24]

In the late 1950s and early 1960s, communities across the country came together to host United Nations delegates. The goal of these events was simple: to bring the international community into the American home, to offer foreign dignitaries a glimpse into the life of the American family. Echoing the ideas of the nation's Cold War prodemocracy agenda, these weekends were meant to showcase American virtue, to sway representatives from nonaligned nations around the world toward the benefits of the democratic system.[25] The UN was not directly involved in such efforts. Rather, the company Private Entertainment for UN Delegations, Inc. served as the liaison for all coordination.[26] Typically planned for the spring or summer, when the General Assembly was not in session, these weekends gave delegates the chance to relax and enjoy the comforts that the democratic system could afford.

One such event took place in the Philadelphia area in 1959, when the Swarthmore Committee for the United Nations hosted sixty delegates in the small college town twenty miles south of the city.[27] Nearly one hundred UN representatives came to Swarthmore in May of that year to spend the weekend with host families from the community, visiting local sites and attending dinners and dances.[28] When West Mount Airy Neighbors learned of the festivities in Swarthmore, the organization decided to host its own UN Delegates Weekend. Working with the UN's private entertainment affiliate, the board sent personal notes to each delegate, inviting them to spend a spring weekend in the community.[29]

In conceiving of the weekend, however, WMAN made one notable change from the model that Swarthmore had put forth three years earlier: rather than offering their guests a quiet weekend away from the frenzy of New York City, the group sought to provide delegates with a glimpse into the experience of an integrated America. As the *Philadelphia Sunday Bulletin* reported during the event, "important and inherent in the plan for this visit is that they will see an integrated neighborhood. Delegates from white nations are staying with American Negroes and African statesmen are the welcome guests of white hosts."[30] Community leaders in Mount Airy viewed the weekend as an opportunity, once again, to position the neighborhood's integration project within the context of the nation's Cold War agenda. Just as the CCRC had, nearly a decade earlier, linked civil rights progress to the international image of democracy, WMAN saw potential in the UN Delegates Weekend to highlight their experiment in interracial living.[31] As the federal government crafted policy initiatives to highlight for the world the nation's progress in civil rights, West Mount Airy Neighbors worked to draw attention to a community putting these integrationist sensibilities into practice; by connecting their own efforts to the international fight for democracy, they were able to gain exposure in front a national audience.

Armed with funding from the Germantown Savings Fund, the Broad Street Trust, Liberty Real Estate Bank and Trust, First Pennsylvania Banking and Trust, and the Girard Trust Corn Exchange Bank, the organization focused in on the weekend of May 12–13, 1962. By selecting this date, the board believed, they could coordinate with the annual Germantown Week celebration, a local festival that commemorated northwest Philadelphia's history and community, and thereby increase their visibility.[32] WMAN established a Delegates Weekend subcommittee, led largely by women who were charged with coordinating housing, food, and entertainment.[33] As was true with efforts toward social change around the country, Mount Airy wives and mothers made up one of the largest organizing forces for the neighborhood's integrationist initiatives.[34] On April 29, 1962, WMAN executive director Anita Schiff sent a press release to regional newspapers and radio and television stations, as well as the Associated Press, UPI, CBS News, and the Voice of America.[35] Through this carefully orchestrated media campaign running alongside the festivities, the organization worked to invite the rest of the country to experience the weekend as well.

All told, sixty-nine delegates and their families visited West Mount Airy that May weekend. Four UN representatives in attendance held ambassadorial rank, those from the Dominican Republic, Ecuador, Madagascar, and Yemen. Four nations from the Soviet bloc participated in the events, as did several from newly independent postcolonial nations in Africa.[36] Local newspapers followed the delegation closely, chronicling the weekend's schedule and echoing the neighborhood's vision of the American democratic ideal that WMAN highlighted in its April press release. "Visitors partook in that old-fashioned American custom, the covered dish luncheon," the *Philadelphia Bulletin* reported, "and at the end of the reception . . . they heard no speeches, political or propaganda, but merely good American folk music. Today, they are lazing through a typical American Sunday. They are likely to see that it's a pretty good life."[37] The *Germantown Courier* noted that the guests were presented with souvenirs, including a charm emblazoned with the Philadelphia seal and a parchment copy of the Declaration of Independence. Above all, the *Courier* said, the weekend was "meant to demonstrate to other countries how people in an urban integrated community live."[38] Indeed, it was this model of interracial city living that West Mount Airy Neighbors sought to present to residents of the Philadelphia region, at a moment when many such homeowners were considering a move to the suburbs.

Responding to WMAN's press release, several national media outlets ran stories about the weekend's festivities. The *New York Times*, in an article printed two weeks before the event took place, touted West Mount Airy Neighbors as "an organization of more than six hundred residents interested in promoting a racially balanced community and integrated schools." The paper gave a rundown of the schedule for the weekend, highlighting a stroll along the Wissahickon Creek and attendance at local religious services.[39] The *Christian Science Monitor*, too, in a larger series on West Mount Airy that was published in the weeks surrounding the UN visit, used the weekend as a lens through which to explore the process of residential integration.[40] Journalist Kenneth Gehret wrote of the early years of transition and the initial efforts to stave off decline and preserve the viability of the community. He highlighted the liberal ethos of race relations and the collective buy-in from residents that created the possibility of stabilization, and he noted the efforts to spread the virtues of interracial living to a larger audience: "So effective has this integration project been, in the eyes of WMAN leaders, that they believe it has value as a model of democratic American life."[41] As he lauded the community for its efforts toward interracial living, he also noted the underlying economic currents that created the conditions for integration to occur. "The people moving into the neighborhood," he wrote, "are very much like those already there. Education and economic backgrounds are similar, although both Negroes and whites are represented. The high level of homeownership has not changed. Properties are well maintained, and an active interest in community affairs is evidence [*sic*] among the newcomers."[42]

Echoing the importance of economic homogeneity in fostering racial harmony, Gehret's depiction of the neighborhood fell in line with the white liberal sensibility of intentional integration that WMAN had worked to invoke throughout their 1962 publicity campaign. In making deliberate decisions about which elements of the Mount Airy narrative to include and to whom to assign the agency in the story, Gehret contributed to a coalescing national image of the neighborhood, one predicated on the combined ideals of racial integration, urban sustainability, economic stability, and lived American democracy. Even as West Mount Airy Neighbors' UN Delegates Weekend offered international visitors a window into the experience of interracial living, the presence of the American press and their coverage of the events brought these idealized images of an integrated, middle-class city neighborhood to a larger national audience.

The United Nations Delegates Weekend and the "Green Country Towne" brochure marked the beginning of a widespread media campaign that highlighted the white-middle-class experience of West Mount Airy's integration project. Through the 1960s, WMAN continued to offer press releases on the community's efforts, and editors around the nation responded, printing stories on the neighborhood and lauding it as an example of what the country could be. The *Christian Science Monitor*, the *New York Times*, *Women's Day*, *Jewish Digest*, and *McCall's* all published stories on West Mount Airy. Many were written by neighborhood residents themselves, uncritically underscoring the democratic ideal that WMAN put forth and applauding the residents for their efforts in the pursuit of racial justice.[43] The founding principles of West Mount Airy Neighbors—the calculated balance between interracial liberalism and economic exclusivity—remained central to the neighborhood agenda.

As white residents saw their vision of the community reflected in the regional and national spotlight, African American homeowners found in the neighborhood the personal security that stable integration could provide. Whereas they certainly valued the inclusion that WMAN's vision of intentional integration espoused, more often than not black buyers made their way to the neighborhood in search of the tangible opportunities that living among whites afforded. Their interest in interracial living came with the dual recognition of civil rights progress and material advancement.

At first, these subtle distinctions between the white and black experiences of integration may in fact have served to foster the economic and social stability that all residents of West Mount Airy so desired. The white-centric push for a common class-based sense of identity complemented well the goals of the professional and upwardly mobile black buyers moving in, who sought the very economic conditions that this class-based exclusivity required. White families, proudly displaying their liberal politics by remaining committed to interracial neighborhoods, welcomed their new black neighbors based on a common socioeconomic identity. According to one African American resident, a white neighbor greeted her for the first time, exclaiming, "I'm very happy to see some nice blacks moving in to get rid of some of these poor whites."[44] And African Americans believed that this economic exclusivity would function to keep their own property investments secure. Mount Airy's residents—black and white alike—overwhelmingly saw their neighbors as similarly situated socially and economically, and they believed that these attributes were an intrinsic part of successful residential integration. Within a decade, however, these ideological differences in the value of integration that were so crucial to the neighborhood's early successes would give way to a heated battle over the experience of daily living in West Mount Airy.

Chapter 4

Integration, Separation, and the Fight for Black Identity

When Juilliard-trained opera singer Gail Tomas returned home after several years of performing, she was ready to settle down. Originally from South Philadelphia, Tomas visited her brother at his house on Johnson Street on the Germantown/Mount Airy border, and found herself taken with the area. Shortly after, she and her new husband rented an apartment east of Germantown Avenue and then another on West Mount Pleasant before purchasing their first house on Westview Street in West Mount Airy in 1963. The area was green and lush, Tomas thought. It was clean and safe. There was space between the homes and private backyards. The twenty-six-year-old black woman did not know until she and her husband moved in that the community was working toward integration.[1]

In 1957, the *Philadelphia Tribune*, the city's largest African American newspaper, declared Germantown (the region that encompassed West Mount Airy) a racially integrated neighborhood. A survey conducted by the paper found that African Americans from North and South Philadelphia, frustrated with growing population density, were relocating to the city's northwest reaches in search of a safe, welcoming, and stable community.[2] By the early 1960s West Mount Airy had become a veritable Who's Who of Philadelphia's black elite. William Coleman, who went on to serve as secretary of transportation under the Nixon and Ford administrations, owned a home on the 500 block of West Hortter Street. Reverend Leon Sullivan, an acclaimed civil rights activist who later formulated the Sullivan Principles for U.S. firms operating in South Africa, lived in the area, as did Joseph Coleman, the first African American to be elected president of the Philadelphia City Council. Sadie Alexander, the first black woman to serve on a presidential commission—appointed by Truman to his Commission on Human Rights—resided with her husband, Judge Raymond Pace Alexander, on the 700 block of Westview Street.[3] These black leaders were drawn to the community because of its strong and growing reputation as a site of interracial living. Through WMAN's media campaign and coverage in both the mainstream and black press, complemented by casual conversations among neighbors and friends, wealthy and upwardly mobile black Philadelphians were becoming familiar with the integration project and looking toward Mount Airy with interest.[4]

But for many such black buyers contemplating a move to the neighborhood, it was not necessarily the democratic ideal that WMAN articulated to woo white liberals that attracted them to the community. To be sure, most African Americans in the years following World War II believed in the fight for civil rights, broadly construed. They agreed that a nation predicated on the ideals of equality and democracy would necessarily bring them close to tangible reform in race relations. Particularly for the nation's black middle class, the equation of racial justice with a philosophy of integration resonated loudly.[5] Black professionals often conceived of a sense of equality of opportunity, in which their own access to housing should be proportional to that of similarly situated white buyers.[6] But their interest in such neighborhoods as West Mount Airy often stemmed as much from the possibility of tangible benefit as it did from these abstract notions of justice and equality. Black buyers saw in residential racial integration the prospect of both the material conditions characteristically attached to economically stable white communities and the opportunity to educate themselves and their children to a mainstream professional culture.[7] For them, there was the possibility of substantive gains in living among whites. In the first decades of integration, then, Mount Airy's black residents lived with a dual consciousness, a simultaneous commitment to civil rights progress and a desire for the assurances of safety and security.

When Ed Henderson and his wife began to look for a house in 1960, they could have afforded to move anywhere in and around Philadelphia. Henderson, a black professional who grew up in a largely African American neighborhood in the city, had recently accepted an engineering position at a plant in Blue Bell. Financially, he could have comfortably moved to the northwestern suburb, but he knew he wanted something different. "There is a richness in urban communities," Henderson reflected. "I didn't want to be out in the suburbs where I had to go a long distance [to find that]. I wanted to be in the city, close to the richness of the city, the culture." Of particular importance to Henderson and his wife was the experience of community that their children would have. "[I wanted for them] the things that happen within a good community that's integrated not only racially but ethnically, culturally," he recalled. "I didn't want them to be a little cork bobbing in the ocean, not knowing where they came from, where they were, or where they were going."[8] The Hendersons sought the cosmopolitan nature of urban life without the frenzy of living in Center City, nor the social and economic problems of the black inner-city of North Philadelphia.

The couple scoured the region, from Germantown and Mount Airy to the far reaches of West Philadelphia. Finally, nineteen months into their search, they received a call from their realtor. He had found them a house on the 500 block of West Mount Pleasant Avenue, an old stone home on the edge of Fairmount Park's Wissahickon Gorge, around the corner from one of the best elementary schools in the city. The property was set back from the street, slightly elevated, with no public thruway running behind. "I pulled up," recalled Henderson, "looked around at the neighborhood, and that was it. . . . Sight unseen, I said, 'this is where we're moving. I could spend the rest of my life here.'"[9]

Henderson's motivations for moving to Mount Airy echoed the attitudes of many of his neighbors, black and white alike. The area boasted old stone homes with big front porches, a quiet refuge from the busy streets yet with strong community ties. And the neighborhood's charm went beyond its tree-lined streets and expansive parks, woods, and trails. Its two elementary schools were renowned across the city for their competent teaching staffs and innovative principals. Just as these factors kept white residents from fleeing the area, they were instrumental in enticing black families to move in.

For many African Americans in Henderson's position, their personal goal was not residential integration itself. In fact, during the postwar decades there emerged a number of self-segregated black suburbs, where financially successful black Americans sought refuge from the pressure and, at times, discrimination they encountered in their professional world. As *Pittsburgh Courier* columnist Eric Springer wrote in 1962, "Assuming that there were decent, safe, sanitary, and pleasant surroundings, is it not possible that some of us would desire to live in such a neighborhood precisely because we know that people with a similar heritage, common religion, or racial background lived there?" The problem, argued Springer, is not when black Americans choose to live together, but when society constructs barriers preventing such mobility.[10] Residential integration, then, offered the black middle class a choice; it provided them with the possibility of positive change.[11] Their perception of integration, though, went far beyond this abstract sense of opportunity. For middle-class African Americans across the country, the prospect of integration offered a fundamental material gain that could not be discounted. An integrated neighborhood meant nicer homes, more stable property investments, better schools, safer streets, and more reliable municipal services. Living among whites meant that the larger city government would pay attention.[12]

The *Pittsburgh Courier* made this connection clear in a January 1957 piece on the "evil" of segregated housing. "Negro housing is expensive," the *Courier* author wrote. "All experts agree that for a comparable facility, the Negro pays substantially more than whites and he pays it all out of a smaller annual income." Segregated housing leads to overcrowding, the article continued: "Old one-family residences have been chopped up to make several apartments. Many families have doubled up, as some of us did during the war, because living space in decent quarters is unobtainable at a price Negro families can pay."[13] In 1964, *Courier* columnist Benjamin Mays offered a similar assessment in his treatment of inequality in the public schools, arguing that integrating housing was a necessary step in the fight for integrated education. Though Mays articulated a call for equal education regardless of racial demographics—school boards, he wrote, "are obligated to see to it that all schools are equally adequate in construction, materials used, and in equipment"—he clearly linked the idea of integration with the promise of better material conditions.[14]

Black residents in West Mount Airy echoed these sentiments. Christopher Edley and his wife moved to the neighborhood from North Philadelphia in the mid-1950s to offer their children a better education. "It is time for my children to begin school," said Edley's wife in 1957, "and the schools in [my old neighborhood] are inferior, as they are in all Negro neighborhoods." An African American man who lived on Sedgwick Street ignored name-calling and snowball attacks when he first moved to the neighborhood because of the stable property investments the community offered. "I had a house I wanted to live in," he said, "and I was determined to stay in it."[15] This relationship between integration and the prospect of better material gain created a substantial and sustainable pull toward these integrating neighborhoods for African Americans.

Perhaps equally important to this secure investment in home and school was the possibility of a window into a majority white culture. For many black homeowners in West Mount Airy, living with whites provided a lens into a mainstream professional culture. According to Ed Henderson, the community provided a space for him to educate his children to a white world.[16] Henderson believed that in raising his kids in an integrated neighborhood, in teaching them to interact with their white counterparts from an early age, he could better equip them to negotiate the largely white professional sphere as adults. His kids would grow up well versed in this mainstream white culture, he thought. They would know how to negotiate it, and how to find success within it. They would get this education on the streets and in the schools. The neighborhood would provide them a sort of orientation, a boot camp for entering the majority white professional world.[17] For those African Americans who could afford it, residentially integrated space offered them the opportunity to educate themselves and their children to a world of relative privilege and stability.

Though by the early 1960s the African American population in West Mount Airy spanned the spectrum of middle-class status, the neighborhood's black community was largely made up of economically stable homeowners in search of better opportunities for themselves and their families.[18] According to the 1960 census, the median income for black families in West Mount Airy was $6,323, compared with $4,248 among African Americans in Philadelphia, and $5,782 among all Philadelphia residents. In West Mount Airy,

22.7 percent of African Americans were categorized as professional or technical workers, compared with 4.7 percent of black Americans in the city and 9.4 percent of Philadelphia residents as a whole. In West Mount Airy, 76.5 percent of black families owned their own homes, compared with 42.9 percent of the black population in the city and 58.7 percent of Philadelphia residents overall.[19] These families chose West Mount Airy in part because it offered them access to a world from which they were often excluded.

Although there undoubtedly existed African Americans who saw it as their ideological mission to pave the way for integrated residential space, many more saw neighborhoods like West Mount Airy as opportunities to leave the dilapidated conditions of the inner city to which they had previously been consigned, and to simultaneously participate in the larger push toward equality.[20] The middle-class African American experience of residential integration in the middle of the twentieth century was not a simplistic assertion of racial justice, nor was it a crude calculation of economic advantage. Just as white integrationists saw the project as a balance between economic viability and racial liberalism, blacks participating in these efforts toward intentional integration did so from a dual recognition of racial justice and material gain.

As the Hendersons settled into their new home on Mount Pleasant Avenue, Ed began to involve himself in neighborhood affairs. In 1963, he joined the Henry Home and School Association, wanting to have a voice in his children's education. Over the next twenty years, he became active in West Mount Airy Neighbors as well. In 1965, he joined the zoning committee, and a few years later became its president. He served as vice president of the physical resources department, and then, in 1979, became vice president of the organization. He was deeply committed to preserving the integrity of the neighborhood, often attending meetings and making phone calls late into the night after long days at the Blue Bell plant.[21] Throughout the community, African American residents became involved in WMAN and attendant organizations, seeking to maintain an active black presence in the Mount Airy integration project.

Of course, not all black homeowners felt compelled to participate in community activities and institutions. A *Philadelphia Tribune* survey conducted in 1957 reported that most African American residents in northwest Philadelphia did not frequent neighborhood restaurants or social clubs. "We do most of our entertaining at home," said one woman. "It's more convenient . . . and that's why we bought a home." Her family moved to the 300 block of

Phil Ellena Street that year but continued to attend weekly religious services at the historically black Church of St. Simon the Cyrenian in South Philadelphia for at least an additional half decade.[22] "I'm more inclined to go [to restaurants and clubs] where I know it's okay," said a man who had recently relocated from North Philadelphia. "I have no fear of the other group. . . . I just don't want to be a pioneer."[23]

But for those that sought out those community connections, involvement in local organizations often provided a vehicle through which to channel the frustrations of segregation and marginalization so common among African Americans across the country. In 1955, when Don Black moved with his wife to the 100 block of Westview Street, he quickly involved himself in such localized efforts.[24] For Black, who grew up as one of the few black residents in the largely white Frankford neighborhood in Philadelphia's Lower Northeast district, West Mount Airy offered the chance to live in a friendly, stable community as he and his new wife looked toward starting a family. Black, like Henderson, was emblematic of this double consciousness that many African Americans experienced in electing to move to integrated communities. First, he saw West Mount Airy as an opportunity for advancement. In talking to friends and family, he learned that it was an economically stable middle-class neighborhood, and he felt that the long-standing (and continuing) white presence evidenced a long-term investment potential. Moreover, because of the widespread attention to the area, he and his wife believed that they would be welcomed. WMAN's publicity campaign had not only opened the eyes of white America to the integration efforts taking place in northwest Philadelphia. Even in the early 1950s, the region was gaining a localized reputation among African Americans who saw that they could find both economic security and a friendly white face in the neighborhood. The Blacks worked with white local real estate agent Nancy Longstreth, and quickly found the place that would become their home for more than fifty years. "I really wanted a fireplace," Don recalled, "but I liked the house so much that I said, 'I can forget the fireplace.'"[25] The move to Mount Airy offered the Blacks that element of material advancement, the prospect of offering his children a better life than his parents had been able to provide to him. He wanted safe schools, a bigger house, and more space. At the same time, though, in moving to the neighborhood, Black saw himself taking part in the larger struggle for racial equality.

Black had a history of pushing the limits of race relations. As a teenager, he ignored cultural mores and took a seat in the white section of his local

Horn and Hardart's, a regional Automat chain. "It was accepted," he remembered, "that you could go to [the restaurant], but you sat upstairs if you were a Negro. . . . One day, I just decided I was going to sit downstairs." He had taken his girlfriend to the eatery with him, and she objected to the gesture. "This is where we sit," he recalled her saying. But he was persistent. "I wasn't breaking any laws," he said, "but I constantly got into a little bit of trouble here and there because of my challenging discrimination."[26]

As his adult consciousness took shape, Black became increasingly angered by the systemic racism that he witnessed across the city. When he and his wife moved to West Mount Airy, he found new ways to channel his indignation. As soon as they settled into their home on Westview Street, Black became active in the neighborhood's integration efforts. He joined West Mount Airy Neighbors as it was getting off the ground, and he served as the president of the Westview Neighbors Association, formed the same year as WMAN to organize the residents of his block. At the same time, he became a leader for one of the neighborhood Boy Scout troops, and remained in the position for nineteen years.[27] Black was able to carve out a sustainable middle-class existence by finding a calculated balance between social action and familial and material comfort.

Even as this conception of middle-class respectability had become an integral part of biracial integration in West Mount Airy, members of Philadelphia's black community took issue with the neighborhood's integration project, and specifically with the African Americans who were moving into the neighborhood. As he became increasingly immersed in the neighborhood's efforts toward stabilization, some of Don Black's friends outside of Mount Airy condemned him as an "Uncle Tom" for his close work with white integrationists and his willingness to criticize segments of the black population.[28] Henderson, too, received censure for his work with WMAN. "There were some black people who had the opinion that I was too white," he recalled. Henderson believed that his focus on the community as a whole at the expense of individual ethnic and racial interests marginalized him from many African Americans throughout Philadelphia. "There were some," he later reflected, "who didn't think I was 'black enough.'"[29]

As WMAN's media campaign in the early 1960s brought widespread attention to the neighborhood's integrationist agenda, many of Mount Airy's black residents were confronted by verbal attacks for their perceived economic and spatial abandonment of the city's larger black community. Amid rising racial tensions in Philadelphia, the local NAACP leadership waged an intense campaign against those middle-class black homeowners working toward residential integration in West Mount Airy.[30] In the mid-1960s, the neighborhood itself became a symbol of racial betrayal, and African American residents found their very blackness challenged with charges of racial desertion.

As much as integration had become the consensus goal of civil rights progress for many liberal Americans, in northern cities economic and ideological differences among African Americans created a fractured vision of the larger movement for racial justice. Around Philadelphia and across the nation, strong black voices were emerging, challenging the efficacy of mainstream efforts toward collaborative change.[31] As African Americans in West Mount Airy spoke of the value of interracial living, more radical activists agitated for black separatism, condemning both the class-based identity and the integrationist ideology as dangerous to the larger African American community.

These tensions between black separatism and interracial collaboration challenged more than simply the viability of modes of social change. The 1963 rise to power of local NAACP president Cecil Bassett Moore prompted the city's African Americans to ponder the existence of a collective black community, and, by extension, a collective black identity. Through heated exchanges mediated by the local and national press, these clashes between separation and integration touched off intense debates over the very meaning of blackness in urban space. In the mid-1960s, Moore and his followers waged a rhetorical war to debunk integrationist claims of black authenticity. Moore directed many of his attacks toward the African American professionals of West Mount Airy. For the NAACP leader, the integrated community in northwest Philadelphia represented a retreat from the realities of black America, a spatial, social, and political dividing line that separated the masses from a disingenuous middle class. In this way, Moore turned Mount Airy into a symbol of the collusion between the city's black elite and the white political establishment. According to the outspoken orator, African American homeowners in Mount Airy gave up their claims of blackness when they fled to the integrationist neighborhood.[32]

The son of a medical doctor and a teacher, Cecil B. Moore was born in Yokon, West Virginia, on April 2, 1915.[33] His racial consciousness began to take shape at an early age. When Moore was a child, the Ku Klux Klan visited his family home; because his father's skin was so light, Klan members believed that he was a white man living with a black woman. A respected country doctor, the elder Moore was eventually able to prove that he and his wife were both, in fact, African Americans. The Klan left them alone, but the experience stayed with Cecil Moore.[34]

Though he moved around quite a bit during college, often registering for classes at one school and finishing the semester at another because he was unable to cover tuition costs, the budding activist ultimately graduated from Bluefield State College in Bluefield, West Virginia.[35] The historically black school had opened its doors in 1895 as the Bluefield Colored Institute to serve the influx of black Americans moving to the state in response to the burgeoning coal industry. By 1909, the college had cultivated a strong teacher-training program, and by the time Moore arrived, it had reinvented itself as Bluefield State Teachers College. Although far removed from the black cultural renaissance in northeastern cities, Bluefield's faculty worked hard to impress upon its students the presence of a cohesive, national African American community. During his time there, Cecil Moore likely interacted with many black leaders and cultural figures; among those who visited the school in the years during and after the Harlem Renaissance were John Hope Franklin, Langston Hughes, Duke Ellington, Dizzie Gillespie, and Joe Louis.[36] Later in his life, he would regale his children with stories of learning from Carter G. Woodson, founder of Negro History Week.[37] Even as Moore went on to become a tireless advocate for the black poor, he negotiated the world from a position of relative privilege, firmly rooted in the educated African American elite.[38]

Moore graduated from Bluefield State a part of a growing black professional class in the United States. After a brief stint as a salesman at the Atlanta Life Insurance Company, Moore enlisted in the military in 1942 and moved to North Carolina. As a member of the still-segregated Marine Corps, he was stationed at the Montford Point base, an all-black training facility adjacent to Camp Lejeune.[39] The outspoken Moore quickly earned a reputation for calling attention to the racial inequity of Corps life. At one point, recalled Cecily Banks, Moore's oldest daughter, a number of black marines were wrongfully accused of a crime for which they would have been sentenced to extended prison terms. Moore stormed down the main corridor of the base headquarters looking for someone to confront about the situation. "And as he went down the hall," said Banks, of her father's story, "all of the white officers would close their doors. None of them wanted to get involved."[40]

Moore's racial consciousness came of age during his time in the service; the international war against fascism fundamentally shaped his understanding of race relations in the United States.[41] In 1945, he left for combat in the Pacific theater.[42] He spent two months fighting his way through Saipan, Tinian, and Okinawa, and when he returned to North Carolina, he married Theresa Lee. The following year, Moore was reassigned to Philadelphia's Fort Mifflin, and the young couple settled into life in the northern city. In 1948, President Harry Truman signed into effect Executive Order 9981, ending legal segregation in the U.S. military. Within the Marine Corps, however, black men continued to encounter stumbling blocks, and when Moore was asked to serve in Korea without elevation to officer status, he declined. "You see," Moore later said, "I made a living killing for this country. I was determined that when I got back, that what rights I didn't have I was going to take, using every weapon in the arsenal of democracy. After nine years in the Marine Corps, I didn't intend to take another order from any sonofabitch that walk[ed]."[43] Moore received an honorable discharge as a sergeant major, the highest rank an enlisted man could attain.[44]

Moore was surprised by the brand of racial politics he encountered in Philadelphia.[45] Having spent much of his life in the rural South, he had grown accustomed to the legal segregation of Jim Crow. He had assumed that the Northeast would be different, and was distressed over the level of entrenched intolerance across the city. In employment, housing, and education, African Americans faced systemic discrimination. The legal separation of West Virginia, Georgia, and North Carolina had given way to a new breed of segregation in Philadelphia. Moore was caught off guard.

In 1960, as Moore, by then a licensed attorney, rose to prominence, there were 535,000 African Americans living in Philadelphia, upwards of 27 percent of the city's total population and an increase of more than 150,000 people from ten years earlier. Although many black families were moving to areas on the outer edges of the city, nearly one-third still lived in North Philadelphia, considered the city's black ghetto.[46] These African Americans had the lowest education and employment rates in Philadelphia, received the poorest medical care, and lived in the worst housing. They were politically marginalized and alienated from the city's power structure. Frustration was high at the same time that expectations of equality were on the

Figure 4. Raymond Pace Alexander (left) trying to calm demonstrators at the
Columbia Avenue Riots, a three-day riot in "the Jungle" of North Philadelphia, home to
nearly half of the city's black population, *Philadelphia Bulletin*, August 28, 1964. The riot
was sparked by escalating tensions between police and residents and widespread allegations
of police brutality. Used with permission from Special Collections Research Center,
Temple University Libraries, Philadelphia.

rise, as civil rights agitation was spreading across the country.[47] In 1964,
Andrew G. Freeman, president of the National Urban League, called the
city a "racial tinderbox." Between high unemployment and widespread substandard housing, Philadelphia had all the ingredients of disaster, said Freeman. "Consigned to street corners," he warned, "the young Negro is building up a store of frustration and resentment."[48]

When Moore was elected president of the local NAACP in 1963, he
promised to empower the black masses of North Philadelphia. He made it
his mission, he said, to move away from a sense of racial justice that counted
its victories in the strides of black professionals gaining token advances. He
decried those individuals like Judge Raymond Alexander of West Mount
Airy, whom he said had fled the black community and focused his energies

on the benefit of an elite few, at the expense of the larger black population of Philadelphia. The judge and his wife, Sadie Alexander, chairwoman of George Schermer's Human Relations Commission, had moved from North Philadelphia to West Mount Airy in 1960. The couple sold their home at 1708 W. Jefferson Street to Cecil Moore and his family. According to the *Philadelphia Tribune*, during and after the Second World War, the 1700 block of Jefferson was known as "Strivers Row," an exclusive elite enclave in the black ghetto of North Philadelphia. Two decades later, the *Tribune* staff writer lamented in 1965, most of these black leaders were moving to Germantown, Mount Airy, Chestnut Hill, West Oak Lane, and other neighborhoods on the outer edges of the city.[49]

Though it would be a few years before calls for black nationalism rose up around the country, in Philadelphia and other northern cities movements for black power and intraracial pride had been central to the civil rights agenda since the years surrounding the Second World War. Such groups as the Nation of Islam, the Muslim Brotherhood, and the Citizens Committee against Juvenile Delinquency and its Causes emerged, challenging the slow pace of liberal reform that had come to define the nation's movement for racial justice. By the late 1950s, Philadelphia's NAACP branch was growing concerned about the possibility of losing its authority as the primary advocate for civil rights progress. The organization, historically viewed as a moderating force catering to the needs of the African American elite, began to shift its focus, embarking on a campaign to work more directly with the city's black neighborhoods.[50] When the NAACP elected Cecil Moore as president, the leader's presence on Jefferson Street signaled to the city's black masses a shift in racial politics and representation in Philadelphia.

Though Moore regularly offered broad characterizations about Philadelphia's black middle class, he reserved particular condemnation for the African American homeowners of West Mount Airy, whom he believed had distanced themselves both spatially and communally from the realities facing the city's larger black population. Responding to Andrew Freeman's reference to Philadelphia as a "racial tinderbox," Moore wrote, "He was asremote [*sic*] in his thoughts from the true situation as it exists in Philadelphia as he was when he made the observation in Louisville, Kentucky, and upon his return to Philadelphia the distance was just as great, for he had no identification, contact, or rapport with the masses he purports to speak about during the eighteen months he had lived in . . . Mount Airy."[51] Speaking of his own decision to remain in North Philadelphia, Moore said, "I'd be lost if I had to move up to Mount Airy . . . where I'd have to be so damned respectable that I couldn't stand on a street corner on Friday night. The Negro is always on the corner on Friday or Saturday nights. That's where you go to talk."[52]

Cecil Moore saw West Mount Airy as a sort of ideological dividing line in the city's struggle for civil rights. African Americans moving to the north-west Philadelphia neighborhood had become symbols of the black middle-class complicity with the white establishment that Moore condemned. As Moore said in reference to Mount Airy's black professionals, "I run a grass-roots group, not a cocktail-party, tea-sipping, fashion-show-attending group of exhibitionists. That's the difference. Those things divide the Negro, sepa-rate him into classes. I want nothing to divide the Negro; I want a one-class Negro community. Your so-called middle-class Negro is a 'professional Negro' who doesn't come into contact with the masses."[53] To Cecil Moore, the black middle-class residents of West Mount Airy represented those African Amer-icans who had abandoned the black masses and thus given up their claims to blackness; Moore used these rhetorical turns to consolidate power and posi-tion himself at the center of the city's fight for racial justice.

In a sense, Moore's conception of blackness was defined by one's commit-ment to the black community. That is, rather than a legal, political, or social construction of race that distinguished black from white, this notion of racial identity was set within the African American world by a hierarchy of black-ness that became inextricably linked to racial allegiance. Moore's thinking reflected a shift in the nature of racial justice more broadly, what cultural critic Harold Cruse defined in his 1967 work, *The Crisis of the American Negro*, as the tension between those seeking to effect change in the white imagination and those working to remake the material and political conditions in which African Americans lived. The central conflict between the integrationist mind-set and this nationalist—or black power—agenda, wrote Cruse, was a "propos[al] to change, not the white world outside, but the black world inside, by reforming it into something else politically and economically." The history of black America, he continued, "is basically a history of conflict between in-tegrationist and national forces in politics, economics, and culture."[54]

In Moore's Philadelphia, then, those working toward change for the black masses were viewed as more legitimate than the liberal black reformers in West Mount Airy, adopting an integrationist agenda. Middle-class African Americans, recalled Cecily Banks, "were seen as not paying attention to what was going on for the black poor. It was a matter of concern for our own people, not trying to fit into a 'white world.'"[55] In this way, an individual's self-identification as African American was less important than his or her commitment to a cohesive black community. For Moore, people who conformed to these standards were identified as black; those who deviated became sellouts.

The concept of "selling out" has longed been linked to a perceived abandonment of race-based interests and the black community. In the wake of the Civil War, when Martin R. Delany, the first African American field officer in the U.S. Army, aligned himself with the Democratic Party, black militiamen condemned him as a deserter, firing shots at him as he campaigned for former Confederate general Wade Hampton in 1876. Abolitionist Frederick Douglass was deemed a turncoat when he married Helen Pitts, a white woman, and W. E. B. DuBois became a "Benedict Arnold" when he rebuked black protestors following U.S. entry into the First World War.[56] In 1920, the moniker of Uncle Tom first became associated with "selling out," when followers of Marcus Garvey and the Universal Negro Improvement Association announced during a parade for the first UNIA convention in New York City that "Uncle Tom is dead and buried."[57] In August of that year, the *New York World* published an account of Reverend George Alexander McGuire's address to the convention, announcing that "the Uncle Tom nigger has got to go and his place must be taken by a new leader of the Negro race . . . not a black man with a white heart but a black man with a black heart."[58]

In the years following World War II, the image of the Uncle Tom became institutionalized in African American popular rhetoric as a synonym for this racialized conception of a "sellout." When Channing H. Tobias took the podium as the keynote speaker at the Forty-Fifth Annual NAACP National Convention in 1954, he declared war on the Uncle Toms of America. "We are not going to deal gently with those congenial Uncle Toms who have a vested interest," Tobias maintained, "and are willing to sell their people down the river to save their own skin."[59] Nobel Peace Prize laureate, Ralph Bunche, speaking later in the week, went further. "Some Uncle Toms are saying that there is nothing wrong with Jim Crow schools," he told a crowd of delegates in Dallas, Texas. "They are saying that Negro teachers will go when segregated schools go. In most instances, this professed love of segregation by so-called Negro leaders is actually a smokescreen, protecting them from the rugged competition of the outside world."[60] On July 20, 1954, the

Philadelphia Tribune reprinted an editorial about the convention from New York's *Amsterdam News*. There, the editors publicly heralded Bunche for his comments. "We think the scholarly UN mediator made a substantial contribution to all right-thinking Americans when they exposed our intellectual Toms," the paper wrote. "We hope other Uncle Toms will be exposed, too. We have more than our fair share of these pitiful creatures."[61]

Although nationally the cries of Uncle Tom were levied against black men perceived to be sabotaging efforts toward equality and desegregation, in the urban North the invocation of the term gained a particular meaning that brought together issues of race and class. For black Americans in such northern cities as New York, Chicago, Detroit, and Philadelphia, "Uncle Tom" became universally understood as shorthand for delegitimizing middle-class claims of black identity.[62] In 1953, sociologist E. Franklin Frazer published his controversial book *The Black Bourgeoisie*. Frazier asserted that members of the black middle class were seeking to shed their African American identities and adopt the culture of the white upper class.[63] Frazier's work argued that the African American leadership in the United States had failed to foster a cohesive black community. These status seekers, he said, were so focused on becoming integrated into the white world that they lost sight of their responsibility toward the black masses.[64] Frazier, chairman of the department of sociology at Howard University and president of the International Society for the Scientific Study of Race Relations, sought to compel the African American middle class to return to their communities of origin, to create cohesion and stability, and to empower the masses and uplift black America as a whole.

By the 1960s, Frazier's language had leaked out of academia, disseminated through the black press and the rising cadre of radical black leaders spreading notions of separatism around the urban North. This tension between race and class became a critical site of contestation in the growing public discourse of black identity. In 1961, black nationalist leader Malcolm X issued a direct call to Ralph Bunche, by that point undersecretary for special political affairs at the United Nations, through the national press. "I'm challenging this International Uncle Tom" he said, "who has become world-famous in the United Nations as a puppet and parrot of the so-called white liberals, to come to [a] mass rally in Harlem on Saturday and prove that his feelings . . . reflect the feeling of the black masses."[65] Malcolm X was condemning what he saw as the disconnect between the black middle class and the larger black community, the *real* black community.

The 1963 election of Cecil B. Moore as president of the local NAACP brought into sharp relief this acute tension within Philadelphia's black population. As Moore rose to power agitating for African American autonomy, he continually came to blows with both the leaders of the national NAACP and local black professionals and integrationists, those whom he saw as pressing for empty civil rights reform. While privately, Moore, in fact, socialized with many of these middle-class black leaders, publicly he staged intense feuds, fueling debates over black identity in the city.[66] By casting the fight for civil rights squarely within the streets of North Philadelphia, Moore was able to galvanize the black working class and, in this way, draw support away from the moderate liberalism that had historically defined race relations in the city. In condemning middle-class integrationists as sellouts, he forced them to defend their blackness, to prove their authenticity as black Americans against charges that they had abandoned their roots for the white world.

Through this lens, the African American homeowners of West Mount Airy came to be seen as "traitors to their race." As Moore put it, "the Negro middle-class . . . subsists on the blood of the 'brother down under,' the brothers they are supposed to be leading."[67] In 1964, he appointed himself spokesman for the black community. "For the majority, anyway," he added, "excluding the 20% who don't want to be Negroes."[68] He condemned those who left the "jungles" of North Philadelphia, referring to them as "warmed over part-time Negroes" and "refugees from the Negro race."[69] They had fled their roots, he cried, for the material comforts of the middle-class white world. Moore was attacking these individuals on two levels: first, for their middle-class economic status, and second, for their beliefs in and actions toward the creation of racially integrated residential space.

As a general practice, these black homeowners of northwest Philadelphia that Cecil Moore so often attacked rarely spoke out publicly against the incendiary NAACP president. Where Moore spoke of a "one-class Negro community," these liberal integrationists believed that it was more important to present an image of a united African American effort toward change.[70] In those instances where they did engage Moore, though, they challenged the leader, asserting that his ongoing condemnation served to disempower the larger black community and curtail their efforts toward racial justice more broadly.[71] In 1964, Reverend Henry H. Nichols of the Germantown region embarked on an unsuccessful challenge for local NAACP leadership. When Moore referred to Nichols as one of the "big

Negro power structure . . . divisive 'Uncle Tom' hatchet boys," the reverend of the James Memorial Church responded with cries that Moore had pitted class against class, and race against race. Describing himself as a "militant moderate leader," Nichols blamed Moore for separating the city's African American population into divisive factions and maintained that his own commitment to racial liberalism would lead to a more productive pursuit of the interests of the entire black community.[72]

Figure 5. Civil rights leaders Cecil Moore (left, in suit) and Stanley Branche (center) lead picketers at Girard College, where the NAACP staged demonstrations after several years of unsuccessful legal actions to desegregate the private institution, *Philadelphia Bulletin*, October 8, 1966. Used with permission from Special Collections Research Center, Temple University Libraries, Philadelphia.

Sadie Alexander, one of Moore's favorite targets, also spoke out against the leader's critique that she and her husband, Judge Raymond Alexander, were "part-time Negroes."[73] The Alexanders had been a force for change in Philadelphia since the early 1920s, waging legal battles on behalf of disenfranchised African Americans. In 1939, after a long campaign, they compelled the Pennsylvania legislature to pass a statewide equal rights law. They fought city and state courts to roll back segregation ordinances in restaurants, hotels, lunch counters, theaters, and coffeeshops. They held demonstrations, organized marches, and gradually saw the separation of blacks and whites in the public sphere begin to erode. It was a tall order, Judge Alexander later recalled, "to make Philadelphia and Pennsylvania a city and state where black people could enjoy the fundamental freedoms guaranteed to them in our Federal Bill of Rights."[74] In 1963, Sadie Alexander responded to Moore's condemnations by establishing a familial line of civic activism for racial justice dating back to the early nineteenth century. She spoke of her work with the Human Relations Commission, in desegregating Girard College, in breaking down the color line in public accommodations across the state, and in serving on Harry Truman's President's Committee on Civil Rights. "I do not intend to be dragged into any personal vendetta with Mr. Cecil Moore," she said, "[but] my contribution to democracy in the U.S. is recorded and cannot be diminished by irresponsible accusations."[75]

Alexander chose to link herself to the black community through a record of struggle for racial justice, rather than through her genealogy, geographic home, or economic status. She spoke of her family not as African Americans but as activists. Like Moore's equation of racial authenticity with racial allegiance, she employed her history as a leader in civil rights to demonstrate her connection to the African American populace. Reverend Nichols, the Alexanders, and the Mount Airy African Americans responding to the cries of Uncle Tom and attacks on their middle-class racial identity believed that they were as authentically black as anyone living in Cecil Moore's North Philadelphia. The city's African Americans, they maintained, could not be limited politically, economically, or spatially. Middle-class reformers in West Mount Airy had been agitating for racial justice as well, they maintained; they were just as legitimately African American as those focusing on the black poor.[76]

By 1966, Cecil Moore's power in Philadelphia—and his authority to dictate who was included within the city's larger black community—had begun to wane, as he continually found himself at odds with the national NAACP. Though early on, the city saw membership rates grow—within six months of his inauguration, Moore boasted that the local branch had expanded from ten thousand to twenty-five thousand members—Moore routinely alienated white members of the organization, and in doing so he drew the ire of the national leadership.[77] One of his primary targets were the northern whites who, Moore charged, "call themselves liberal but in fact do nothing but bleed the Negro." Six months after taking office, Moore told *Pennsylvania Guardian* reporter G. A. Wilkens, "They are a bunch of phonies. . . . I'd rather deal with any southern racist than the unscrupulous bigots living in Chestnut Hill," he asserted, referring to the wealthy community in the far northwest reaches of the city, bordering Mount Airy to the south and suburban Montgomery County to the north.[78] In the same interview, Moore attacked Jewish activists, maintaining that their interventions in the struggle for racial justice were insincere. "If people of a Semitic origin continue to exploit Negroes, as they do, I'll exploit them as anti-American," he cried, channeling the language of Cold War anticommunism.[79] Moore believed that Jewish landlords and business owners were taking advantage of the black residents of the city.[80]

Letters flooded the national NAACP office, calling for Moore's immediate removal. On June 20, 1963, Philadelphian Herman Price wrote to Roy Wilkins, the national organization's executive secretary, to express his concern:

> The NAACP has always been the true representative in this fight.. The superlative efforts of Reverend Martin Luther King, Jr. will always be a pillar of strength to those of us who laud his great work. For many who have given their time and resources to further the cause of justice, I will always be greatful [*sic*]. My annual contribution will be doubled, but unless something is done to correct [the] terrible wrong [of Moore's comments] here in Philadelphia, I shall send my check to your New York office.[81]

Burton Caine, a Jewish attorney in Philadelphia and member of the Board of Directors of the American Civil Liberties Union, took his frustration a step further. "I am a member of the NAACP and have been a contributor to the Committee of One Hundred for many years," he wrote, referring to the association of educators and attorneys that was founded in 1941 to raise money for the ongoing operations of the national office. "However, I am resigning from the NAACP and I am discontinuing all further contributions to the Committee of One Hundred until Cecil Moore is removed as president of the local branch. I am sure that you understand that the reckless, irresponsible, and completely unjustified pronouncements of Moore can set back the movement for Negro rights quite considerably. For this reason, I, for one, greet the toleration of Moore by the national NAACP with extreme sadness."[82]

Moore's inflammatory anti-Semitic proclamations in June 1963 were the first hints of the breakdown in his relationship with the national office. In December 1964, several Philadelphia residents filed a complaint against Moore to the national board, alleging that the president was "guilty of conduct not in accordance with the principles, aims, and purposes of the NAACP as set out in the constitution and bylaws for branches, and as defined by the national board of directors and convention." Petitioners accused Moore of unauthorized disbursement of funds, violating fund-raising procedures, and failing to "properly exercise general executive authority on behalf of the branch."[83] As the *Philadelphia Evening Bulletin* reported in late 1964, "Moore has been up to his ears in controversy since he assumed office almost two years ago." The paper called the hearing a self-investigation of alleged corruption, and said that it marked a growing maturity and responsibility on the part of the organization.[84]

The charges were ultimately dismissed, but ten months later the national office made a move to curtail Moore's power, proposing to disband the central Philadelphia NAACP in favor of a multibranch system that would establish local offices in four regions of the city, each under its own leadership and budget and with the authority to carry out its own initiatives. In a letter to Moore, the national board advised him that the plan followed a larger decision to create these multiple branches in cities with populations over 250,000 people. If you resist, the board told Moore, "the national office has authority to lift [Philadelphia's] charter."[85] Though similar plans had been implemented previously in such cities as Atlanta, Chicago, New York, Dallas, and Los Angeles, Moore believed—likely quite justly—that the board was using the decentralization scheme as a vehicle to usurp his authority. After intense public battles, the national office succeeded, naming directors to the four new branches on July 6, 1966. Moore had been run out of office.

But even as Moore's authority in Philadelphia faded, the battles between the NAACP president and the city's liberal middle-class community highlighted rising tensions within the fight for racial justice. In West Mount Airy, these strains evidenced new external pressures to the neighborhood's integration project. As larger cultural and structural forces began to intervene and intrude on their grassroots efforts, community members struggled to redefine their mission and to maintain a sense of control over local institutions. Cecil Moore's condemnation of the neighborhood's black homeowners in the mid-1960s hinted at new forces at work in the larger civil rights movement in northern cities and new powers asserting influence over West Mount Airy's idealized notion of integrated space.

Chapter 5

"WELL-TRAINED CITIZENS AND GOOD NEIGHBORS"

Educating an Integrated America

On April 26, 1971, Bernard C. Watson of Temple University offered the keynote address at the West Mount Airy Neighbors' thirteenth annual meeting. A scholar of urban education and former deputy superintendent of planning for the School District of Philadelphia, Watson spoke of the challenges facing the city in public education. "If we cannot deal openly and honestly with the problems," he said, "we had better be prepared to be run over by them. Time is short, and the road is tough, but it has to be traveled. If not us, who? If not now, when?"[1]

Watson spoke of the choices that individuals make every day in how they respond to the problems within a community. West Mount Airy residents had chosen to react to racial transition with concerted campaigns promoting genuine interracial living, said Watson; their commitment to maintaining the viability of local schools, however, had waned in the face of local, citywide, and statewide battles over how best to manage the immense Philadelphia school district. Parents who professed tolerance and liberalism were withdrawing legitimacy from public education. "The fundamental problems in the schools," he urged, "have not been, and are not being, addressed by these sorts of individual decisions . . . What people want from the schools differs from person to person, community to community, and the result is conflicting demands, diverse expectations, and constant pressure on school officials." According to Watson, the quality of education must be the responsibility of the community as a whole. Residents of West Mount Airy, he said, have to decide that education is worth fighting for. People cannot wait for citywide improvement; "self-interest is not only alright, but may be the only thing you can trust."[2]

In many ways, the early efforts toward residential and social integration in West Mount Airy were successful in spite of economic pressures and formal policy directives aimed at perpetuating segregation on a structural level. WMAN integrationists had embarked on an interventionist grassroots movement to overcome what many viewed as the natural tendency toward residential separation. But while community leaders saw tangible results from efforts toward block-by-block integration, many residents struggled to contend with conflicting ideas concerning the value of education and city, state, and national policies that were often at odds with local efforts. The successful negotiation between local autonomy and external support in the realm of neighborhood integration did not translate to the realities of urban public education in the decades following the Second World War. What began in the mid-1950s as a hopeful campaign to integrate neighborhood elementary schools had become, by the early 1970s, a desperate plea for local control over an increasingly precarious educational climate.[3]

When West Mount Airy experienced its first rumblings of residential transition in the early 1950s, the neighborhood was served by two elementary schools. Charles W. Henry School and Henry H. Houston School offered local children a quality public school education for decades with little turmoil. Built in 1908 and 1926, respectively, both schools were overwhelmingly white through the middle of the twentieth century. As African American families began to move into the community, though, the school demographics shifted rapidly, significantly faster than the neighborhood itself. The Henry School, at the corner of Carpenter Lane and Green Street in the center of the integrating core, experienced this change particularly acutely. Because the first African American families tended to be wealthier black professionals purchasing larger homes with more land, it was the sprawling region around

Henry that saw the demographic swing first. The Houston School, sur-rounded by more densely populated blocks and smaller row homes, did not experience a significant transition until the late 1960s.

These striking shifts in student population resulted both from new black residents moving into the area and from official redistricting initiatives by the Philadelphia Board of Public Education. In 1953, the Henry School was home to four hundred white and ninety-five black students.[4] That same year, in an effort to cope with changing residential patterns in northwest Phila-delphia's sixth district, a subsection of the larger city school district, and to ameliorate early hints of overcrowding at some local elementary schools, the school board transferred nearly two hundred children to Henry.[5] Although some of these new students were residents of the community, the vast ma-jority came from adjacent neighborhoods. Nearly all of these new transfers were lower-income black students from the Eleanor C. Emlen School at the corner of Upsal and Chew streets on the Mount Airy/Germantown border.[6] The policy brought sudden changes to both the racial and economic land-scape of Henry's predominantly middle-class population. By the end of the decade, as the racial dynamics of the school shifted and the overall popula-tion grew, enrollment of white students plummeted to 35 percent, and by the middle of the 1960s, there were 275 white students at Henry and 560 African American.[7]

Henry School parents protested the redistricting plan, arguing that the new boundaries "would be injurious to the school."[8] But their cries were met with little acknowledgement from the school board. As soon as the 1953 policy took effect, Henry's student body was transformed, and class sizes increased dramatically. In WMAN's estimation, the potential consequences of this rapid transition were dire for both the elementary school and the community at large. As new black students moved to Henry, the organiza-tion feared, white families would begin withdrawing their children. While initially such a scenario would result in the school operating under capacity, the WMAN Education Committee warned, quickly "there [would be] sub-stantial gains in student population . . . and this increase [would be] almost entirely a Negro increase."[9] More broadly, board members believed, segre-gated educational facilities would threaten the very core of the residential integration that neighborhood activists had been working so hard to main-tain. Not only would the schools lose the coveted resources that came with the investment of middle-class white families; WMAN leaders feared the loss of white families from the neighborhood altogether.[10]

Though West Mount Airy Neighbors had expressed internal anxieties about this potential loss of white families in the community, in their public pleas the group framed their arguments around concerns for the recently enrolled students from the redistricted zone. One of the fundamental issues facing the Henry School, the Education Committee said in a November 1959 report, was that the new boundaries had introduced students who were ill-equipped to handle the academic rigors of the school. "The boundary extension several years ago," they reported, "has brought in a large number of students from a small corner of the zone who, because of economic and educational background, are not able to keep up with the majority of the students in the school."[11] Several members of WMAN approached the Board of Education informally, inquiring about the prospect of relocating some of the Sharpnack students at Henry back to the Emlen School to conform with the pre-1953 boundaries.[12]

In response, school superintendent Allan Wetter told the community group that he would consider the relocation plan, provided that he could place the responsibility for such action on West Mount Airy residents. If he shifted students, he said, he needed to be able to make it clear that he was doing so in response to pressure from WMAN and the Henry Home and School Association. In a subsequent exchange, Wetter reiterated such sentiments. The board will recommend six new portable classrooms at Emlen and new district boundaries lines, if, as Schools Committee chair Henry Wells recounted at an April 1960 meeting, they receive "a strong letter from WMAN urging it and asking for a meeting with him to press him further for it."[13] The group considered the superintendent's offer. Many members believed that it was in the best interest of the community as a whole to remake the elementary school in the image of the neighborhood. But not everyone on the board agreed.[14]

Citing the already overcrowded conditions at Emlen, George Schermer firmly opposed the measure. Local integration should be a goal only insofar as it does not create discriminatory conditions elsewhere, said the Human Relations Commission president. This type of short-term solution, he cautioned, would only increase tensions in the larger northwest Philadelphia community. Matthew Bullock, who went on to serve as WMAN's first black president in 1961, agreed with Schermer. He believed that Henry could serve as a sort of "beacon of light" for the community, but he questioned the ethics of sending children back to the Sharpnack area school. Emlen is a "disgraceful situation," said a third board member, well beyond physical capacity and operating with an established precedent for shuttling white children within its boundaries to other schools. "We still have a responsibility of balancing issues," he implored. Still others expressed unease about "looking out for our own interests at the expense of others not in a position to look out for their own."[15]

Although rarely part of public or institutional conversations, the question of WMAN's responsibility to the surrounding region underlay many of the decisions the organization made. When the group began its campaign to drive out corrupt realtors from the area, a number of the offending agents resettled in adjacent neighborhoods, exacerbating the rate of transition and intensifying patterns of flight.[16] Although some members of the WMAN leadership acknowledged the need to consider the impact of their efforts on other parts of the city, for others the impulse to protect and preserve West Mount Airy as a vibrant, economically stable community took precedence over the potential consequences of their actions for those outside of the neighborhood. In education, resource allocation, and institutional muscle, the ongoing vigilance within West Mount Airy had profound effects on the stability of the larger northwest Philadelphia.

In the 1959 boundary dispute, Schermer and Bullock held firm in their conviction that the stabilization of the Henry School could not come at the expense of students from neighboring communities. Thus, the WMAN Schools Committee abandoned the proposal to redraw district boundaries and relocate the Sharpnack students, and called instead for the school board to undertake a comprehensive study of the Sixth District. The group sought analysis of the region's six elementary schools and two junior high schools in order to assess all potential improvements in concert. The goal, WMAN mandated, would be to foster integration throughout the district.[17] As the committee later wrote in a follow-up report, "[We wanted to] obtain optimum classroom conditions for all schools, regardless of racial composition, with the firm conviction that out of the optimum educational environment [would] come well-trained citizens and good neighbors."[18] The board accepted the new proposal, and during the fall of 1960 it set out to examine the demographic trends facing the district.

In July 1961, WMAN issued a report analyzing the school board's findings. The information, the group said, confirmed what they had suspected: the institutions making up the Sixth District of the Philadelphia School District were experiencing marked demographic shifts as a result of both administrative redistricting and rapid changes in the residential landscape of the neighborhoods. Henry was in the running for the greatest turnover. The group's findings echoed the conclusions of a similar study around the country: on a percentage basis, there were more black students in the public schools than black families in these integrating neighborhoods.[19]

In a familiar pattern that community leaders had established in their earliest exploratory meetings about the prospect of residential integration, the group took a measured approach to this data, assessing the various explanations for these larger trends. WMAN at first focused on the city's policy of intradistrict school choice. It was possible, the committee wrote, that there were students from outside of the neighborhood enrolling in local schools.[20] Although children in the Philadelphia School District generally attended the elementary school that served their immediate community, from its inception the Board of Education had adhered to a policy whereby students could request a transfer to another institution. Though some opted to take advantage of this open enrollment program for the sake of convenience or because of a prior connection to a particular school, most saw the policy as a means through which to attend schools with stronger teaching staffs, better funding, and superior equipment. More often than not, those schools also had majority white student enrollment.[21] In practice, however, few families took advantage of the policy. According to Board of Education reports, in 1960 approximately five thousand of the district's 245,000 children, or roughly 2 percent, were attending schools outside of their neighborhood boundaries.[22] Though the proportion was higher in the Sixth District, even there only 7 percent of students—approximately thirteen hundred in total—lived outside of the district's boundaries, not nearly enough to account for the dramatic disparity in overall district enrollment. WMAN concluded that it was not worth their energy to attack the long-standing policy.[23]

Instead, returning to the strategy of Myrdalian moral suasion that had served to stabilize the community in the middle of the previous decade, WMAN chose to focus organizational resources on enticing individual families to send their children to Henry School. To combat the demographic trends in the Sixth District, the board determined, integration had to be actively fostered within the schools. Board members thought that if parents in the neighborhood took proactive measures to bring the commitment of residential integration into the elementary school, they could stave off both the panic that was beginning to take hold among white families and the perceived potential negative consequences of racial transition for the school itself. Integrationists believed that they could rely on the same tactics that had been so successful in the realm of residential stability to achieve educational stability. Through grassroots efforts, they maintained, they could extend their strategies in dealing with white flight to local schools, so as to offset the effects of the larger structural forces and city-mandated education policies.[24] What community leaders failed to realize was that these early initiatives geared toward stabilizing Henry were strikingly similar to the early neighborhood policies toward integration. They focused on individual choice at the expense of structural change, and, as such, their efforts ultimately resulted in the same shortcomings as the Church Community Relations Council.

Under Marjorie Kopeland's leadership, the Henry Home and School Association (HHSA) implemented programming designed to bring neighborhood families, black and white alike, into the schools. The organization called on parents to donate time, money, and skills to draw the community together and supplement the support from the school board.[25] HHSA member Don Black served on the committee to hold a school fair. Others used personal and professional connections to bring in local television and radio stations to cover their efforts. Within four years, the school was operating at physical capacity, and students enjoyed access to a gymnasium, an auditorium, home economics and shop facilities, and a central library. "It was really fun," Black later recalled, "because everyone participated."[26]

Around the country, urban, middle-class professionals were pooling individual resources to protect their local schools. In Washington D.C.'s Takoma neighborhood, parents affiliated with the integrationist community organization Neighbors, Inc. spent money on construction materials and donated their time to build new classrooms. It was easy, parent Janet Brown later reflected. "Here we were, college educated people in striving families with well-disciplined children. We all had the same interests and the same values [about education]."[27] This sense of optimism led families to believe that with enough individual contribution and community effort, they could ensure the viability of local schools.

To support and facilitate this new interventionist approach to school stabilization, West Mount Airy residents saw that it was time to usher in new
leadership at the Henry School. In 1957, following the influx of Emlen students and the early threats of white exodus to local private and parochial
schools, the HHSA and WMAN board members Marjorie Kopeland, Bernice Schermer, and Matthew Bullock led a drive to petition the school
board for a new principal at Henry. "Principal Hargraves wasn't able to
cope with [the changes]," Schermer remembered. "He was a very fine gen-
tleman but it was more than anyone would be able to handle without prepa-
ration."[28]

The newly appointed principal, Beatrice Chernock, saw it as her mission
to recraft the culture of the school. A slight white woman with a short shock
of black hair, Chernock believed that as a strong leader, she could help to
facilitate the creation and maintenance of a stable, integrated school. The
new principal sought to bolster the spirits of the entire Henry community:
students, parents, and teachers alike. She developed new school-wide programming and instituted "D-Days," or dress-up days, where children were
required to come to school in ties and dresses.[29] Chernock adopted a philosophy of dignity and security, hoping to boost morale by instilling in the
students a sense of decorum that she believed had been lost in the years of
transition.

The principal's agenda went beyond strengthening morale, however; soon
after she arrived at the school, she began a coordinated campaign to recruit
white families from the neighborhood, seeking to convince them to send
their children to Henry. "You have no idea what I went through that first
year," Chernock was reported as saying. "The neighborhood had just begun
to integrate. My white parents were running like frightened chickens! With
a few sensible white parents, I organized a group to visit homes and sell the
values of integration. I talked to realtors about our wonderful schools. I got
publicity for us."[30] In both public campaigns and conversations with individual families, Chernock invoked the ideas of the Church Community
Relations Council, summoning the language of middle-class respectability
to convince them that her school would be carrying on the lessons that their
children were learning at home, that she could instill such respectability in
loco parentis.

Lois Mark Stalvey, a white woman who moved with her family from
suburban Omaha to Philadelphia in the early 1960s, settled in West Mount

Airy because of its reputation as an integrated community. "We moved into our new house on June 18, 1962, after the schools had closed [for the year]," Stalvey wrote in her 1974 memoir, *Getting Ready: The Education of a White Family in Inner-City Schools.* "As soon as our phone was connected, it rang." It was Beatrice Chernock on the line, and she was calling to introduce the Stalveys to the local elementary school. The principal spoke of dedicated teachers and a dynamic Henry Home and School Association. She highlighted advanced teaching techniques and the high quality of the families sending their children to the school. "I was impressed with a principal who used her vacation to welcome all the new parents to the neighborhood," Stalvey wrote, unaware at the time that Chernock's list was largely limited to Mount Airy's white residents.[31]

The Stalveys had already decided to send their three children to Henry. When Lois arrived at the school for registration that September, the principal escorted her past the lines of African American parents and offered her a private tour of the facilities and her choice of first-grade teachers for her oldest son. They visited classrooms and met with students and teachers, and when they returned to registration, Chernock asked, "Have you noticed how our school is rebalancing itself racially? Fifty percent of the *younger* students are white" (original emphasis).[32] Stalvey did not realize that this speech was being repeated countless times to white parents around the neighborhood.

Chernock's policies aimed at allaying the fears of white parents had serious consequences for the school's African American population. As the principal directed her resources toward recruiting white students and ensuring that they had a satisfying experience at Henry, many of the school's black students, particularly those who had arrived following the 1953 redistricting plan, fell victim to lower tracking, an inattentive administration, and, at times, physical mistreatment. Some members of the Henry School community condemned these practices, which served to coddle the school's white population. Stalvey expressed discomfort with such policies, and several parents charged Chernock with creating racial tensions within the neighborhood. As kindergarten teacher Eve Oshtry later reflected, "There [was] some resentment on the part of some people who [felt] that you shouldn't bend over backwards too far for this and you shouldn't give special privileges to white families or special inducements for them to come."[33]

Similar problems, of course, existed in public school systems throughout the country. Deeply ingrained racism continued to pervade American thought across geographic and socioeconomic lines. Though the nation was looking at the problem of racial inequality with an increasingly critical eye, individuals and institutions were often not able to escape the culture of racism that had been normalized in the United States for centuries. Even West Mount Airy, a community so intentional in its efforts to defeat a system of racial hierarchy and create a genuine interracial society, could not break free from the entrenched bigotry. Bowing to the pressures of maintaining a white presence at the school, Chernock and her staff, perhaps subconsciously, granted special treatment to the minority of white faces in the hallways while relegating many of her black students to second-class status.

Still, the efforts of the HHSA and the policies that Chernock implemented at Henry did serve to stabilize the community in the early 1960s. By 1961, the school had balanced out to approximately 70 percent black and 30 percent white.[34] Though the numbers were not reflective of the overall population of the neighborhood—in 1960 roughly 15 percent of West Mount Airy residents were African American—the transition appeared to have stalled as families began to reinvest in local public education.[35] For a brief moment, it seemed as though integrationists in the community had successfully stemmed the panic and halted the rapid transformation at Henry School.

But these individual efforts were not enough to overcome the institutional mandates of the Philadelphia Board of Public Education. In the early 1960s, the board once again implemented new redistricting initiatives and set updated class-size guidelines; between the fall of 1962 and the fall of 1964, enrollment at Henry swelled. Over those two years, the population of white students grew by 70 percent, while the African American student population expanded by 165 percent.[36] Even as the school was, as Chernock had boasted proudly to Stalvey, beginning to recalibrate, the institution could not support its expanding student body. By the end of 1964, Henry, constructed at the turn of the century as the city's first modern fireproof school building, was operating out of sixteen permanent classrooms and four temporary units.[37] During the previous two years, the school's population had expanded from 590 to 835 students.[38] Whereas the earlier instability at Henry stemmed more from the fear of transition than from actual depreciation in quality, the district initiatives in the middle of the 1960s brought concrete changes to the classrooms. The teacher-to-student ratio soared, special activities were eliminated to accommodate growing class sizes, school personnel were increasingly overworked, and desks and books and equipment began to fall into disrepair as the school struggled to provide for the influx of students.[39]

HHSA president Robert Rutman believed that these numbers would only continue to increase. According to his projections, 25 percent of the homes in Mount Airy were owned by young families with more children than the previous occupants.[40] In effect, said Rutman, the current enrollment figures, which had briefly stalled, represented a skewed sense of stasis. Realistically, he believed, within a few years the population would slant toward a younger mean and median age and an increased ratio of children to adults. "Accordingly," Rutman wrote to C. Taylor Whittier, school board superintendent, in the fall of 1964, "the overall prospects are for continued enrollment which exceed the Board of Education standards. . . . This situation cannot but adversely affect the school and severely limit the opportunities for improvement."[41]

According to newspaper reports, by the end of that year Henry had become the most crowded school in the Sixth District, itself the most crowded district in the city.[42] In one-third of the school's classes, more than forty students crammed into the overflowing rooms. The classroom ceilings and stairwell railings were crumbling. There was a widespread teacher shortage. Students seeking to enroll were being turned away. The district was renting space for the school from the Germantown Jewish Centre and Summit Presbyterian Church, but they needed a more permanent solution.[43] In a proposal put forth to the Board of Education, WMAN called for district support for the expansion of the Henry School grounds. The report emphasized that the neighborhood had successfully alleviated the problems associated with racial transition through an effective interdependent effort by a committed parent base and an innovative faculty, but it noted that the swelling student body was endangering the precarious balance that the community had achieved. "The increases in enrollment," the WMAN Schools Committee wrote, "have placed a severe strain on the school and have caused some curtailment of essential educational activities. The conservative projections for the future leave no doubt as to the danger to both the school and the community. Failure to counteract this danger can be expected to destabilize both school and community."[44]

WMAN and the HHSA launched a campaign to convince the board to expand the school's budget and build additional classroom facilities. They called for the addition of twelve permanent classrooms to be constructed on two adjoining lots. Applying a combination of threat and flattery, the organizations sought to garner support for the school's middle-class base. Although some members of the school board thought that these demographics meant that Mount Airy required less institutional backing, the community groups argued that, in fact, the neighborhood's economic makeup entitled the region to greater assistance for what residents brought to the district as a whole.[45] In a 1963 WMAN statement on the district's budget, the school subcommittee had linked the city's tax base to the very residents sending their children to Henry School. "To a great extent," the committee wrote, "the schools of Philadelphia are being financed by real estate taxes collected from the more desirable areas [of the] the city." The report went on to implore the board for additional funding, arguing that the integration efforts in the neighborhood and the local institutions that supported them could not be sustained unless the district allocated to them the resources necessary to keep their schools competitive with the adjacent suburbs. "If integration fails in Mount Airy," the report concluded, hinting at the ominous demise of the community without district support, "the Board of Education will witness an extension of that creeping process of social and economic blight, overcrowding of housing, overcrowding of schools, and decrease in tax values of real estate on which the school income is derived."[46]

Throughout the young history of West Mount Airy's integration project, community leaders had relied on a coordinated collaboration with governmental agencies and institutions in order to preserve and maintain the character of the neighborhood, racially and economically. These relationships were critical to the community's success; the careful balance of internal control and external support had created the structure for stable integration. When the quality of the schools began to erode, WMAN attempted to employ this same model to raise standards and restore the standing of Henry School throughout the city. Mount Airy residents wanted a neighborhood school supported by district resources. The Board of Education, however, operated under a different model of organization and policy implementation; this external management by the board shifted that equilibrium, and the grassroots liberalism that had worked so well in the community's early efforts at creating residential integration began to break down as local organizers fought for control over neighborhood schools.[47]

In the years that followed, Mount Airy community leaders sought to prove to the school board that it was in the district's best interest to provide the necessary support for the elementary school. By the mid-1960s, the neighborhood had become a nationally recognized model of a successfully integrated community. Liberal organizations around the country looked to West Mount Airy as an ideal worthy of emulation, an example of what racial justice could be. Through this publicity, Philadelphia, too, had gained positive attention. Accordingly, WMAN believed, the Board of Education could not ignore them.[48] Mount Airy residents inundated Superintendent Whittier's office with letters and phone calls, urging him to consider the school's unique potential as a model of successful racial integration. The neighborhood's population had expanded precisely because parents were attracted to the prospect of an integrated community, they reminded him. But this influx of new young families brought with it the need for increased institutional support. "The neighborhood strongly desires that the school maintain its high quality of education so that [it] can continue to serve as an attraction for people of all races," wrote WMAN president Louis Levy. Without the district's assistance, said Levy, the potential existed for the momentum to shift in the efforts toward stabilization.[49]

Such sentiments echoed a letter that HHSA president Rutman had submitted to the school board months earlier, imploring the committee to consider taking over a large property adjacent to the school, where a local realtor had applied for a zoning variance to build an apartment house:

> The Henry School has the good fortune of remaining a key point of attraction in the entire school system. Certainly this attractiveness, which offers a proper example for the other schools in our district and in the city, cannot be sacrificed lightly without engendering serious questions as to the underlying educational philosophy . . . Can citizens and community organizations be expected to seriously participate in the solution of urban education if their efforts are not cultivated and assisted by the school system?[50]

Rutman's statement was a clear indication of the tension between the desire for local control and the need for citywide support. Even though WMAN pushed for community autonomy, it required institutional resources and assistance in order to keep the neighborhood integration project from collapsing. A year later, in 1966, the board heeded local complaints, approving a permanent annex for Henry School on Carpenter Lane, at the site of the previous zoning variance.

These increased efforts on the part of WMAN to court the assistance of the school board came during a moment of radical transformation for the Philadelphia public school system. In 1965, the city passed a new home rule charter that shifted fiscal control from the state legislature to the city school district. The legislation reduced the school board from fifteen members to nine and called for seats to be filled with people with fresh energy. Superintendent Whittier struggled with how to implement these new initiatives, and in 1966 he resigned from his post. Calls for district support from West Mount Airy parents were passed on to his successor, Mark Shedd.

Shedd, a graduate of the Harvard University Graduate School of Education, had cut his superintendent teeth in Englewood, New Jersey. His mission when he had arrived in the integrated Manhattan suburb five years earlier was to stabilize a district up in arms over a state-mandated desegregation plan. His success at managing the transition in Englewood and avoiding racial agitation gave the Massachusetts native a national reputation in school reform; by the end of his tenure there, every school in the Englewood district had seen black enrollment figures between 38 percent and 50 percent of their total populations.[51] Still, many questioned whether Shedd was equipped for the larger and more volatile Philadelphia district. As the *Philadelphia Tribune* reported, Shedd was "leaving a position where there [were] only 4,000 school children out of a population of 28,000 and [taking] over a system that has 270,000 pupils in 256 schools with close to 20,000 professional and non-professional employees."[52] But former Philadelphia mayor Richardson Dilworth believed he was ready. Shedd came to Englewood "amid racial turmoil and tension," said Dilworth. He worked hard there to bring black and white families together to find quick and meaningful solutions to the growing racial divide. "He's dedicated," the politician continued, "and he knows how to get things done."[53] In 1967, Shedd came to Philadelphia to become the highest paid public official in the city.[54]

In his first year in office, the new leader crafted an agenda so comprehensive and innovative that it prompted journalist Henry Resnik to write, "Philadelphia . . . seemed to be well on the way, more than any other American city, to coping successfully with the failures of urban education."[55] Shedd proposed a plan to redefine the relationship between the city and its schools. With an eye toward racial integration and a drive for improved quality across the district, the superintendent worked to create what he termed a "Model School District," bringing Philadelphia residents into conversation with the Board of Education and calling on them to make decisions about what should take place within local schools. As Shedd wrote in an open letter published in the *Philadelphia Tribune*:

> New channels must be set to involve the community and satisfy it. . . . So what we are really talking about when we use the word 'responsiveness' is creating an open, trusting, and accepting climate for human relationships: a tolerance not simply for race or religion, but a respect for ideas, feelings, and concerns of those above and below in the school hierarchy and those outside it. Without this climate the unlocking of talent and the mobilization of resources needed will simply not be possible.[56]

Shedd's push for local control of schools raised broader questions about the nature of community within a large urban metropolis. As WMAN made clear in both its bylaws and its brochures and mailings, the physical space supported by the organization was bounded by Wissahickon Creek to the west, Germantown Avenue to the east, Cresheim Valley Road to the north, and Johnson Street to the south.[57] The area east of Germantown Avenue became known as East Mount Airy. In 1965, when East Mount Airy Neighbors was formed, the organization drew its eastern border at Stenton Avenue. In imagining the community as this confined entity, East Mount Airy Neighbors was able to regulate the activities within its internally defined borders, without contending with the region just to the east of Stenton, a neighborhood known by official designation as West Oak Lane that went on to experience rapid white flight and economic downturn in the late 1960s.

By naming their neighborhoods and drawing concrete geographic boundaries, community leaders could craft a sense of identity within those walls. Although socially, politically, occupationally, or religiously, residents could, by choice, engage with members of other communities around the city, it was only through the educational system that broader segments of one neighborhood would come into contact with broader segments of a separate neighborhood, often beyond the control of the individual students and parents involved. In this way, educational communities at times differed from neighborhood communities; where parents sent their children to school was largely dependent on how the school board drew its boundaries.[58] In Philadelphia, the continual shifts of district lines within, around, and through

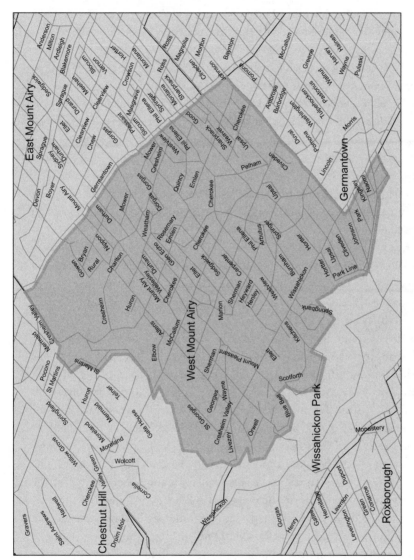

Map 2. Street map of West Mount Airy. Prepared by David Ford, assistant director,
Temple University Social Science Data Library.

residential communities made it impossible to maintain a sense of cohesion among homeowners and a sense of demographic control over local schools. Thus, as West Mount Airy Neighbors tried to manage the progress of the Henry School, the organization could not avoid the larger issues facing the Philadelphia public education system and the city at large.

In 1966, as one of the final initiatives of Whittier's term, the school board put forth two new proposals to deal with the problems of overcrowding in the city's public schools. That year, Henry was chosen for inclusion in a pilot program that would convert selected kindergarten-through-eighth grade elementary schools into K–4 institutions.[59] The plan included new construction of additional facilities that would serve grades five through eight. The initiative, meant to alleviate congestion in neighborhood schools, was offered as an alternative to the board's earlier failed attempts to implement a mandatory busing system.[60] Residents in West Mount Airy worried about the destabilizing effects that the initiative would have on Henry. Though transforming the K–8 school into a K–4 would ease many of the capacity issues, it would also bring in an entirely new—likely poorer and blacker—population from outside of the neighborhood boundaries. Parents feared that another period of transition would push the precariously integrated institution beyond the point of recovery.[61]

As the community began to mount a campaign to protest the proposal, though, their attention was quickly redirected. In July of that year, the school board informed the HHSA of its interest in acquiring through eminent domain six additional properties adjacent to the schoolyard on Sedgwick Street for an additional play facility and increased parking for the faculty. Sedgwick, one of the most organized blocks in the neighborhood and one of the most stable, quickly rallied to halt the district's plans. More than one hundred residents signed the circulating petition. The project was unnecessary, local homeowners maintained, in light of the likely conversion of Henry School to a K–4 facility. And even if the pilot program did not take off, they continued, the newly constructed annex would provide ample space for a yard and parking facilities, as it negated the need for the four temporary trailers that had been occupying the grounds.[62]

Moreover, petitioners argued, it would be a step backward to break up such a thriving block community. "These homes do not represent urban blight," one resident wrote, "but rather middle-income housing whose owners, together with the remainder of Sedgwick Street, exemplify the city, state, and national goals toward democratic living." A decade before, as the Church Community Relations Council was just getting off the ground, the Sedgwick Neighbors Association had provided an example on a microlevel of what the larger organization hoped to accomplish for the whole of West Mount Airy. The block, by 1966, was well-integrated economically, racially, and religiously, populated by lawyers, teachers, cabdrivers, salesmen, and city employees. Many of the homeowners sent their children to Henry and even those who did not, petitioners maintained, served as an example for the students who looked out onto the block adjacent to the schoolyard. "The unusual harmony of this street provides the school children of Henry a dramatic lesson in living and working together," the signers concluded.[63]

Ultimately, neither the K–4 plan nor the Sedgwick proposal came to fruition, but these threats, both to the school and to the neighborhood, fostered increasing anxiety among residents and families as they struggled to maintain stability. The apprehension took its toll on the Henry School community. Parents worried that the day-to-day experiences of their children were being compromised. Some white students reported feeling physically threatened by their minority status.[64] Teachers struggled to maintain a sense of continuity. Gradually, the tangible problems of underfunding and over-enrollment, paired with this looming concern over institutional change, prompted many West Mount Airy families to reevaluate their commitment to the public school system.

Though Mount Airy parents had a long history of sending their children to the area's several prominent private and parochial schools, through the 1960s neighborhood enrollment at these independent schools spiked.[65] At Germantown Friends School, which opened its doors in 1845 to provide a progressive coeducational foundation for Quaker children, the number of enrolled K–12 students from the 19119 zip code swelled from 178 in the 1956–57 academic year to 253 in 1967–68.[66] At Chestnut Hill Academy, an all-boys college preparatory school, enrollment from 19119 climbed from thirty-eight in 1955–56 to sixty-seven in 1967–68.[67] Though these two schools attracted different demographics of students, both were drawing new families from West Mount Airy, who were leaving local public schools in search of a sense of security for their children.

Historically, these private institutions in the area largely catered to a white constituency. However, in the years following the Second World War, middle-class black families from West Mount Airy began seeking admittance for their children, and by the mid-1960s a number of the schools saw rising applications from African Americans. In 1948, Joan Cannady became one of the first black students to enroll at Germantown Friends School.[68] The oldest child of an upwardly mobile African American family who had moved to northwest Philadelphia in 1944 and to West Mount Airy in 1951, Cannady began kindergarten at the Emlen School in 1945. When she was in second grade, she later recalled, she and her best friend were punished for reading ahead in their schoolbooks. Cannady's father, a mathematics teacher at Bok High School in the city's Germantown neighborhood, was enraged by what he saw as Emlen's overall approach to education. His longtime friend, a teacher at Germantown Friends, encouraged him to speak with admissions personnel at the school.[69] The Germantown Friends School, which had received censure a decade earlier from Raymond and Sadie Alexander for its refusal to admit minority students, sat down with the Mount Airy parents.[70]

Cannady became the first black student to enroll in the elementary school at Germantown Friends, and the first to graduate from the upper school, in 1958.[71] For several years, she was the only African American student at the Germantown Friends School. By the mid-1950s, though, other children of color were beginning to trickle in. According to school yearbooks, in 1959 there were five black students in grades seven through twelve. By 1967, there were upwards of twenty.[72] That same year, Chestnut Hill Academy had six black students, nearly all of elementary school age. In 1965, Norwood Academy, an all-boys K-8 Catholic school in the city's Chestnut Hill neighborhood, had as many as half a dozen African American students enrolled, up from zero prior to 1961. Many of these black children attending area private schools were coming from the 19119 zip code.[73] Although the actual numbers were small, the larger trends are telling; by the mid-1960s, middle-class residents of West Mount Airy, black and white alike, were growing disillusioned with the Philadelphia public school experience.

Witnessing this retreat from local schools, the WMAN board once again grew concerned about the impact of educational instability on the viability of the larger community. In the spring of 1968, the Schools Committee undertook a new study to understand why local families were leaving public schools. Results echoed the concerns that families had brought before the school board earlier in the decade; surveys indicated that parents were frustrated by the large class sizes and the lack of personal attention.[74] They spoke of inadequate equipment and facilities and noted that their children were not feeling sufficiently challenged.[75] Some worried that by sending their children to Henry School, they were setting them up to be ill-prepared in college and the professional world. As one Jewish mother reportedly remarked, "[Non-Jewish white parents] can afford to be liberal. My kids need the best education I can afford. They'll have plenty of job discrimination when they grow up."[76]

Although community leaders saw many of these concerns as legitimate, at a basic level the WMAN board believed that parents simply lacked sufficient information about what was taking place at Henry School.[77] As Lois Stalvey later wrote, many white parents believed that black students were aggressive. Some were concerned that their children would pick up poor grammatical tendencies from black teachers. Others worried about lice, about slang, about bullying. Principal Chernock suspected that white parents also harbored significant fear about the prospect of interracial dating, an issue that by the late 1960s occupied an active presence in the public imagination.[78]

In 1967, in the landmark case of *Loving v. Virginia*, the U.S. Supreme Court took up the question of whether a 1924 Virginia antimiscegenation law violated the Fourteenth Amendment of the U.S. Constitution. Writing for a unanimous court, Chief Justice Thurgood Marshall held that the freedom to marry is a basic right in American society. "To deny this right on so unsupportable a basis as racial classifications embodied in these statutes, classifications so directly subversive of the principle of equality at the heart of the Fourteenth Amendment," wrote Marshall, "is surely to deprive all the State's citizens of liberty without due process of law."[79] Though the legal implications of the decision were felt only in discrete areas of the country, the cultural ramifications reverberated across America. A new consciousness was beginning to emerge; white parents around the country, who had not previously considered the possibility that their children may marry outside of their own race, suddenly feared placing their daughters in close proximity to black youth.[80]

Three months later, Americans witnessed what *Ebony* magazine described as "the unprecedented interracial marriage involving the highest ranked

American public official in history," when eighteen-year-old Margaret Rusk, daughter of U.S. Secretary of State Dean Rusk, married Guy Smith.[81] Rusk was white; Smith, African American. The event prompted editorials and articles in publications throughout the country. The September 29 cover of *Time* featured a black-and-white photo of the couple as they left the Stanford University chapel following their ceremony; the headline read "Mr. & Mrs. Guy Smith—An Interracial Wedding."[82] The corresponding article spoke of the marriage as a symbol of racial tolerance. "In a year when black-white [*sic*] animosity has reached a violent crescendo in the land," the magazine reported, "two young people and their parents showed that separateness is far from the sum total of race relations in the U.S.—that to the marriage of two minds, color should be no impediment." Following that utopian vision of color-blind liberalism, however, the piece chronicled the widespread censure that the couple had received, the hundreds of critical calls and letters that were inundating the State Department, and the concern over the possible impact of the relationship on President Lyndon Johnson's bid for reelection the following year. For many, the wedding seemed to highlight a growing anxiety over interracial romance and, even more distressing, the children that could result.[83]

On December 11 of that year, this cultural unease became fodder for a new drawing room comedy from Columbia Pictures. Stanley Kramer's *Guess Who's Coming to Dinner* featured a young white woman who arrives at her parents' house with the news that she is engaged to the African American doctor whom she met on vacation. The award-winning film, which grossed nearly $57 million domestically and was named by *Variety* in 1968 as the eighteenth-highest-grossing film of all time, portrayed the exact situation that Henry School's Beatrice Chernock believed many Mount Airy residents feared: the white, liberal parents of the bride-to-be, who had raised their daughter on the principles of equality and justice, struggled to come to terms with the prospect of a black son-in-law.[84] Ultimately, Spencer Tracy, as the distraught father, gave his blessing to the union, leaving the audience to consider what they might do in the same situation. At Henry School, administrators attempted to alleviate concerns by temporarily suspending the school dance program for seventh and either graders, but, recalled Chernock, the policy did little to quell such fears.[85] For parents of students in their final years at the elementary school, the question of interracial romance also highlighted new concerns: What would happen to their children when they graduated from Henry and had to navigate junior high and high school outside of West Mount Airy?

As officials at Henry struggled to maintain a sense of stability, eight miles away at the school board offices Mark Shedd and his team were working on a plan to decentralize the district, allowing for greater local control and community input. In the midst of cries for black power in Philadelphia, the fall of 1967 saw growing agitation in schools across the city. For several months, the Black People's Unity Movement had been organizing for greater representation, increased resources, and intraracial solidarity and empowerment among black youth. Though members of his administration were wary of relinquishing control, Shedd believed that by bringing local residents into the conversation, he could quell the demonstrations and avoid further confrontation.[86]

The superintendent's concerns proved prescient. At 12:30 p.m. on November 17, more than thirty-five hundred black students from as many as twelve city high schools converged on the main administration building at 21st Street and the Benjamin Franklin Parkway, in the northwest corner of Center City. The students had staged walkouts earlier that morning from schools in Germantown, North Philadelphia, West Philadelphia, and South Philadelphia, and many marched through the city with gold "Black Power" buttons pinned to their chests.[87] At first, Shedd invited protest leaders into the building to negotiate. For nearly two hours, the groups deliberated on matters of curricular representation and school reform. But talks were interrupted when Police Commissioner Frank Rizzo dispatched 111 officers, dressed in full riot gear, into the crowds.[88] By the end of the day, fifty-seven protestors had been taken into custody and upwards of thirty students, twelve officers, and twenty-seven bystanders had been treated for injuries.[89] Though negotiations failed that afternoon, in the weeks and months to follow Shedd reaffirmed his commitment to negotiation and rehabilitation. The superintendent sought to work with black students and their parents, both to ameliorate tensions and to usher in tangible reforms in neighborhood schools. The board created ad hoc committees for curricular development and race relations and worked to pass legislation swiftly.

Still, the earlier standoff between the school board and protestors and the subsequent clash with police spread outward to animate racial hostilities among students at integrating and transitioning schools across the city.

Figure 6. Police officer grabs protester at November 1967 school board demonstration, *Philadelphia Bulletin*. Used with permission from Germantown Jewish Centre, Philadelphia.

With the increased focus on racial empowerment and separatism, schools in the Sixth District became sites of acute tension as students, parents, and administers struggled with how to negotiate the changing cultural landscape. In West Mount Airy, even parents who remained committed to keeping their children in the public elementary schools were becoming increasingly anxious about the prospect of academic life after Henry.

Germantown High School, which served the Sixth District elementary and junior high schools, saw a primarily African American student body emerge by the late 1960s. Because many of the white—and black—middle-class families in the region took advantage of the educational alternatives available to them, enrolling their children in one of the many secular or religiously affiliated college preparatory schools in northwest Philadelphia or applying to one of the city's prestigious magnet schools, Germantown's students were often less academically prepared and from less economically stable families. The school struggled with widespread gang activity and rampant teacher turnover.[90]

One of the feeder schools for Germantown, Leeds Junior High was experiencing swift white flight in the waning years of the 1960s, and the attendant turmoil spilled over to impact the whole of northwest Philadelphia. A white ethnic enclave that had sprung up in the post–World War II years, the neighborhood surrounding Leeds had had the potential to be a "great neighborhood," reported the *Philadelphia Tribune* in 1972.[91] Like West Mount Airy, West Oak Lane was within the city limits but sheltered from the rush of downtown. It offered dependable public transportation and a close-knit community, and it was bound by parkland that seamlessly blended the neighborhood with Germantown to the southeast and the inner-ring suburbs to the northwest. Though transition started slowly in the middle of the 1960s as the first black families began to move east, by 1970 the community had decidedly tipped. Mount Airy parents, just a few miles away, looked on as white flight took hold, particularly concerned with the impact on the neighborhood's schools.

As West Oak Lane native Jeff Zimmerman later recalled, "There was a sense of trepidation amongst the adults in the neighborhood that blacks were moving closer to the area. They didn't know what to expect, but they had a sense that it wasn't anything good." Zimmerman, who grew up on the 8500 block of Michener Street and attended Leeds from 1967 to 1969, remembered a rising sentiment of fear throughout the community. "There were police around all the time. . . . More and more stores began installing bulletproof glass in their windows. . . . My friends and I didn't want to walk around by ourselves at night anymore." By the end of the decade, Leeds Junior High was suffering the trying effects of the educational instability that such residential upheaval brought with it. "The school became a tough place in the late 1960s," Zimmerman reflected. "There was a real growing sense of animosity. . . . When we were in elementary school, we were all friends, black and white . . . [but] by junior high, people didn't trust each other."[92]

In 1967, several classrooms at the junior high school were vandalized. When four black students were arrested three days later, one teacher kept her white students in class during recess, warning them that they might get hurt on the playground. A black West Mount Airy resident, who sent her daughter to Leeds, reported that the same teacher, an African American woman, had told her primarily black class, "It's your kind of people who cause all the crime in the city. You make it harder for decent Negroes."[93]

Three years later, racial antagonism erupted at the school once again. On the morning of Wednesday, April 8, 1970, a black student at Leeds reportedly assaulted a white eighth grader. According to one witness, a teacher who had watched the episode unfold turned and walked away. Later that day, reported the *Philadelphia Bulletin* of the bystander's account, "a group of black youth, not students from the school, went through the corridors roughing up white pupils."[94] In response, the paper said, several white teenagers drove past the school that afternoon, shouting racial epithets and waving guns at younger black children. The following day, older African American students at Leeds formed a "protective unit" around those who had been threatened.[95] By the end of the week, members of the Philadelphia branch of the Jewish Defense League (JDL), described by the *Bulletin* as a militant organization that had formed in the city a year earlier, invaded the school to defend the minority of white, predominantly Jewish, members of the student body. The national JDL had been founded in New York City in 1968 with the expressed intention of protecting American Jews around the country "by any means necessary." At Leeds, the activists—five adults and four students—took over the school office for more than an hour and unsuccessfully attempted to commandeer the building's public address system. As the *Bulletin* reported, they sought "to dramatize what they called a need for greater protection of students from violence."[96] The principal reportedly locked himself in his own office and refused to come out. Later, all five adults involved, including the JDL's administrative director, a Spanish teacher at Olney High School, were charged with disorderly conduct.[97]

These incidents of violence and turmoil in the Sixth District had significant implications for West Mount Airy parents wrestling with whether to send their children to Henry School. A week after the JDL episode, a group of one hundred parents and students gathered at the Grace Episcopal Church in East Mount Airy. "We can't send our children to school and be sure they'll be safe there all day," said moderator Aaron Silverstein. Silverstein recounted for the crowd the steps taken by the Leeds administration to safeguard against further violence within the school. Following the April incident, he said, the district established a special security force made up of ten guards to patrol the halls. But, Silverstein lamented, the force was set to remain in place only so long as the principal deemed their presence necessary, and they would be removed if the school board felt that they were more urgently needed elsewhere.[98] Those in attendance at the Grace Episcopal meeting sought a greater institutional commitment to protecting the Leeds student community. Many feared that the instability in the secondary schools would seep into the local elementary schools. Others worried about the decision they would have to make once their children graduated from Henry; they questioned whether their commitment to integration should eclipse their concern for their families.

Of course, some parents held firm to the belief that maintaining a white middle-class presence in the schools was critical to the integration project and to the larger fight for racial justice. "If [my children's] being there helped make things better for [poorer black students] . . . it was worth it," Lois Stalvey later wrote of her steadfast commitment to keep her three children enrolled at Henry.[99] Superintendent Shedd, too, sent his children to Germantown High School. For others committed to residential integration, though, the structural problems of the education system forced them to reconsider how far they were willing to go in their efforts to create an interracial society. As historian and Mount Airy resident Dennis Clark later reflected, many parents "[were] willing to put themselves on the line in different ways, but they [were] not willing to gamble with their children.[100] Such sentiments were commonplace in these intentionally integrated communities by the late 1960s. Marvin Caplan, cofounder of the Washington, D.C.-based Neighbors, Inc., moved his younger children out of the neighborhood elementary school once he learned that his older daughter felt bullied and alienated as one of the few white students in her class. Caplan had at first been willing, he said, to "sacrifice [my] children for [my] beliefs," but he reconsidered when he saw the impact those beliefs were having on their lives.[101]

By 1970, even as Mount Airy's residential integration remained stable, the crisis of confidence over neighborhood schools had resulted in dramatic declines in enrollment. According to urban planner Leonard Heumann, that year more than 63 percent of white parents and 32 percent of black parents of elementary-school-age students in West Mount Airy reported sending their children to private schools or to nonlocal public schools. Even more striking, 93 percent of parents of white high-school-age students and 36 percent of their black counterparts were sending their children either to private schools or to special magnet schools within the district.[102]

And then, on Monday, February 1, 1971, a shot rang out that many later said killed any hope for public education in Philadelphia. Samson Freedman, a longtime Leeds teacher and member of the West Oak Lane community, who had decried the actions of the JDL a year earlier, had just entered the Leeds schoolyard when fourteen-year-old Kevin Simmons approached him.[103] At 3:00 p.m., Simmons raised a .45 caliber handgun, reportedly yelled, "Look out, y'all," and pulled the trigger, shooting the fifty-six-year-old ceramics teacher once in the head.[104] Two days earlier, Freedman, a card-carrying member of the Philadelphia NAACP and the president of the interracial organization Northwest Neighbors, had punished Simmons with detention for cursing in the hallways. Leeds was the eighth school that Simmons had attended in nine years. His parents moved frequently, his grandmother later told reporters, "to try to do a little better for their children." The boy transferred to Leeds a year earlier, following an incident at his previous school when he was struck by a teacher. Simmons's father had gone to the school later that day threatening to kill the offending faculty member. Officials called the police, and Simmons looked on as his father was led away in handcuffs.[105]

According to newspaper accounts, Simmons returned to Leeds the day after Freedman had issued the detention to steal the dreaded pink slip that would have sent him to the local reform school. When the ceramics teacher caught him, he took Simmons to the principal's office. The student left soon after and went looking for Freedman.[106] He only wanted to scare him, Simmons later said.[107]

A collective wail arose around the region. Freedman's death marked a historic event in Philadelphia; it was the first time in the city's history that a student had shot and killed a teacher. Superintendent Shedd made the unprecedented decision to close all city schools the following day in memory of the slain educator. Newspapers featured the story for days after the incident. Everyone mourned the loss of a beloved member of the Leeds faculty and a long-standing leader in the transitioning neighborhood of West Oak Lane.[108] Many called the teacher's violent death a senseless tragedy—senseless, but perhaps not surprising. Around Philadelphia, people seemed to understand that Samson Freedman's murder was part of a larger battle for the very survival of the city. And while communities offered varying explanations for the causes of the crisis, everyone seemed to agree that Philadelphia was quickly losing ground.

The *Philadelphia Tribune* reported that Freedman was a leader in his community, trying to bring peace and stability to the ever-changing landscape of West Oak Lane. The paper quoted Bertram Bernard, a community activist and longtime friend to Freedman, who described the incident as a three-car collision. Freedman was in the first car, said Bernard, and Simmons was in the second. The school district represented the third. The accident began with the district striking Simmons from behind. Simmons, in turn, skidded into Freedman.[109] Wrote one *Tribune* columnist, "Mr. Freedman was not the victim of a gun but the victim of a cold, selfish, and decaying system. Was the expulsion of that boy who is accused of death, and the expulsion of many more disturbed children, the answer to a nation of unwanted and disturbed youth? White Racism, Black Selfishness, and overall Greed. These are the culprits that created the conditions for the death of Samson Freedman."[110] Many mourners pointed to a broken educational system and entrenched cultural and structural racism as the root causes of the violence at Leeds. Although Simmons may have been the catalyst, they said, Freedman's death was a product of deeply embedded institutional problems that needed to be addressed.

East Mount Airy Neighbors board member Gisha Berkowitz described the shooting as an explosion. "I think both are victims, Samson and the boy," Berkowitz told reporters. "The incident is a total breakdown in education and human relations. Even if it is just a matter of a sick kid, it is a sign of a serious problem."[111] West Mount Airy Neighbors quickly released a statement urging the community to remain calm. "We are . . . aware of those who would exploit tragedies such as this to disrupt the quality of life in Mount Airy and the general community," WMAN president Oliver Lancaster said. "We call on all our neighbors to take a calm, rational approach to facing up to the many problems that have existed and will continue to exist, should we be swayed by emotion rather than reason, by fear rather than determination."[112] Lois Stalvey, too, saw Simmons as the victim of larger systemic inequality. "[He was] a human bomb," she later wrote, "triggered by other teachers, [who] had killed someone who was trying to help."[113] She believed that the root of the problem was a decaying system that would let a young black man fall through the cracks.

For many other whites around the city, though, this blame was misplaced. The *Philadelphia Bulletin* reported that the crime evidenced the growing unruliness of black youth. There will be a "crescendo of panic," predicted Cedarbrook Area Neighbors president Edward T. Feierstein. "We have been working so hard to stabilize the community and a fourteen-year-old dumps all our efforts into the garbage truck."[114] To some fearful white families, this explanation was too generous. Freedman's murder by a young African American troublemaker proved what they had believed all along: black kids were violent and aggressive. They could not be trusted.

Samson Freedman's death marked the end of any hope of an integrated educational system for many Philadelphians. "This killing has made all of our work for the school go for naught," said William Carter, West Oak Lane Coordinating Council president. "Now there will be a howl for a complete police state in the school, and under the circumstances, what can you say?" Michael Feinman of the Mount Airy Community Action Council (a neighborhood organization focused on stabilization in West Oak Lane) called the event a turning point for the Philadelphia School District. "It has been one violent occurrence after another at Leeds," said Feinman. "Leeds is eighty percent black this year. Next year, with parents concerned about the safety of their children . . . ," he reportedly trailed off.[115]

The years following Freedman's death brought a marked decline in elementary school enrollment for the Philadelphia School District, from 171,324 in the 1968–69 school year to 143,432 in 1975–76.[116] In West Mount Airy, the 1970s saw educational resegregation rates climb, aided, too, by a budgetary crisis and teachers' strike that left local elementary schools in a state of turmoil that community leaders could not assuage. By the 1972–73 academic year, more than three hundred students from the 19119 zip code were attending Germantown Friends School, an increase of more than fifty students in five years. At Chestnut Hill Academy the numbers had swelled as well, from sixty-seven in 1967–68 to roughly ninety in 1972–73 and more than 110 in 1973–74.[117]

By 1979, as WMAN celebrated its twentieth anniversary, more white parents than ever before were choosing not to send their children to Henry School. "For all their apparent liberalism," *Philadelphia Inquirer* staff reporter Howard Shapiro wrote, "a large number of parents do not put their money where their mouths are. They put it, instead, in private schools. Some critics say these are the very people whose support could greatly enhance public education."[118] For WMAN, the impact of Freedman's murder was emblematic of the organization's inability to manage the local schools amid larger institutional and cultural forces. But perhaps more significant, the response of community leaders to the crisis was reflective of larger threats to the neighborhood's viability. By the early 1970s, residents of West Mount Airy were struggling with how to adapt to widespread political, economic, and social changes to the country's urban landscape, as established community leaders worked to maintain the postwar liberal ideal on which they rested their integrationist mission.

Chapter 6

Confrontations in Black and White

The Crisis of Integration

On June 9, 1975, George Schermer once again addressed the WMAN board at its seventeenth annual meeting. In recent years, the organization had found itself in the midst of an institutional crisis. The rising culture of black power and the growing hostilities in area schools were, by the late 1960s and early 1970s, also giving way to racial clashes within the West Mount Airy community. At the same time, the city of Philadelphia was experiencing a political and economic crisis as deindustrialization drew resources away from the northern urban center, resulting in intensifying decline and increasing incidents of crime. As West Mount Airy Neighbors struggled to reorient its institutional mission to negotiate this growing racial divide, the crisis of crime became the battleground on which racial strife in the neighborhood was fought. "Some groups still resist change," Schermer told the crowd, "but change is an inherent part of the life process. Racial change is just one example. . . . We must now focus on conservation and preservation. We now *must* deal with the problems of our community. A degree of disagreement is a good thing, but we must be able to deal creatively with change" (emphasis in original).[1]

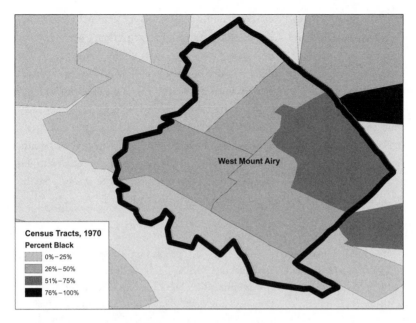

Map 3. Map of West Mount Airy by percentage of black residents, 1970 census data.
Prepared by David Ford, assistant director, Temple University Social Science Data Library.

After a decade of vigilance to protect and preserve the neighborhood's residential, educational, and economic stability, WMAN was, by the late 1960s, experiencing a sense of organizational fatigue. Throughout the community, homeowners were growing frustrated with what they saw as the association's stale organizing tactics and a sense of virtuous self-righteousness. In an editorial published in the WMAN newsletter, one resident wrote:

> West Mount Airy Neighbors is now nine years old, and our community has gained national recognition for its work in the areas of integration, zoning, housing, and schools, but has it gone to our heads? Are we still the leading community organization in Philadelphia? I question . . . what we are doing to alleviate overcrowding in our schools and to improve the quality of education? . . . Isn't it about time we all took steps to make this the community we will continue to be proud of?[2]

"I feel that WMAN once had a goal," wrote another member, "to bring together all sorts of people and to help them live harmoniously. Now that this end has been achieved, WMAN tends to rest on its laurels."[3] For many homeowners in Mount Airy, the long-standing clearinghouse seemed to be struggling to remain relevant in the face of broader changes in the fight for racial justice and new challenges to urban America. WMAN, critics seemed to be saying, was not keeping up with the realities facing the nation's cities.

African American residents in the neighborhood expressed more pointed concerns over a perceived racial hierarchy that was beginning to emerge in the community. Black homeowners of the eastern section of West Mount Airy—the area between Lincoln Drive and Germantown Avenue—hinted at feelings of alienation, a sense of frustration that WMAN was not paying attention to their interests in its programming initiatives.[4] As Don Black later recalled:

> It seemed . . . to me and [several] of the black people [in the neighborhood] . . . that the focus changed. . . . White members began to say, "Let's keep that side [west of Lincoln Drive]. It was almost like, 'we are going to keep this thing the way we want it. . . .' But they didn't really work hard to keep it the way Schermer . . . and some of the earlier members had, and some of us openly accused West Mount Airy Neighbors of forgetting that there [were] twos side to Lincoln Drive.[5]

Another black resident, a WMAN board member, later remembered a community meeting where a neighbor cried, "We need to have two West Mount Airy Neighbors . . . because there is a differentiation in the way we are treated."[6] Whether because institutional shifts in WMAN resulted in a sense of marginalization or because the rising emphasis on racial consciousness and racial pride brought into focus a new recognition of existing unequal practices and policies, by the late 1960s many of Mount Airy's African American residents began voicing protests over WMAN's emphasis on the wealthier, less populated area near Wissahickon Park.

In the summer of 1968, the WMAN board sat down to address these emerging tensions in the neighborhood and to breathe life back into the organization. At a June 8 executive committee meeting, President Jerry Balka spoke of the need for fundamental changes in the organization's vision of community organizing. WMAN, said Balka, needed to move away from the "nitty-gritty of making the community a better place to live . . . to think of the larger picture."[7] That evening, the board agreed on a new long-term goal for the organization: for perhaps the first time, community leaders sought to move beyond the Myrdalian vision of white-centric racial liberalism to examine cultural and institutional racial prejudice in the region. "We need to see ourselves before we [can] try to change attitudes in the white communities," said one member.[8] Through open dialogue and discussion, the group determined, they could work to unearth the problems of racism that existed both within the organization and throughout the larger West Mount Airy community.

WMAN, in consultation with the Wellsprings Ecumenical Center, planned a series of workshops for that fall, events that would bring together white and black Mount Airy residents to discuss the growing racial divide in the community. Wellsprings, located at the southeastern edge of the Germantown/West Mount Airy border, had been working throughout Philadelphia for a number of years to promote a program of guided intervention, "[bringing] various groups into meaningful contact with each other."[9] The organization promoted itself as "an ecumenical group of laymen" and "a community—open to persons from all religious, racial, ethnic, political, and economic groups—which establishes relationships of mutual respect and trust enough to permit and quest for personal and spiritual renewal."[10] By bringing the group in to facilitate conversation among Mount Airy residents, community leaders believed they could create a culture of meaningful communication and collaborative change within the neighborhood.

Though Wellsprings presented itself as an open, community-based organization that ground its teachings in religious liberalism, a number of WMAN board members expressed unease over a perceived undercurrent of radicalism in the group's mission. As one person asked, "Would the course be slanted in one direction—favoring 'black militancy' over 'moderation'?" The questions may have been warranted. For an event that the organization cosponsored with the Junior League of Philadelphia, participants were encouraged to read, among others, the *Autobiography of Malcolm X*; *Black Power*, by Stokely Carmichael and Charles Hamilton; *Black Power and Urban Unrest*, by Nathan Wright; *The Report of the National Advisory Commission on Civil Disorders*; *Black Rage*, by Price Cobb; and *The Race War*, by Donald Segal.[11] Still, other WMAN members gave assurances that Wellsprings had "made a fair representation and kept tight control over the discussions to prevent them from becoming one-sided." The debate prompted one WMAN member to pose what he called "the unanswerable question:" Were the residents of West Mount Airy moderate? Did WMAN serve as a moderating force in the community?[12] With local tensions intensifying and broader changes emerging in the nature of racial justice and activism, residents were beginning to question what role the longtime clearinghouse should have in the community.

Ultimately, the board concluded that in order to serve the residents of Mount Airy, in order to foster genuine community cohesion, the group needed to challenge the racial prejudice within the neighborhood. WMAN, in concert with Wellsprings, set up a six-session course titled "Face to Face: Black-White Confrontation." Wellsprings promised to adapt their offerings to the needs of the West Mount Airy community. The organization would offer a list of suggested readings and provide carefully chosen moderators to facilitate each session.[13]

That fall, WMAN sent out letters to area residents, inviting them to the upcoming workshops:

> Behind the stones and bricks of the houses in West Mount Airy live your neighbors. Many of them have harsh, racially hypocritical feelings toward others in the community. Black and white, none of us is above such feelings. Worst of all, few of us admit that we feel this way. . . . You might be surprised how many people share your view of others. Perhaps you should talk about them . . . openly. Talk about what you really think about your neighbors and your neighborhood. . . . Come to talk, come to listen. We're not sure you'll enjoy it; but we're not sure that you're supposed to.[14]

The letter hinted at Balka's efforts to reshape the conversations surrounding race relations and community cohesion. The increasingly complex urban environment in which they lived necessitated a reorientation of WMAN's goals and strategies; the organization was moving into a new era, one that Balka hoped could abandon colorblind liberalism in favor of race-consciousness and open dialogue.

The organization also signaled this evolving ideology in the corresponding press release that WMAN issued to regional media outlets. "Confrontation in Black and White," the publication read. "West Mount Airy is integrated, but is it stable? Could there be civil disorder here? What can a neighborhood do to lessen the potential for racial explosion within it? These are among the sensitive questions that a progressive community must ask itself today, and it must be prepared to act on the answers—whether it likes it or not."[15] Through direct mailing and media publicity, WMAN had issued a challenge to the residents of West Mount Airy. The organization was imploring homeowners to admit to their own racial biases, to acknowledge their deep-seated prejudices.

In response, several homeowners affirmed their commitment to liberal race relations, returning their invitations to the Face to Face classes with accountings of interracial friendships and professional relationships. Their replies implied a subtle defensiveness, challenging the need for such conversations in the community. "I am very happy being among both my white and colored neighbors," wrote Lillian Williams in a letter to WMAN. "I feel just as kindly to the colored people as I do the white folks, and anywhere that I can convey this message to my friends and associations, I do so with all my heart."[16] Sybil Watson, who noted that she was unable to attend the series because of her shift work as a nurse, wrote:

> I am returning the enclosed literature in order that it may be used for someone else. I want to state that the only reason I am still working at this business of bedside nursing . . . is because I like people and am concerned for their welfare. . . . I have <u>never in my life</u> entertained any form of racial prejudice, and do not now. As a child in school, the only one I attended school with, over fifty years ago, was a Negro named Hilda Carter and I'd love to know what became of her. I have nothing but complete respect for the numbers of Negro nurses with whom I work and am always happy when I am fortunate enough to have anyone of several of them, working for me. (emphasis in original)[17]

Other residents expressed fear that the Wellsprings workshops would have the effect of exacerbating racial tensions within the neighborhood. As Helen Worfman wrote:

> I can think of no better way to stir up trouble than this that you are preparing to do. . . . Why not leave well enough alone? I know enough of Wellsprings to know that it is a biased group, bent on presenting one side of a question. If WMAN is launching into this kind of trouble making, please remove my name from your membership list. . . . I'm convinced that the

more you talk about race relations, the more intolerant each race becomes. If you can <u>live</u> peacefully in an integrated neighborhood, that does more good than all the words in the world. I shudder to think what these six evenings will produce. (emphasis in original)[18]

Such responses hinted at a push back against WMAN's new agenda; even as some in the community were agitating for institutional change, there were others who expressed wariness over the prospect of a race-conscious orientation. This growing divide in West Mount Airy cast in sharp relief conversations taking place across the nation about the evolving nature of racial justice and the potential limitations of civil rights liberalism to effect meaningful change.

For others still, WMAN's public challenge offered the opportunity to air feelings of hostility. Said one resident, who wrote that she was withholding her name out of fear, "I don't think it is any good to try to talk about some of those people. . . . There are a few of those people [who are] alright, but I think the community should divide the neighbors—divide and see what it is like. We have some ghettoes and those <u>are</u> the people that are making them, so I don't think it would do any good to attend those meetings" (emphasis in original).[19] A West Upsal Street homeowner wrote, "Kindly do NOT send me any literature from your group" (emphasis in original). The woman described in detail her experiences during the six years that she had lived in West Mount Airy—rape, robbery, assault, and theft—noting that each crime had been committed "by NEGROES." "I have had Negroes up to my teeth," she continued, "and I am afraid to sign my name because of Blackie. . . . I was very tolerant until I experienced your conduct, which is SAVAGE. So be SAVAGES—we are going to pay plenty of taxes in support of your SAVAGES. It will take another hundred years to civilize you and then you MONKIES will still want more" (emphasis in original).[20] Though such responses were rare, they served as a reminder of the diversity of thought and interest within the neighborhood; while the loudest voices in West Mount Airy continued to affirm a zeitgeist of interracial living, there were many for whom racial justice played no role in their choice to move into the community. The increasing focus on race-consciousness may have unwittingly alienated those homeowners who lived in Mount Airy simply because of the amenities and resources the neighborhood offered.

Still, even with these condemnations, tickets for the Face to Face program quickly sold out.[21] Through November and December 1968, Mount Airy residents attended evening workshops on topics including "white racism in an integrated community," "institutional racism," "urban poverty," "black humanism," and "where do we go from here?"[22] Some sessions were moderated by race relations experts from the neighborhood, and others by representatives from city organizations and community groups. After each meeting, participants were encouraged to continue their conversations over a "relaxing coffee hour," which Wellsprings maintained was "an integral part of the program."[23]

Following the third session, WMAN board member and past president Matthew Bullock approached current president Balka with a proposal. "I personally feel it is very important that the Face-to-Face audience at the conclusion of the present association adopt some kind of statement that could serve as a rallying point for 'liberal' groups," he wrote. Bullock went on to offer a six-pronged statement, which he believed could serve as a starting point for thinking about such an institutional mandate. The draft articulated a mission for the future of West Mount Airy Neighbors, one that supported the possibility of a harmonious interracial society and placed the primary responsibility of eliminating racism within white America. "Their basic responsibility is not to 'help' black people," he wrote, "but to reexamine themselves and the organizations and institutions they control with the object of purging themselves of racism and seeking its elimination in institutionalized form." The proposal spoke of the principles of the "Black Revolution" and expressed support for notions of intraracial cohesion and empowerment while maintaining the necessity of interracial collaboration. Bullock advocated both nonviolence and active resistance as he highlighted the link between racial and economic inequality. "We believe," he concluded, "that racism is a convenient tool for the exercise of economic discrimination in an economic system which does not afford at least a minimum standard of living for all its citizens."[24] With this proposed institutional commitment toward a race-conscious agenda and an acknowledgement of a clear link between race and class, Bullock attempted to push Balka's vision of WMAN's mission further. He sought to use Face to Face as a platform to reinvigorate West Mount Airy Neighbors and to push the organization, and the neighborhood it served, to play a role in the new culture of racial justice in the late 1960s.

It seemed that many residents, however, were not ready for such radical transformation. When the organization held its postworkshop evaluation, many participants focused on the problems they experienced with the program, leaving little room to contemplate WMAN's future. Though some participants expressed appreciation for the opportunity to learn about one another through personal interaction and human contact, many more voiced frustration over the trajectory of the conversations. Some believed that Wellsprings had been unable to manage the group effectively. "There was no dialogue," one participant said in the postworkshop debriefing. "The moderator was so aggressive and antagonistic that no one could express his opinion." "The group [was] too diverse for Wellsprings to handle," said another. "They did not know who they were talking to." One attendee noted, "At the first session I was astounded at the moderator. . . . I came to learn and update my understanding of the black-white relationship. It was impossible to learn in an atmosphere of such hostility."[25] Other white participants felt as though they had not been heard, that their experiences had been minimized. "I went to the first session only and found that the course wasn't designed for me," said one homeowner. "It was designed to get Whitey. . . . It gave whites a chance to hear how a large majority of black people feel and think. . . . I didn't hear anything new, anything I don't hear everyday, things whites don't hear." "My black friends delight in taking off on me," said another, "saying it is impossible for me to understand the black situation and acting as if I were a stupid white person. They discard a lifetime commitment to equality."[26]

Above all, there emerged a consensus among participants that Face to Face unearthed a fundamental disconnect within West Mount Airy. "[The workshops] show we don't know about our own community," one resident reflected, "and what our people are thinking."[27] Rather than conceiving of the moment as an opportunity to reorient the focus of WMAN, to follow Matthew Bullock's challenge to make the organization relevant to the changing aims of racial justice, many homeowners believed that the group simply could no longer function as a community association, that it had lost its ability to bring the people of Mount Airy together. Residents, it seemed, were not interested in reshaping the institutional aims of the community clearinghouse. Even as the original goals of the integration project, first articulated in the postwar culture of possibility and optimism, faced becoming anti-

quated as the neighborhood entered the 1970s, many white residents resisted WMAN's attempts to recast the organization's mission. They perhaps
failed to see that the early efforts to stave off transition and protect the viability of the historically wealthy enclave in northwest Philadelphia were no
longer relevant in a city facing rapid economic transformation.

Across the nation, urban centers were in crisis. Deindustrialization redirected millions of jobs to the American South, and then out of the country
altogether.[28] Chicago lost one-third of its manufacturing capacity between
1967 and 1977.[29] The growth of suburbia and the trends toward white flight
were depleting urban centers of thriving tax bases. In 1970, for the first time
in the nation's history, more Americans were living in suburbs than in cities.[30]
Shopping districts closed and crime rates swelled as gang activity intensi-
fied. In Baltimore, downtown retail sales dropped 48 percent; in Boston, 38
percent. In Detroit, homicide rates rose 345 percent between 1965 and 1974,
stabilizing at these heightened levels.[31]

In Philadelphia, particularly in the industrial districts at the north and
south end of the city, factories shut their doors, leaving thousands of residents out of work. The middle-class exodus sent public schools into crisis as
funding dipped to record lows. Though Frank Rizzo, the nation's most in-
famous law-and-order police commissioner turned law-and-order mayor,
kept the area from following in the riotous footsteps of such deindustrializ-
ing cities as Detroit and Newark, New Jersey, crime rates soared as the
economy plummeted and discontent surged. Even the liberal enclave in northwest Philadelphia experienced the effects of such turmoil.

In the early 1970s, West Mount Airy began to see an upsurge in dilapidated
homes, abandoned cars, gang-related violence, and criminal activity.[32] WMAN
leaders worked to issue a response, wanting at once to protect their community
and to minimize the possibility of panic and further instability. In 1971, the
organization canceled a series of planned open house tours, out of fear that
would-be burglars might use the event to scope out properties. A year later, the
Chestnut Hill Local reported that the neighborhood was "locking up."[33] These
growing concerns about upheaval, combined with the unresolved racial tensions in the community, prompted more families to leave the area. By 1970,
West Mount Airy had shrunk to 15,365 residents, losing approximately one-
sixth of its population over the previous twenty years. Though the neighborhood had settled at a near even racial balance in population, only 58 percent of

residents lived in the same home in 1970 that they had owned in 1965.[34] As incoming WMAN president Edwin Wolf said at a 1971 board meeting:

> I think West Mount Airy is in trouble. It is beginning to be beset by those marks of urban decay—the slackening of city services; growing tension between police and community; intensifying conflicts, including the use of arms, between groups of our young people; deterioration of our schools; and overall, a slow decline in the confidence we all have in our public institutions to do the job we require of them.[35]

Wolf's critique brought into focus a broader crisis of confidence in the ability of government to alleviate the effects of deindustrialization on the nation's cities. Across the country, neighborhoods saw a renewed interest in the creation of local centers of control. Cooperatives, collectives, and community centers served to bolster neighborhood autonomy and decrease reliance on state institutions.[36] In West Mount Airy, it seemed like a moment in which WMAN would flourish; however, the resistance toward the proposed institutional shift three years earlier meant that for the group to reemerge as a stabilizing force in the neighborhood, leaders needed to return to early organizing tactics and the historic colorblind integrationist mission.

In another attempt to promote community cohesion, WMAN set out to revitalize its then-defunct Block Captain Program. The initiative was modeled after a 1969 effort that appointed organizers for each of the area's two hundred residential streets. Block captains were to act as the neighborhood's cheerleaders, the town watch, the cleanup crew, and the educators.[37] Though the program saw initial interest, just as in 1969, residents soon tired of the commitment required to sustain the effort. As WMAN settled into its second decade, more and more families were moving to the area not to be activists but simply because they wanted to live among like-minded neighbors.[38] These incoming residents had not experienced the instability of the 1950s and were unfamiliar with the number of hours that earlier integrationists had dedicated toward building and stabilizing the community. Thus, at the same time that West Mount Airy Neighbors needed more institutional support to carry on as a community clearinghouse, there were fewer people who wanted to serve in such a capacity. The requirements of the Block Captain Program were cumbersome, and they quickly took their toll. Many who signed on as block leaders chose not to continue to serve, and even fewer volunteered to replace them.[39]

Still, community leaders in Mount Airy believed that, with this increased attention to crime and its attendant causes, they could stave off the problems of urban decay that were devastating cities across the country. In addition to the Block Captain Program, organizers embarked on a neighborhood beautification project and began to focus their energies on engaging neighborhood youth.[40] WMAN member Len Persley led a camping trip for local teens. The Allens Lane Arts Center offered use of its facilities, and boys flocked to the basketball courts. A group of high schoolers held bake sales to raise funds for a block newspaper.[41]

But these efforts were not enough to protect the community from the effects of citywide deindustrialization and to heal the growing racial divide within the neighborhood. Over the next two years, Mount Airy saw petty and violent crime continue to creep up. Residents remained uncertain of the viability of the area, and WMAN struggled to maintain a sense of stability for the community and utility for the organization. By the middle of the decade, the neighborhood had reached a point of crisis. According to figures from the Mayor's Criminal Justice Improvement Team, during the first six months of 1974, incidents of larceny in the Fourteenth Police District, of which West Mount Airy is a part, rose from 499 to 630; homicide, from 9 to 12; and aggravated assault, from 89 to 140. Reports of rape climbed from 18 to 34. The percent increases from the first six months of the previous year were dramatic: accounts of larceny had risen 26.3 percent; homicide, 33.3 percent; aggravated assault, 57.3 percent; and rape, 88.9 percent. Rates of robbery, burglary, and car theft were up as well, though less acutely.[42] The escalation throughout the region, particularly of violent crime, sent residents into a panic.

Echoing recent concerns over the responsiveness of West Mount Airy Neighbors, some residents called into question the organization's historic approach to crime prevention. Their long-standing tactics had become inappropriate, WMAN past president Oliver Lancaster later reflected, for the current problems the community was facing. Over the previous decade, the organization had worked to craft a calculated balance, trying to address internal problems of increased criminal activity while at the same time condemning the erosion of police-community relations.[43] In 1972, the Philadelphia Police Department had come under the leadership of Frank

Rizzo, and his tough-on-crime agenda and bullish bravado struck many in the city, particularly African Americans and white liberals, as both inhumane and counterproductive. But in 1974, with the growing fear in the neighborhood, a group of homeowners asserted that the organization's recent response to the practices of the Philadelphia police force was confounding its agenda and hindering efforts geared toward increasing street safety.

Born October 23, 1920, Francis Lazarro Rizzo became a proud member of the Philadelphia Police Department just before his twenty-third birthday. One of the few Italian officers in an outfit dominated by second-generation Irish and Germans, Rizzo quickly earned a reputation as a public servant who would take extraordinary measures to help someone in danger. On April 22, 1944, the *Philadelphia Bulletin* first introduced the city to the new officer. "Frank Rizzo," the one paragraph blurb reported, "a patrolman attached to the 22nd and Hunting Park Avenue Station, was burned on the hands last night when he tried to extinguish a fire in an awning of the drug store of I.M. Ostrum at Tulpehocken and Baynton Streets." According to the report, someone had thrown a lit cigarette into the drugstore overhang. The off-duty Rizzo, who was a few blocks away at his father's house, put out the fire with his bare hands.[44]

Rizzo approached disorder with the same fervor. Cutting his teeth in the northeast Philadelphia neighborhood of Tioga, he routinely charged into buildings unannounced, breaking windows and crashing through doors and knocking around his targets before taking them into custody. When he was named acting captain in 1952, he was reassigned to the Sixteenth District at the corner of 39th Street and Lancaster Avenue, on the border of the city's Powelton and Mantua neighborhoods. It was the first time he had worked in a predominantly black area, and within weeks the police commissioner was fielding complaints about the young captain's harsh tactics. Cecil Moore, prior to his rise to power in Philadelphia's NAACP, was an active member of the Young Independent Political Action Committee, the legal team representing African American community members in complaints against Rizzo. As fellow YIPAC attorney Harvey Schmidt later recalled, "The reports we kept getting was that [he] was using strong-arm tactics, ... breaking doors down and being extra tough because ours was a black neighborhood."[45]

Still, throughout the city, Rizzo's popularity grew. Many white home-owners, anxious about the rising postwar neighborhood instability and the increasing black expansion into their communities, lauded the captain's efforts to maintain a sense of order. Local media outlets nicknamed him the Cisco Kid, referencing the popular 1950s television vigilante who brought his own brand of justice to the Old West.[46] While white liberals and African Americans assailed the gunslinging officer, no one in city government would touch him.

By the early 1960s, Captain Rizzo had become a national advocate for this law-and-order approach. In 1962, he was invited to address the Senate Permanent Subcommittee on Investigations. Speaking before presiding Senator John McClellan, Rizzo condemned liberal advocacy groups for their soft-on-crime philosophies. The Philadelphia officer believed that safeguarding civil liberties should not come at the expense of personal and community security. It was the victims of crime that needed protection, he testified, not the criminals. "The [ACLU] should become as concerned with the good people of the community," Rizzo said. "Their constant scream is police brutality. When they cannot reach the top police officials, when they cannot get them under their wing in other ways . . . there is only one other way they can reach us, and that is to scream police brutality against minority groups."[47] It was the first time that Rizzo had publicly linked the rhetoric of race with the rising crime rates and growing allegations of police mistreatment. As Rizzo biographer S. A. Paolantonio writes, "Frank Rizzo instinctively understood what was happening out on the streets: from a political standpoint, skin color was the dividing line in America's cities, especially on the issue of crime."[48]

These tactics, of course, proved contentious, particularly to those working toward racial justice. Though many believed him to be impartial in his actions as an officer—"he was an equal opportunity tough guy," Cecil Moore was once quoted as saying—by the time he rose to the rank of commissioner, Rizzo had made no secret of his disdain for black agitators.[49] He believed that the civil rights struggle was slowly killing American cities, and he sought to do everything in his power to stanch the bleeding.

Rizzo's rise to prominence paralleled a broader shift in Philadelphia, away from the liberal agenda of the city's postwar reform-minded politicians. Democrat Richardson Dilworth succeeded Democrat Joseph Clark as mayor of Philadelphia in 1955, and both the policies and the administration that Clark had established in the early 1950s remained in place until 1962. When Dilworth resigned as mayor that year to run for Pennsylvania governor, however, city council president James Tate stepped in as acting mayor, and the political climate in Philadelphia changed at once. As Tate worked closely with city unions to create jobs and secure safe working conditions, the civil rights agenda of the previous decade quickly lost favor. In March 1963, following Tate's close electoral victory, both the Congress of Racial Equality (CORE) and the NAACP held rallies at schools and work sites, protesting what they saw as systemic discrimination that kept black workers off construction crews.[50]

Then, in June of that year, George Schermer stepped down as director of the city's Human Relations Commission. According to Schermer, Tate's administration had weakened the commission by undermining its authority and engaging in backroom deals.[51] Schermer charged that the mayor was holding meetings with the NAACP and CORE one day and the labor unions the next, without ever informing the Human Relations Commission. "We had the best operation of its kind in this country," Schermer told the *Detroit News*. "But we reached the point where we were being so badly undercut that if I hadn't taken some dramatic move, we'd have been squeezed out into a little complaint bureau."[52] For Mount Airy residents in particular, Schermer's threatened departure drove home the sharp break in city politics and prompted widespread unease over the city's evolving approach to race relations.

Hundreds petitioned Mayor Tate, imploring him not to accept the Human Relations Commission director's resignation. Writing on behalf of 748 Henry School parents, West Mount Airy's Philip Turner, president of the HHSA, issued a public statement to Tate through the *Philadelphia Inquirer*. "Philadelphia is entering a period of crisis in human relations, which reflects critical changes throughout all of America," he wrote. "George Schermer's outstanding skill, judgment, and leadership is needed here as ever before."[53] The ACLU called the resignation "an ominous signal that the city government is losing its leadership in civil rights." The organization declared Schermer's exit a "tragedy" that had the effect of placing the onus of action on private groups rather than the city government. "We rejoice, of course, that thanks to private efforts the walls of prejudice are tumbling down," the group continued, "but we think the mayor should be out there blowing the trumpet, instead of stuffing cotton in his ears."[54] The letter-writing campaign did little to sway the mayor's response; that June, Tate accepted Schermer's resignation. The exiting director left his post in city government and worked as a freelance expert on race relations. In 1965, he and his family moved from West Mount Airy to Washington, D.C., where Schermer opened his own consulting firm. The mayor appointed Clarence Farmer to head the Human Relations Commission, and Tate and Rizzo continued to run the city with a heavy hand.

When demonstrations broke out in the city in 1967, following riots in Newark and Washington, D.C., Rizzo quickly rounded up the protestors. That summer, Philadelphia police arrested 328 demonstrators. Mayor Tate called for the city council to pass an emergency proclamation prohibiting residents from gathering in groups of twelve or more. With the support of Rizzo and Human Relations Commission director Farmer, the council passed the ordinance.[55] Rizzo and his cadre broke the will of the protestors that summer, and in the process they broke heads as well. That fall, Rizzo once again entered the public spotlight, this time following the violent clashes during the November protests at the Philadelphia School Board offices. The aggressive force that Rizzo had authorized caused an uproar across the city, as community leaders and residents alike levied charges of police brutality at Rizzo and cries of incompetent, soft leadership at Shedd and Dilworth.[56]

It was in the context of these 1967 conflicts that Rizzo's reputation as a racist reactionary began to coalesce. Over the next few years, the commissioner's officers attacked black student protesters in the city's Fairmount neighborhood. They raided the home of several members of the black power organization, the Revolutionary Action Movement, and infiltrated the group. Finally, in 1970, in perhaps the most divisive incident of his long career as both police officer and politician, Rizzo ordered the arrest and public strip search of several members of the local Black Panther Party, following a bloody week that had seen the killing or wounding of six police officers and a number of black activists.[57]

Integrationists in West Mount Airy repeatedly condemned Rizzo's tactics, asserting that the commissioner's brand of leadership threatened to disrupt decades of efforts on the part of city government and neighborhood institutions to foster mutual respect and general order throughout Philadelphia. Beyond the outcry over his systematic targeting of African American agitators and violation of their civil rights, WMAN board members believed that Rizzo's approach was further exacerbating the growing crisis of crime across the city. Police brutality, they argued, served to alienate its victims, making them more suspicious of authority and increasingly frustrated by the established social channels.[58] And within West Mount Airy, WMAN said, that suspicion was pitting neighbor against neighbor. "There are incidents by police that are undermining community relations," said one board member at a June 1969 meeting. "Neighbors that were once friends are having neighborhood problems. . . . The forced pressure and violence of the people has changed the attitudes of many people. On the job, in the schools, in the stores, in business, your neighbors, friends, and even relations. The warm feeling is gone."[59] Rizzo's style of leadership, they believed, was threatening the very foundation of community on which the neighborhood was built fifteen years earlier.

While WMAN's statements served to align the organization with a liberal coalition across the city and reaffirm the community's commitment to racial justice, some Mount Airy residents believed that the agenda was subverting local efforts to protect the neighborhood. In January 1974, a splinter group began to emerge. That month, several homeowners came together at the Germantown Jewish Centre to organize volunteer auto patrols to survey the area and report suspicious activity to the police. Though local business owners at first reported progress, by summer the volunteer structure of the new group had weakened, and the leaders of the effort believed that a formal organization was necessary to move forward.[60] Described by the *Chestnut Hill Local* as a group of black men seeking to "give the community, particularly its youth, some attention," West Mount Airy Action, Inc. (WMAA) quickly focused in on the problem of increased crime in the neighborhood.[61]

In reality, WMAA did have some white members. But the predominantly black-led organization evidenced a continuing and evolving divide in the experience of living in the interracial community. In the mid-1970s, the issue of crime brought together the cultural turn toward racial pride and self-help of the 1960s with the long-standing disconnect between many of Mount Airy's white and black residents over the meaning of integrated space. Some upwardly mobile African American homeowners in the neighborhood made the decision to organize on their own behalf, to attempt to achieve through their own innovation what integrationist community activists had not been able to through more formalized channels. They saw the need for a new type of leadership in the community and a new approach toward preserving the viability of the neighborhood.

These black leaders had not moved to Mount Airy simply to live out an abstract sense of justice. They believed that the integrated community could offer them stability and safety, protection from the problems associated with the decay of the Philadelphia's black inner-city areas. If liberal white community leaders were more focused on fighting police brutality than on preserving the neighborhood, these black residents believed, then they would fill the void by safeguarding against criminal activity. In this way, the crisis of crime in the region became a lens through which local black residents could assert their own autonomy; the creation of a crime prevention program became the terrain on which the battle over local control and racial representation was fought in West Mount Airy.[62] For the largely black membership of West Mount Airy Action, by working toward crime prevention, they sought to challenge what many perceived as the obsolete tactics of West Mount Airy Neighbors and present an alternative vision of race-conscious community control.

With WMAN past president Oliver Lancaster at the helm, WMAA wasted little time in making its presence known in the neighborhood. Lancaster, a longtime Philadelphia educator, brought to the new organization a well-documented history of pushing for integrationist reform. Serving in the school district's Office of Integration and Intergroup Education before being appointed in 1970 as director of the Office of Community Affairs for the school board, Lancaster believed in the goal of an integrated society. However, the Temple- and Yale-educated leader argued that integration for the sake of integration could not solve the problems of racism in the United States. Interracialism alone would not ameliorate the structural economic and racial inequity that had besieged American cities, Lancaster said; the nation needs fundamental, systemic change in order to break the historic patterns of injustice. In a 1969 discussion on school desegregation, Lancaster advocated for curricular changes over bussing. "Bussing is an incidental thing," he told the *Philadelphia Bulletin*. "All it does is provide a physical mixing of blacks and whites. If we focus only on . . . bussing, then we miss what is real."[63] By adopting a more comprehensive and community-oriented approach to intergroup dynamics, Lancaster said a year later, "We're getting to the core of the problems. We're treating diseases now and not just the symptoms."[64]

By the mid-1970s, Lancaster seemed to believe that social dislocation was the root cause of the increase in crime throughout the country, and he felt that a concerted and focused effort toward alleviating those issues was the key to finding a community solution. Highlighting police relations only confounded the issues and made finding solutions all the more challenging.[65] It was with this in mind that he signed on as president of West Mount Airy Action. "There are presently growing problems in West Mount Airy of increasing crime and disruptive youth," WMAA leaders said in an early report. "Our goal of community crime prevention, in cooperation with existing city and private agencies, will be to reduce the number of active anti-social gangs, and gang members, and to help reverse the rising crime rate in our area." The fledgling community organization, incorporated as a not-for-profit in October 1974, gained the support of the Philadelphia Police Department as the board developed a town watch program to patrol the streets and alert officers at any sign of disturbance.[66]

As official policy, West Mount Airy Neighbors endorsed the new organization. On November 27, the WMAN board adopted a statement of support for the goals and programs set forth in WMAA's mission. "While we [WMAN] have had many successes in dealing with community problems," the declaration read, "the problems of anti-social juveniles and an increasing crime rate have frustrated our entire community. We have spent a great deal of time and effort working on the problem and have realized that our organizational resources are insufficient."[67] WMAN pledged ongoing support and collaboration with West Mount Airy Action. Within six months, though, some members of the WMAN board began to fear that their authority within the neighborhood was coming undone. Concerned that they were losing their place as the voice of the community, that spring a group came together to stage a covert takeover of the burgeoning crime-fighting group.

In early April 1975, WMAA peppered the neighborhood with a flyer publicizing an upcoming meeting. "Don't Be a Victim!" the announcement read. "Because we believe you love your family, home, and neighborhood and are concerned about their safety, we are asking you to join us in a well-organized massive and sustaining effort to make our streets safe from the destructive and terrorizing activities of misdirected youth." The meeting was to be held at the Germantown Jewish Centre on April 7.[68] The day before the scheduled event, four members of WMAN, acting independently of the organization and without any institutional authority, printed their own flyer, on WMAN letterhead, and distributed it in the affected area:

> Don't Be a Victim of Scare Tactics. West Mount Airy Action tells us we are in the heart of a high crime area. But are we? The Fourteenth Police District doesn't think so. WMAA claims to have an answer on April 7. But will they? Are vigilante patrols and funding of repressive programs the answer? West Mount Airy Neighbors thinks not. There are better ways to deal rationally with community concerns of all kinds. WMAN urges you to attend the meeting and counteract this negative approach to our neighborhood.

The flyer was signed by the renegade WMAN board members, which included former executive secretary Ruth Steele and current board president Douglas Gaston III.[69] The following night, a large group of Mount Airy residents gathered at the Germantown Jewish Centre for the WMAA meeting. While the meeting began peacefully, by the end any sense of order had broken down, with representatives of the two dissenting factions screaming at each other from across the room. Community members, unaware of the rising tensions, were alarmed by the display of aggression, and many left believing that the two organizations were butting heads at an institutional level.[70]

On April 8, WMAN executive secretary Flora Wolf issued an internal memo to all board members, calling for an emergency meeting. She described the events that had transpired over the previous two days, leading up to the confrontation at the WMAA meeting. "The quarrel between the two organizations was aired in a noisy, public way that cannot fail to lessen our image in the community," she wrote.[71] According to Wolf, this misguided conduct by four rogue board members was threatening to break the organization apart. WMAN had to form a united front to maintain its position as a viable community clearinghouse, she continued. The board had adopted a policy of support with regard to WMAA and nothing had changed to mitigate that pledge. The rest of the West Mount Airy Neighbors board met on April 14 to issue a unanimous reprimand to President Gaston and the three other offending members.[72] But the incident, and the attendant fallout, continued to follow the organization.

That spring, WMAA applied to the Governor's Justice Committee for the disbursement of $24,906 in federal funds to help implement its community initiatives. According to the grant proposal, the organization was seeking support to develop programming geared toward educating residents on security; implementing a comprehensive town watch program; developing a properly trained, unarmed patrol team equipped with two-way radios; promoting police-community relations; and offering counseling and referral services to young people with drug, family, or peer problems.[73] Individual residents of the neighborhood—many with ties to WMAN but acting outside of the bounds of the organization—mounted a campaign to oppose the governmental support, reportedly declaring that WMAA was invoking "unnecessary emotionalism on the issue of public safety in [the] neighborhood."[74] The critics submitted a petition to the Governor's Justice Committee on April 24, at which point Judge Harvey Schmidt, a champion of civil rights and chair of the state's Community Crime Prevention Committee, called for a community-wide effort to resolve the tension before the funding body would consider the request.

Once again, on an institutional level, WMAN and WMAA worked together to craft a series of guidelines for a collaborative relationship between the organizations. But still, individual members of WMAN protested. On May 8, the Regional Council of the Governor's Justice Committee announced an unprecedented public hearing to allow both sides to defend their positions. President Lancaster began his testimony by addressing the discord in the neighborhood. "Unanimity in a community of 7,000 people is not going to be possible," he said, "but West Mount Airy Action, Inc. and West Mount Airy Neighbors are growing together."[75] He went on to describe the ongoing efforts by the two organizations to reach a collaborative coexistence. They had agreed to exchange board representatives, to develop mutual block associations, to coordinate meeting and event calendars, and to review each other's work, he told the committee. Having two community organizations could rip the neighborhood apart, said Lancaster. Or, through mutual exchange and innovative partnership, it could make it stronger.

Opponents of the funding laid out three critiques. First, they said, WMAA had not articulated a concrete strategy with regard to the problems of youth of the neighborhood. Second, they argued, the organization could not provide the necessary matching funds. Finally, they maintained, the roving WMAA volunteers would cause hostility between police and teenagers. "I have no personal hang-ups about the people in WMAA," testified WMAN member Edward Simms, "but they're going to put people in cars driving around and they're going to see kids—my kids—and think they're acting suspiciously."[76] The new organization, Simms and others maintained, would create a culture of fear in the community. Even as his remarks hinted at a sort of institutional turf war between the two organizations—with some members of WMAN bristling at the prospect of having their authority tempered—Simms's invocation of fear called to mind the apprehension that many white Americans felt toward black militancy, a sense of unease over the concentration of black control. In linking the largely black-led WMAA to a growing anxiety throughout the neighborhood, then, his comment implied a patently racialized conception of local control.[77]

At the end of the May 8 meeting, the state provisionally approved WMAA's request for funding, pending the mending of relationships within the neighborhood. Residents feared the fallout from the confrontation. In an anonymous editorial published in the May 22 *Germantown Courier*, one community member called for an end to the hostility:

> The bonds between neighbors that made West Mount Airy a vital community must not be allowed to dissolve as a result of recent controversy that divided the neighborhood. The people of both factions and all groups must wipe the slate clean and rationally discuss the direction West Mount Airy is to take. It will take all the resources of the community to heal the wounds and find the best answers for everyone concerned. The people of West Mount Airy have worked too hard at making their community a healthy place to live, to let their efforts go down the drain in the wake of a single dispute. The fight must be forgotten and brotherhood remembered.[78]

Though such comments did not overtly mention racial strife, the invocation of a sense of "brotherhood" hinted at the desire for a return to the postwar integrationist ethos on which the community was originally built. The speaker may have been calling on the black leadership of WMAA to temper their perceived militancy in the interest of restoring a sense of stability to the neighborhood.

On May 23, West Mount Airy Action surprised residents by withdrawing its request for funding. "With 7,000 people living in Mount Airy," said President Lancaster, "it's going to be very difficult to stop them from raising objections or circulating petitions. We're going to dissolve the corporation and let it go."[79] The next day, Lancaster issued a public letter to the community, formally declaring the end of WMAA. "In spite of West Mount Airy Neighbors' enthusiastic expression and actions of support as an organization," he wrote, "several of our neighbors and members have been very successful in their strategies to destroy the formalizing of the fifteen months' efforts to more ably serve our community with a positive thrust at crime prevention." Lancaster went on to name individually the WMAN members who had derailed the organization. "Our board does not wish to be a party to the extension of the disruption and destruction of our community that has been so carefully orchestrated," he continued. "We love West Mount Airy and because we do, we take immediate steps to de-escalate our efforts, fulfill our contracted obligations, and fade quietly into the night."[80] The dissolution of WMAA effectively put an end to the institutional struggle for control in West Mount Airy. For WMAN leaders, the episode appeared to legitimate their rightful place as the official voice of the community, and to prove that their time-honored integrationist agenda and governing principles could effectively lead the neighborhood into the waning years of the twentieth century.

Throughout the country, once-integrated communities were beginning to tip. Shaker Heights, Ohio; Takoma Park in Washington, D.C.; and Oak Park, Chicago, were all witnessing creeping population changes.[81] Whereas half a decade earlier the integration movement had seen the formation of National Neighbors, a broad-based umbrella organization to coordinate localized efforts to monitor open housing and fair housing policies, neighborhood trends around the country evidenced that many such areas were experiencing shifts from intentionally integrated toward middle-class black enclaves.[82] West Mount Airy, though, had managed to avoid such a fate and was maintaining its role as a national example of interracial living. WMAN believed that the defeat of WMAA proved the success of their own continued vigilance in maintaining community cohesion and racial and economic stability.

Tensions within West Mount Airy, however, were not as quick to abate. In June 1975, Doug Gaston, who had been at the center of the WMAA debacle, stepped down as WMAN president, following the completion of his term. Chris Van de Velde, a member of the organization since 1972, was elected to fill the position. "I wasn't planning to run for public office," Van de Velde later recalled, "but then there I was [at the meeting when Gaston stepped down] . . . Sometime during the evening's discussion, someone decided to nominate me as a compromise alternative to the divisiveness of the previous administration."[83] The new president had served for two years as the director of field operations in the New York regional office of the Department of Housing and Urban Development. Prior to that, he had worked under New York mayor John Lindsay as deputy commissioner of the Department of Rent Control and Housing Maintenance, and while in graduate school he had interned at the Philadelphia office of the Housing and Urban Development Department.[84] When he returned to the city in 1970, he and his new wife chose to live in West Mount Airy because of the community's reputed commitment to racial integration, and he brought with him a belief that community groups like WMAN could serve as a solution to the problems facing America's cities.[85]

Many, it seemed, hoped that he would be able to bring closure to the events of the previous spring. "The time has come to mend the differences that have tested the West Mount Airy community," wrote a *Germantown Courier* reporter. "The election of Van de Velde . . . is an encouraging beginning, but he can only be effective with the cooperation of all concerned."[86] The new president, who arrived with a demonstrated commitment to urban sustainability, sought to usher West Mount Airy into a new era, but first he had to restabilize the community. As his first official act, he set out to bring together for the first time the three opposing parties to the recent controversy—WMAN, WMAA, and the renegade WMAN board members—to try to find a common ground from which to move forward.

To many residents, the election of Van de Velde seemed to evidence a recalibration of the long-standing community organization and a welcome reprise of its earliest integrationist mission. The new president's résumé looked strikingly similarly to that of WMAN cofounder George Schermer, and, like Schermer before him, Van de Velde's election coincided with a pressing need to create stability out of upheaval. But Van de Velde inherited a fractured community, a vastly depleted Philadelphia, and a much-evolved movement for racial justice, and he was aware that West Mount Airy Neighbors required a new model of organizing if the neighborhood was to maintain a sense of economic and communal stability and a reputation for interracial tolerance and liberal politics. The new president set out to reframe community conversations, to move away from the rhetoric of integration and bring homeowners back together through concrete projects geared toward cohesion and improvement. "Integration had been a very conscious effort in West

Mount Airy," Van de Velde later reflected, "but by this point, it was a fact. It had happened. We were all there, so now it was a question of, how are we all going to get along?"[87] As one of his early acts as president, Van de Velde initiated a series of neighborhood beautification projects. Under his leadership, WMAN worked to plant trees, to clean up Germantown Avenue, to refurbish the Allens Lane Train Station, and to bring residents out of their homes with the idea that "when you have projects and things for people to do, they stop arguing."[88] The organization believed that they could heal the wounds of the previous year through concrete, collaborative community projects that transcended questions of race.

In place of the decades-old interracial mission of the neighborhood integration project, during the later years of the 1970s, WMAN under Val de Velde's leadership worked to recast West Mount Airy from a site of interracial living to a model of alternative urbanity, a deracialized compromise toward diversity.[89] The new manifestation of WMAN heralded the community as a place for liberal- and progressive-minded families to live intentionally. It did not focus on repairing racial hostilities, nor did it minimize racial differences. As *Philadelphia Inquirer* staff writer Howard Shapiro wrote in 1979, "If neighboring Chestnut Hill is home for the well-to-do, then West Mount Airy is the home of those who could be and, in many ways are, but choose to live differently."[90]

Chapter 7

THE CHOICE TO LIVE DIFFERENTLY

Reimagining Integration at Century's End

In 2005, Patricia Henning became the newest member of the Germantown Historical Society Hall of Fame. Henning, who moved to West Mount
Airy in 1967, was a realtor, a part-time librarian at the Germantown Historical Society, and WMAN's longest-standing board member, serving from
1968 to 2003.[1] Henning also founded the West Mount Airy Neighbors Historical Awareness Committee in the early 1980s, through which she worked
to cultivate an active and living history of the community. At her induction
ceremony, WMAN executive director Laura Siena spoke of Henning's
commitment to spreading that historical narrative. The neighborhood has
thrived not simply because of its long-standing dedication to intentional integration, said Siena, but because of the legacy that has been created through
the memorialization of that dedication. "As we have been studied and written about," said Siena, "we have gained insights into just how rare and pre-
cious our community is. Communities like Mount Airy are bucking powerful institutional arrangements when they seek to create different narratives

for themselves, narratives which value integration over segregation, community involvement over alienation."[2]

As Siena noted, over the previous half century, public representations of West Mount Airy had been an integral part of the neighborhood's identity formation, serving at once to create internal community cohesion and to attract new, like-minded homeowners to the region. At first, such depictions helped to solidify the community's reputation for biracial interracialism. In the three decades preceding Henning's induction to the Hall of Fame, however, as WMAN reoriented its mission away from intentional integration, the representations of West Mount Airy about which Siena spoke took on new significance, infusing younger residents with a consciousness toward early activism through which organizers hoped to galvanize residents going forward.

By the late 1970s, amid economic instability, a rapidly shifting national political culture, new conceptions of community-making, and the internal need for healing, Mount Airy was beginning to take a new shape, moving away from the focus on interracial living of the previous decades and toward a more generalized ethos of diversity.[3] As Marilyn Nolen, WMAN executive secretary, wrote in an October 1978 letter to the editor of the *Philadelphia Bulletin*, "We believe that our neighborhood is like the city taken as a whole in being socially, economically, racially, religiously, and ethnically diverse. Diversity, however, as we have seen it in Mount Airy, need not yield division."[4]

This rhetorical shift in the neighborhood paralleled larger national trends that saw a retreat away from the race-based pride and self-help that had dominated the fight for racial justice in the latter half of the 1960s. Fearful that these calls for racial separatism and identity-based power would threaten the progress of race relations, institutions began to deploy the language of cultural pluralism, speaking of the need to bring individuals from a diversity of backgrounds together to combat inflammatory racial clashes.[5] By the 1980s and '90s, policymakers, educational administrators, and human resource managers around the country were implementing that tactical shift away from the language of affirmative action and biracial identity politics, favoring instead a celebration of difference and diversity. In West Mount Airy, the strategic turn took place a decade earlier, with the election of Chris Van de Velde; in 1975, in the wake of the WMAN/WMAA clashes, the new president worked to move the mission of West Mount Airy Neighbors away from biracial integration and to instead commemorate the value of a community in which everyone was welcomed.

The institutional rebranding of West Mount Airy both coincided with and fostered a gradual demographic shift in the area, as new groups of people found their way to the neighborhood. By the late 1970s, Mount Airy was becoming attractive to a new and emerging cohort of residents: leftist religious scholars and their students, multiracial and same-sex families, and a new generation of activists seeking to establish community roots in a space long known for its political and social tolerance. These newcomers seemed to validate Van de Velde's push to broaden the scope of the neighborhood's reputation, recasting West Mount Airy as a haven for those who chose to "live differently."[6]

At first, this influx of new residents enlivened the community. Through the middle of the 1980s, Mount Airy experienced a marked upsurge in both institutional energy and community cohesion. But, as the decade wore on and the tangible effects of the postindustrial recession facing the nation's urban centers and an increasingly violent war on drugs spread into the neighborhood, instability and mass exodus once against threatened. While newcomers had brought fresh energy into the region, community leaders believed, many lacked the consciousness of intentionality necessary to retain its place as the city's beacon of diversity and tolerance. In an effort to preserve its viability as a progressive urban space, West Mount Airy Neighbors embarked on a community-wide historical memory project, seeking to merge the neighborhood's evolving culture of diversity with its historic legacy of intentionality. WMAN saw utility in employing the collective remembrance of the community's integrationist past as an organizing tool for the future.

Growing up in North Philadelphia's Logan section, Ellen Tichenor had always known of West Mount Airy as a site of racial tolerance. She went to school with Wendy Schermer, daughter of the famed founder of the Philadelphia Human Relations Commission, and, as the girls became friends, Tichenor grew familiar with the work of the Schermers and the efforts toward integration in the neighborhood. "I thought of George as something of a hero," she later recalled. "They were doing good, important work over there [in Mount Airy]." Tichenor graduated from the Philadelphia High School for Girls and completed her undergraduate degree at the University of Pennsylvania, finding community in West Philadelphia's Powelton Village neighborhood. Powelton was a hotbed of activism in the early 1970s. "It was an antiwar chanting, folk-music playing, new-age hippie, ever-expanding pot of spaghetti, always enough for anyone who showed up," Tichenor reflected. The revolutionary in her felt at home there. When she and her husband divorced, though, she felt lost. In the mid-1970s, Tichenor came out as a lesbian. Though her split from her husband had been amicable—they had one of the first pro se divorces in Philadelphia and agreed on shared custody of their two boys—she felt destabilized and confused. "I didn't know how to shift identities like that," she later recalled. "It was perhaps the most vulnerable that I had ever been."[7]

Not long after, Tichenor joined a women's radio collective, singing and playing guitar on the local public radio station, and through that she met Sharon. "She was a friend of a friend, living in a lesbian feminist cooperative in Mount Airy," she said. "We fell in love." A year later, Tichenor moved into the twin house at 515 W. Carpenter Lane that Sharon shared with several friends. "I didn't know who I was or what I was looking for," she remembered. "Mount Airy was the perfect place for that." The director of the day-care center at the Rutgers University School of Law in Camden, New Jersey, Tichenor moved into the cooperative with a carpenter, a writer, a law student, the director of the University of Pennsylvania Women's Center, and the director of a collective childcare facility in the area. "Mount Airy felt like a place for liberal, young, hip people," she reflected. "It was a place for rising professionals who thought of themselves as revolutionary."[8] For Tichenor, the move to northwest Philadelphia served as the spatial manifestation of her new identity; Mount Airy offered her a safe, inviting community as she reoriented her sense of self.

Since the early 1950s, Mount Airy had been home to a small but persistent lesbian community, women who were attracted to the area for many of the same reasons that enticed African American buyers to move in and compelled many white homeowners to remain: affordable homes, old stone architecture, and parks and green spaces. "I liked being on the edge of Fairmount Park," remembered Laurie Barron, who moved to the neighborhood in the 1960s. "I liked being up where it was a little quieter and greener." The neighborhood's reputation for racial justice was a significant draw as well.[9] For many such women, the quieter, more residential culture of Mount Airy was attractive because of the lifestyle it afforded. It was a community with a reputation for tolerance, but it also brought with it a sense of independence and privacy; it was a place to purchase a home and start a family. Tichenor echoed such sentiments. "Unlike in Powelton," she reflected, "we weren't jumping around from house to house every night. We felt relieved to come home in Mount Airy. There was a sense of ease there . . . It was like what grown-ups did when they left Powelton."[10] While by the mid-1960s there were a number of lesbian collectives in the community, recalled Barron, "[it was mostly] individuals and couples . . . moving to Mt. Airy." Becky Davidson, a longtime resident of Center City and West Philadelphia, described a lesbian "flight" to the northwest. "The Germantown dyke crew," she said, referring collectively to the northwest Philadelphia community of which Mount Airy was a part, "is very different. . . . They all have kids, they all like to be near the park, they're all professional lesbians."[11] The physical character of the neighborhood that had served as a stabilizing force in the early years of transition continued to provide a strong pull for liberal, upwardly mobile buyers through the rest of the twentieth century, helping to ensure the economic stability of the community.

By the early 1980s, West Mount Airy had gained a regional reputation as a gay-friendly community. In 1983, the *Philadelphia Gay News* proclaimed Mount Airy a "gay neighborhood" in the city. The area, the paper said, was home to a concentration of gay and lesbian residents and professed a strong gay identity. It fostered progressive politics, strong community ties, and a sense of independence particularly important to young lesbian families. "The sense of coming home to quiet is one of the important elements of life for many Germantown and Mount Airy residents," wrote reporter Marc Killinger.[12] For Tichenor, who was interviewed for the article, it was precisely that balance of community involvement, progressive activism, and personal space that drew her to the neighborhood.[13] Mount Airy offered "a sense of being able to live with your politics," she told Killinger.[14] The community offered day-care cooperatives, study groups, and community concerts. There were pacifists, feminists, and those committed to economic justice. Sharing the party wall of their Carpenter Lane twin was Jules Timmerman, founder of the Weaver's Way Food Cooperative. The co-op, which had opened for business in January 1973 at 555 Carpenter Lane, the site of the old Sid's Deli, boasted five hundred member-households by 1975. Six years later, the store was supporting more than two thousand families with hundreds of additional membership applications to process.[15] Mount Airy was an open community, said Tichenor, and that made it feel safe, welcoming, and exciting.[16]

Figure 7. Woman and child on steps of Weaver's Way Food Cooperative, *Philadelphia Bulletin*, January 29, 1979. Used with permission from Special Collections Research Center, Temple University Libraries, Philadelphia.

With its growing reputation as a gay-friendly space and a home for "grown-up Powelton revolutionaries," Mount Airy's population of young progressive professionals grew precipitously in the early 1980s, with little visible pushback from older residents. According to Rabbi Linda Holtzman, "Mount Airy, by the mid-eighties, was the place to be." Holtzman, who grew up in the West Oak Lane neighborhood of Philadelphia and began the process of coming out in the late 1970s, moved to the neighborhood in 1982, not long after she began dating her partner, Betsy Conston. The area was an easy commute to downtown, to Temple University, and to the University of Pennsylvania. It was still a place of racial tolerance, Holtzman later reflected, but that early reputation of racial integration had been transformed, paving the way for a truly diverse community in the 1980s. Within a few years, she said, it was home to a growing gay community and a rising feminist presence, and, equally importantly, an increasingly young and progressive Jewish population. The rabbi, who graduated from the Reconstructionist Rabbinical College (RRC) in 1979, wanted to settle in an area with a strong Jewish identity. She didn't have to look far. In 1982, RRC relocated from Temple University to the suburban neighborhood of Wyncote, located just across the city boundary from northwest Philadelphia. The move helped to position Mount Airy as, said Holtzman, "the Jewish center of the world in Philadelphia . . . , a beacon for progressive Jews in the city."[17]

Founded in 1968, for the first fourteen years of its existence RRC made its home in two brownstones at 2308 Broad Street in North Philadelphia. The school was set up to train rabbinical candidates in Reconstructionist Judaism, a philosophy established in the 1920s by scholar and rabbi Mordecai Kaplan, who advocated that Judaism should be grounded in contemporary cultural and social values.[18] As the only Reconstructionist school in the country, RRC brought to Philadelphia a concentration of progressive Jews, all eager to create a community in the city. The problem, recalled Rabbi Rebecca Alpert, was that the school was not relating to the neighborhood.[19] By day, students and faculty studied together at the North Philadelphia campus, but each evening they returned to their homes in Center City and Powelton Village. "There was a disconnect," said Alpert, who graduated from RRC in 1976 and became the first alumnus to take on a full-time administrative role at the college. "Many of us felt that if we were going to make our home in North Philadelphia, we needed to be working with the community, but no one at RRC was doing any sort of intergroup relations."[20]

As RRC struggled to situate itself within the local community, many students and faculty found themselves attracted to a developing movement in American Judaism more broadly. The national Havurah (or Fellowship) Movement, born out of the counterculture of the 1960s, brought together young Jews in search of an egalitarian alternative to the hierarchical structures and institutionalized practices of organized religion. In small clusters around the country, students of the movement congregated in grassroots gatherings for prayers, study, and celebration.[21] The political and countercultural ideas were central to the organization's mission. The group decried suburban bourgeois culture, offered sanctuary for members seeking student exemptions from the draft, and sought to recast Judaism as "a revolutionary force . . . toward liberation [and] greater freedom for the individual and the society."[22] Still, members viewed these ideas through the lens of contemporary Jewish thought. They came together for ritual and prayer, and they engaged in deep study of religious texts and teachings. They called for a renewal of American Judaism, situated within the world in which they lived.

By the 1970s, that Jewish Renewal movement had found its way to Philadelphia and West Mount Airy. As followers began to move into the region, though, the neighborhood's long-standing Jewish population experienced hints of a generational divide, with new residents struggling to find common ground with the older integrationists of the Germantown Jewish Centre. On one level, the newcomers had been attracted to the region because of its legacy of inclusion. "One thing that was important to me," recalled economist Michael Masch, who was twenty-two years old when he moved to the neighborhood in 1973, "having grown up in a racially segregated neighborhood in Philadelphia, was to find a place where black and white people could live in a community together." Still, for Masch and others like him, it also felt important to establish a break from the older residents who had first created and fostered that tolerance. "I'm not sure we even knew what we wanted," he recalled. "We were people coming out of college in the late 1960s, feeling there couldn't possibly be anything we would have in common with the institutions run by our parents' generation."[23]

In 1974, Masch and his wife joined a group of other young Jewish couples who approached Rabbi Charry at the GJC about the prospect of starting a minyan, a lay-led prayer group, at the synagogue. Charry's response, welcoming the group into the community even as their presence pulled members away from the main sanctuary, was, according to *Philadelphia Inquirer* staff writer Julia Cass, crucial to the survival and growth of a cohesive Jewish community in the neighborhood. "The growth of the Havurah Movement in Mount Airy," reported the paper, "and indeed, the rebirth of its Jewish community in general, is closely tied to the Germantown Jewish Centre in a way that reveals the interdependence of institutions, neighborhoods, and generations."[24] Recalling the neighborhood's earliest integration efforts, Cass linked the emergence of this new Jewish force in the area to the region's historic success in merging grassroots innovation with institutional accountability.

It was these complementary forces that created the space for a sustainable progressive Jewish presence in the neighborhood through the end of the twentieth century. In 1981, when Rabbi Ira Silverman became president of RRC, said Alpert, he brought with him a new vision for the community, one very much grounded in the Havurah tradition.[25] As one of Silverman's first acts in office, he invited Rabbis Zalman Schachter-Shalomi and Arthur Green to join the faculty.[26] A short time later, he solicited Rabbi Arthur Waskow to teach there as well. These three men brought with them a new level of cachet to the school. Schachter-Shalomi, an Austrian immigrant who was imprisoned at a detention camp in Vichy France before escaping to the United States, was one of the foremost leaders of the national Jewish Renewal movement. Green, then a professor of Jewish studies at the University of Pennsylvania, was a leading scholar of Jewish mysticism and one of the founders of Boston's Havurat Shalom. Waskow, a prolific writer and activist and the founder of the Washington Havurah, was a nationally renowned champion of leftist causes.[27] "These were three very powerful personalities," remembered Rabbi David Teutsch, an active havurah leader in both New York and Philadelphia who went on to serve as executive director of the Federation of Reconstructionist Congregations and Havurot (later the Jewish Reconstructionist Federation) from 1982 to 1986 before joining the faculty at RRC and serving as president from 1993 to 2002. All three settled in West Mount Airy. "Because of its history as an integrated neighborhood," said Teutsch, "it was a neighborhood that was attractive to progressives. . . . By the late 1970s, it was a community that attracted a certain kind of Jew. These men moved there in part because of that legacy of integration."[28] Quickly, recalled Alpert, students began to look toward the neighborhood. "They wanted to live near the star faculty," she said. "Zalman [Schachter-Shalomi], in particular, was the center of all Jewish change in Mount Airy during this period."[29] "By the early 1980s," echoed Teutsch, "there was a national Jewish leadership right in West Mount Airy."[30]

Just a year after Silverman took office, he also began plans to move the college away from North Philadelphia. In 1982, RRC relocated to Wyncote. The move refocused the Reconstructionist community of Philadelphia away from Center City and Powelton. Mount Airy, recalled Alpert, "started making sense as a place for people to look for housing."[31] In 1986, when Arthur Green took over as president of the college, he began a self-conscious campaign to bring still more members of the RRC community to the neighborhood. "One of the things that was most important to Art," said Teutsch, "was for people to have a shared living experience. He started to push the college to cluster students and faculty in West Mount Airy."[32] In 1987, the *Philadelphia Inquirer* reported that Sedgwick Gardens, an apartment complex at the corner of Sedgwick and McCallum Streets, had become a de facto dormitory for RRC students. "So many of these students are staying in after they become rabbis," the paper noted, "that it is said that Mount Airy has more rabbis per square mile than any other neighborhood in Philadelphia."[33] This confluence of the relocation of the rabbinical college, the concentration of nationally renowned scholars and rabbis, and the growth of the Havurah and Jewish Renewal movements worked to position Mount Airy as the progressive Jewish epicenter of Philadelphia.

These demographic shifts in the neighborhood in the late 1970s and early 1980s served to complement Chris Van de Velde's vision of a West Mount Airy predicated on the idea of diversity, rather than biracial integration. And long-standing neighborhood institutions responded, at once working to foster a sense of community for recent transplants and to remain relevant to their new constituents. The Germantown Jewish Centre began offering full-day daycare services in the early 1980s, "telegraphing," reflected Teutsch, "women professionals and two-parent working households."[34] In March 1981, the Summit Presbyterian Church welcomed activist Maggie Kuhn, founder of the Gray Panthers, to speak at a special service.[35] Three months later, the church hosted an evening workshop on the nuclear arms race and the international challenges of peacemaking. "From Europe, Africa, Asia, and Latin America," proclaimed the invitation posted in a WMAN newsletter, "leaders in the worldwide struggle for peace and justice will share their perspectives about the escalating arms build-up on the world. . . .

Please come and hear Mr. Clark Smith and together we will begin to understand the far-reaching implications of peacemaking in the world today."[36] That September, the West and East Mount Airy Neighbors organizations launched a collaborative community newspaper, with free monthly delivery to all residents.[37] Once again, WMAN saw a need to reorient its mission to maintain its place in the community, and these new programs and initiatives served the long-standing clearinghouse well. In the spring of 1984, as WMAN entered its twenty-fifth year, the organization saw a 43 percent increase in paid membership from the previous year and a 26 percent increase over the average paid membership numbers in May of the preceding six years.[38]

This rebranding of West Mount Airy began to filter out of the neighborhood as well, as local media outlets started to define the community not as a haven for dignified interracialism but as a reflection of the counterculture coming of age. The neighborhood "is a hotbed of post '60s activism," said co-op staffer Ed Thomas in a 1985 *Inquirer* article, with the Weaver's Way Co-op serving as the community's "social movement."[39] A year later, in an article about the founding of a new community learning center in Mount Airy, staff writer Beth Gillin wrote, "In this liberal laid-back neighborhood, whose inhabitants have been known to furnish vast Victorian homes with little more than peace posters, banana plants, and overflowing bookshelves, intellectual curiosity is a prized community virtue, ranking right up there with saving whales, growing sprouts, and voting in primaries."[40] This new tone both reflected and facilitated the changing demographics of the area; by mid-decade, Mount Airy was attracting more and more young, progressive professionals to the neighborhood.

Of course, WMAN couldn't—didn't want to—abandon its integrationist agenda completely. It was on the issue of schools that questions of race consciousness continued to persist in local and regional conversations. In 1982, the Philadelphia Board of Education appointed Constance Clayton as the city's first black superintendent. Clayton wasted little time in ushering in a new era of school reform, specifically targeting the issue of educational segregation. One of her first initiatives was to implement a program that would direct nearly $5 million annually to schools in mixed-race neighborhoods with disproportionately African American enrollments. West Mount Airy's Charles W. Henry School, with 80 percent African American students in a community that, according to the 1980 census, boasted a 56–42 percent white-black ratio, was one of the beneficiaries of the new program. The goal of the initiative resonated with the strategy that Beatrice Chernock had employed two decades earlier: "to assure white parents that those . . . schools provide safe, high-quality education. No buses needed."[41]

Henry received funding for free after-school care, learning specialists, computer and math labs, a well-supported music program, additional teachers to reduce class size, and a second full-day kindergarten. This was one of the very first requests from Principal Frederick Donatucci, who also stepped into the role in 1982. "Knowing the realities of this neighborhood," said Donatucci, "it's important for us to be able to provide a program that is comparable to what parents can get in private schools, because they're our main competitor." In addition to recruiting neighborhood families, the district offered busing to Henry and other participating schools for white children whose neighborhood schools were not part of the desegregation plan.[42] "You did what you had to do to keep children who had a choice," recalled Ralph Smith, Clayton's chief design strategist. "Basically you had to figure out what the draw was."[43] For much of the next of the decade, the program served to bolster Henry's white enrollment, galvanizing parental support and drawing local families away from the private schools. By the end of the 1980s, Henry had settled into a 60–40 percent black-white ratio. "The school was becoming a community hub," recalled Judith Baker-Bernstein, an immigration lawyer and Henry parent, "and that was a wonderful thing."[44]

The stabilization of Henry provided an additional boost to the region, particularly for the new waves of young families moving to the area. By 1987, home values in Mount Airy were soaring. "Suddenly," reported the *Inquirer* that February, "the neighborhood has become red-hot property. There have been bidding wars over desirable homes, sending real estate skyrocketing. . . . The neighborhood is now so hot, in fact, that some residents have small fears that Mount Airy's cherished traditions might, over time, be altered." In that same article, Bob Elfant, president of Martin Elfant Realtors, described the boom as "a frenzy." According to Elfant, the demographics of the neighborhood showed signs of shifting. "I do have a little bit of fear—and I think a lot of people do—that Mount Airy, ten years from now, will be a white, upper-middle-class neighborhood."[45]

Elfant's concerns foretold growing anxiety in the community. Some of the neighborhood's older residents worried that these new homeowners were no longer steeped in the narrative of intentional integration. "Those days," reported *Inquirer* staff writer Michael Ruane in 1987, "while still strong in the memory of many residents, are becoming more and more distant from modern Mount Airy. . . . [There is a] new generation of Mount Airy residents: young, professional, and very successful, still attracted to Mount Airy's liberal tradition but with a keen eye for investment and architecture as well."[46] When the local housing market was strong, these shifts presented no problems. As the decade wore on, however, and the trying effects of the economic downturn of the early 1980s found their way to the region, long-standing community leaders feared that the "new" Mount Airy was ill-equipped to preserve the stability of the area. Without the institutional memory of the integration project, they worried, the newcomers were unable or unwilling to fight for the neighborhood.

Across the country, the 1980s ushered in a significant departure in American domestic policy.[47] Ronald Reagan, elected to the presidency at the start of the decade, ran on a platform of lower taxes and limited governmental intervention. When he took office, the liberalism that had defined the American presidency to varying degrees for the previous five decades began to fray. Thus, at the same time that the nation was contending with the impact of the deindustrialization and disinvestment of the 1970s, Reagan pushed to reduce funding for job training, food stamps, and Medicare.[48] Though some experienced significant financial gain during these years, the disappearance of a manufacturing economy resulted in acute crises for cities in the Northeast and Midwest.[49] Blue-collar employment rates dipped to their lowest rates in decades. African Americans in urban areas felt the decline particularly sharply. By 1987, the rate of industrial employment among black workers had dropped to 28 percent, down from roughly 70 percent as late as 1970.[50]

This widespread unemployment coincided with a rapidly expanding drug trade in the United States. In the middle of the decade, new technologies, political and military alliances, and immigration patterns brought crack cocaine into inner-city communities at unprecedented rates. With dwindling opportunities for legal employment, an underground drug economy ballooned. This growing drug trade paralleled a rapid expansion of federal support— financial and political—for drug enforcement. Rising unemployment rates, the introduction of crack cocaine, and President Reagan's War on Drugs, introduced in October 1982, came together to assert further pressure on

American cities. Urban blight persisted and neighborhoods saw increasingly violent clashes in the streets.[51]

Mount Airy was not immune to these larger national forces. In the late 1980s, the neighborhood began to see rising drug activity and increasing rates of attendant violence. On the evening of March 16, 1989, three people were wounded in a drug-related street shooting on the 100 block of West Weaver Street. The street, according to the *Inquirer*, had become a known trafficking hub over the previous two years, with dealers congregating on corners and lingering traffic through the night. Curtis Duff, a sixth grader at Henry School, was sitting on his porch when the shooting took place, and was caught in the cross fire. He was hit four times.[52] Two months later, two men were found dead in the back parking lot of the Mount Pleasant Arms apartment complex on Lincoln Drive. In the preceding weeks, residents of the surrounding blocks had reported unusual activity in the lot. "It could be a cool spot to hook up with drugs, because you can run up on the railroad tracks and escape if anyone comes," said seventeen-year-old Sambuka Brown, who lived around the corner from the Arms. Police concluded that the deaths were likely the result of a failed drug deal.[53]

At the same time, residents fought back over the proposed opening of a forty-three-bed AIDS patient facility at the old Arden Hall at the corner of McCallum Street and Mount Airy Avenue and a sixteen-bed residential treatment center for emotionally troubled youth on Wissahickon Avenue. "It's grossly unfair for them to dump this kind of problem in a family neighborhood," resident Barry Zern charged of the AIDS home. "I'm concerned about my children. We have hardly any strangers that come into the neighborhood, and now we are going to have the worst kind of strangers, IV drug users. We never bargained for that."[54] Homeowners expressed concern over issues of safety in the neighborhood, drawing distinctions between the long-standing emphasis on tolerance and the prospect of unseemly encroachment into the community. "This is Mount Airy; we are hardly an elitist crew," resident Jaki Katz Adler said at a protest of the youth treatment center. "This has been a successfully integrated neighborhood for thirty years. It's a credit to humanity that everyone can live together. But when it comes to safety issues, that's another matter." Others echoed Adler's sentiments. "I couldn't care less about housing value," said George Newman, reportedly one of the most strident opponents of the facility. "I plan to stay in my house and raise my kids. I am happy there, but if there is a physical threat to my kids, I'm gone."[55] The language the residents used in protesting the opening of both facilities evidenced new and growing fears in the neighborhood that outside influences would compromise the security and stability of the community.

As homeowners wrestled over these perceived threats to the neighborhood, city schools began to feel the effects of Reagan's hands-off economic policies. The desegregation plan that Superintendent Clayton had introduced in 1982 was, by the end of the decade, beginning to come undone. With federal support waning, the state legislature enacted a new school funding formula, cutting per-pupil aid across Philadelphia. Henry lost its math lab, its full-day kindergarten aides, and its learning specialists. The acclaimed music teacher transferred to one of the city's esteemed magnet schools, where his funding would be safe. The annual school show, which had become a highlight of the academic year for the Mount Airy community, was shut down.[56] Across Philadelphia, twenty-three hundred new students entered city high schools in the fall of 1992, twelve hundred more than the school board had anticipated. At Germantown, the feeder public high school for West Mount Airy, classrooms were reportedly filled beyond capacity, many with sixty students or more, and some with ninth graders who were passed through to the high school level after failing seventh or eighth grade. At the lower school level, the *Inquirer* reported, there were twenty-two hundred students on waiting lists for kindergartens, eight hundred more than the previous year.[57]

Mount Airy parents who had briefly enrolled their children in neighborhood public schools were once again turning to area private schools, which at the same time were experiencing double-digit inflation in tuition and fees. At the William Penn Charter School, for instance, West Mount Airy resident Louis Natali saw his daughter's tuition go from $6,680 to $8,150, a 22 percent jump as the girl moved from elementary school to middle school. The increase was nearly 15 percent more than reportedly projected by Penn Charter officials. "It's a real wallop," Natali, a law professor at Temple University, lamented. "It is just pushing middle-class people out of that kind of quality education for their children. I think it is important that the staff get paid decent wages, and I am sure it is all related to that, but it makes you wonder."[58] Since the early years of transition in the neighborhood, private and parochial schools had afforded those families who had retreated from the Philadelphia education system the chance to live out their commitment to residential—if not educational—integration. However, rising tuition costs, combined with economic recession and exacerbated volatility at neighborhood schools prompted some to question their decision to live in West Mount Airy.

For the WMAN board, this new cycle of unease once again prompted growing concern over the stability of the region. It was time, they believed, for a reinvigorated campaign geared toward promoting residential cohesion and community building. Unlike previous episodes of volatility, though, when leaders could draw on the work of long-standing residents who had been steeped in neighborhood organizing, in the early 1990s board members feared that the swell of new residents over the previous decade had left homeowners ill-equipped to contend with the external forces asserting power on the area. The recent flurry of in-migration to Mount Airy had, in a sense, resulted in a vacuum of organizational memory, a loss of the intentionality that community leaders believed was so critical to the long-standing viability of the neighborhood.

WMAN felt that in order to stem recent concerns and bring residents together, the organization needed to build awareness about the region's acclaimed integrationist reputation; if community leaders could teach current homeowners the lessons of the neighborhood's early organizing efforts, they could merge the region's historical legacy with its future potential. By documenting the development of the integration project of the 1950s, they believed, they could infuse Mount Airy with a new collective consciousness. In creating a community-wide memory of what had come before, they could provide residents with the analytical framework and organizational toolkit necessary to uplift the neighborhood going forward. In this way, WMAN leaders worked to deploy storytelling as a mechanism through which to re-create sustainable, structural change.

In 1992, the West Mount Airy Neighbors Historical Awareness Committee embarked on a sweeping oral history study of the neighborhood's past. The committee, established a decade earlier by Patricia Henning, was charged with helping to document the neighborhood's historical narrative.[59] Early efforts of the Historical Awareness Committee had been relatively ad hoc, pulling together programming as opportunities for historical celebration arose.[60] But by the early 1990s the group was ready to play a proactive role in reinvigorating the community through deliberate historical representation. That June, the organization applied for more than $15,000 in funding from the Pennsylvania Historical and Museum Commission. In conjunction with the Pelham Centennial Celebration, commemorating the hundredth anniversary of the Pelham subsection of West Mount Airy, the committee proposed to collect the stories of some of the region's earliest integrationists.[61] The group, led by WMAN members Vida Carson, Betty Ann Fellner, and Henning, envisioned the project as "a step toward understanding the experiences of the participants—the established residents and the newcomers, those who stayed and those who left, and learning more about the process used by those who intervened to break the all too common pattern of fear, flight, and racial succession in favor of trust, understanding, and integration."[62] Through the oral history initiative, organizers sought to translate the ideals of the midcentury efforts toward interracial living into a roadmap for contemporary community-building.

The committee proposed to commission scholars and experts, to employ transcribers and interviewers, and to purchase recording equipment in order to collect the stories of thirty past Mount Airy residents. Their grant application highlighted plans to include "ordinary" citizens, in addition to community activists, and committed to ensuring racial, gender, and religious diversity among the participants. According to the original proposal, following the initial interview process, the committee would select the fifteen "best" interviews for professional transcription and indexing.[63] There was no indication of how such ranking would occur.

Although the grant application focused on the importance of reclaiming the stories of the past, the language in the proposal hinted at additional motivations for the initiative. "The potential value of the project," the statement said, "reaches beyond Pelham and Mount Airy, because it will attempt to shed light on what actually happened during the 1950s at block meetings and neighborhood coffee klatches that succeeded in calming fears of many residents and began the process of developing a community built on trust. The success of those efforts set the tone for all of Mount Airy in the intervening forty years. This is an opportune time for Mount Airy to revisit that legacy."[64] With instability growing and uncertainty lingering about the future viability of the community, Mount Airy activists saw the remembrance of the early efforts to create "a community built on trust" as a crucial tool in recalibrating the neighborhood going forward.

In the fall of 1992, the Pennsylvania Historical and Museum Commission responded to WMAN's request with the allocation of $3,000 in support.[65] With funding in hand, organizers began to finalize interview subjects and publicize the project. "From the 1950s on, there were assaults on many neighborhoods across the country," said committee member Betty Ann Fellner in a December article for the *Mount Airy Times Express*. "When they were 'threatened' with integration, people left in wholesale numbers. That's typical," said Fellner. "Mount Airy is not. What happened? Why is it that this neighborhood has such an extensive history of maintaining integration?" These subtle language choices—of maintenance over creation, of present-tense sentence construction over past tense—were critical in framing the oral history project as an effort toward renewal and rejuvenation, rather than solely commemoration. "Young people need to know how the neighborhood came to be," said committee member Vida Carson in the same article, "especially today, since there is so much racism. It's important for young people to know that this can be done, that it *has* to be done" (emphasis in original).[66] The very act of sharing such stories, the committee seemed to say, would be sufficient to empower and energize residents, to compel them toward neighborhood rejuvenation.

In the months that followed, the group selected twenty-seven people who had lived in the community in the early 1950s. According to reports, the committee worked hard to get a wide cross-section of the community. All told, there were ten men and seventeen women. Fourteen were black, and thirteen, white. Six were Jewish, and twenty-one of various Christian denominations. The list included teachers, homemakers, judges, realtors, and social workers. There were human rights specialists, clergy members, politicians, and bank tellers.[67] But even as the group sought out those "ordinary citizens" whom WMAN had described in the original grant proposal, the interviews that ultimately made it from tape to transcription were with some of the most vocal and active members of the community.

There was Don Black, who moved to the neighborhood with his wife, Vivian, in 1951 and served for decades on various committees of WMAN and other local community organizations. There was Joseph Coleman, the first African American president of the Philadelphia City Council, and Marjorie Kopeland, past president of the Henry Home and School Association and one of the founders of the neighborhood's Allens Lane Arts Center. There were Shirley Melvin and Doris Polsky, twin sisters who started one of the first female-owned real estate agencies in the country, to drive out blockbusting agents from the neighborhood. There was Jeremiah Wright Sr., the integrationist pastor of Grace Baptist Church.[68] And finally, there was George Schermer, founding president of the Philadelphia Human Relations Commission, who moved to West Mount Airy in 1953 and was critical to the success of the neighborhood's effort toward residential integration.[69] Taken together, these personal histories told a carefully constructed story of activism, intentionality, and public engagement.

Certainly, the oral history initiative did capture the narratives of some of the less prominent members of the community. Patricia Henning interviewed Frank Harvey, a white man born at his grandfather's Mount Airy house in 1922, who spent his entire life on W. Hortter Street. Harvey recalled white residents leaving after the introduction of black homeowners into the neighborhood, but he recounted more memories of attending local church services and frequenting area bars than of engaging in community organizing.[70] And interviewer Vida Carson spoke to Gladys Norris, an African American woman who moved to West Mount Airy as an adult in 1955 on the recommendation of her brother-in-law, a prominent attorney in the city, and had no recollection of many of the key neighborhood organizers and integrationist institutions.[71] But such stories as Harvey's and Norris's never made it from tape to paper; instead, the histories that were transcribed were those of the neighborhood's most active leaders and organizers, the ones who situated themselves on the front lines of the fight for genuine interracial living.[72]

These decisions on transcription selection and editing resulted in a narrative very much tailored to the goals of the Historical Awareness Committee and of West Mount Airy Neighbors more broadly. The group presented a community that was, in a sense, homogeneous in its diversity, a neighborhood drawn together by the activist ethos of its residents and by the mutual benefit and satisfaction they received from that mission. As a November 1993 progress report read:

> People interviewed told us that they felt enriched by the inter-group associations they experienced here. . . . Children received an education in intergroup relations, interpersonal growth, that they would not have gotten elsewhere. . . . Over and over people spoke of certain personal qualities of the residents that made a difference, that promoted good inter-group and interpersonal relations, such as: respect for one another, open-mindedness, progressive attitudes, graciousness and courtesy, a sense of social justice and

fairness, hope and optimism, trust and good will. . . . Virtually everyone interviewed said that the decision to move to Mount Airy, or to stay in Mount
Airy, was a good one. . . . They said they had no regrets, but some expressed
dismay at some negative changes that have occurred in the neighborhood [in
recent years].[73]

The project summary offered an impression of historic Mount Airy as a
community made up exclusively of people of good will, of people who were
enriched by living there, of people who never regretted moving into the
neighborhood. Here, the community was a place and a group of people that
believed that their work was vital to the creation and maintenance of a
democratic society.

Project coordinators made clear the lessons that the Mount Airy of the
1990s could learn from the historic efforts toward integration in northwest
Philadelphia; they highlighted the role that the experiences of the neighborhood's earliest activists could play in pulling the neighborhood together in
the current moment of instability. As the report continued:

> One name came up over and over again. That name was George Schermer . . .
> Friends of George Schermer like to tell stories about going on camping trips
> with the Schermers, and they tend to recall how at the end of their stay at a
> campsite, George would provide a little lesson about the fact that they had to
> find some way to improve the site, to make it better than they had found it.
> Well, George and the other good citizens of Mount Airy in the 1950s applied
> that same campsite philosophy to Mount Airy. That's not a bad thought for
> us to keep in mind as we move into the second century of the Pelham neigh-
> borhood. From time to time we might reflect on this and ask ourselves if we
> are being sufficiently good stewards on the legacy we enjoy in this commu-
> nity today . . . Many see the Pelham Centennial Celebration as a catalyst in
> pulling people together, energizing a new spirit of participation, and re-
> awakening awareness of the kind of diversity we have here in Mount Airy.[74]

The Historical Awareness Committee, through careful editing and deliberate presentation decisions, played a critical role in shaping the historical
narrative of the community. With WMAN serving as the mediator in the
storytelling process, the West Mount Airy Oral History Project curated the
story of a neighborhood born out of democratic impulses and lived racial
justice.[75] Though individual interviewees did discuss issues of economic

exclusivity, complicated identity politics, and subtle power struggles, the public account that emerged was one of neighborly good will, meaningful friendship, achieved liberalism, and, perhaps most significant, strong leadership. In distilling individual interviews into a seamless narrative, WMAN emerged as the stabilizing force in the community. As the invocation of George Schermer's camping trips indicates, through the oral history project West Mount Airy Neighbors leaders developed a consciousness of the past that cast themselves as central to the neighborhood's success and viability. In the hands of the long-standing organization, the story of the community became the story of the unflinching guidance of WMAN through the latter half of the twentieth century. Through this carefully managed telling, the group ensured that it would retain its position in the community going forward.

Of course, WMAN often did serve as the voice of the neighborhood; the organization was the central clearinghouse for West Mount Airy, and over the first forty years of its existence, it was, indeed, a moderating force for the community. By casting the Oral History Project narrative as such, however, WMAN, in a sense, uncomplicated a very complicated story. Lost were the stories of WMAA and cycles of decline; lost were the cries of Uncle Tom and the heated exchanges between Cecil Moore and Raymond and Sadie Alexander; lost were the controversial policies of Beatrice Chernock and the death of Samson Freedman. The collective consciousness that emerged out of the West Mount Airy Oral History Project was one that minimized historical tensions within the community and threats and challenges from outside. Here, by crafting such a sanitized history, WMAN offered current residents a model for successful community organizing—but it perhaps failed to provide them with the tools to withstand the inevitable trials of long-term stability in the future.

Throughout 1993, members of the Historical Awareness Committee took their findings into the community, offering presentations throughout the region about the neighborhood's integrationist past. On January 12, 1993, they spoke to ninety residents at the Lutheran Theological Seminary. On March 31, historian (and project participant) Dennis Clark lectured to seventy-one people at the Lovett Memorial Library, an event captured on tape and disseminated throughout the area. In September, they held a teacher workshop for twenty-one educators at the Cook-Wissahickon School. In November, they held two events for a combined 136 audience members, on interfaith service and neighborhood history. Although the numbers were relatively small, the committee was succeeding in spreading the findings of its study to neighbors and residents throughout the Mount Airy community.[76]

By the middle of the decade, there emerged subtle hints that these efforts were beginning to create a new consciousness, throughout the city, about the neighborhood's integrationist past. In a January 1993 *Inquirer* article chronicling the centennial of the Pelham section of the neighborhood, Patricia Henning situated the origins of the West Mount Airy efforts toward interracial living in the years following World War II. "In 1951," said Henning, "people here say, Pelham became the first area of the city to be successfully racially integrated, as African American doctors, lawyers, and judges began buying homes. Residents and churches organized to get people to sit down and talk and develop a community that was open to change."[77] A year later, in March 1994, *Inquirer* reporter Roxanne Jones wrote, "In the 1950s, when most of the nation's neighborhoods were trying to discourage integration, a small group in West Mount Airy was working against the tide to encourage it." Jones described in detail the efforts of WMAN in effectuating grassroots change, and once again cited Henning. "It drew upon the religious roots and fellowship of man," she said, to urge support from residents.[78] Whereas the 1980s saw features on West Mount Airy that spoke of the community's reputation for diversity as timeless, painting racial tolerance there as a truism rather than a historical process, by the mid-1990s local coverage returned to celebrating the early intentionality and activism toward interracial living.[79]

In 1998, three scholars published an article on West Mount Airy in a special issue of *Cityscape: A Journal of Policy Development and Research*, examining "racially and ethnically diverse urban neighborhoods."[80] Here, Barbara Ferman, Theresa Singleton, and Don DeMarco chronicled the community's early efforts to create an integrated space, and while much of their research drew on secondary literature and analysis of census data, the authors also made use of both the transcripts and reports of the Oral History Project and the *Inquirer* articles of the mid-1990s.[81] In assessing the effectiveness of organizing in Mount Airy, Ferman, Singleton, and DeMarco cited the region's institutional and communal historical awareness as a key factor in the neighborhood's success. A self-consciousness toward integration—and the ability to translate that self-consciousness about the past into meaningful lessons for the present—became a key step in the process of integration itself, wrote the authors.[82]

The narrative created by the West Mount Airy oral history initiative thus entered into public, scholarly, and policy conversations on the community's integrationist legacy. The WMAN board invoked a sense of institutional authority to create an officially sanctioned memory of the neighborhood's past, seeking to celebrate the historic effort toward interracial living, and to position the organization as the keystone of that effort. In this way, oral history became a dynamic vehicle through which to assert control over what came before and to call for community-wide grassroots change in the future. Here, neighborhood leaders worked to build a self-perpetuating engine, whereby this mindfulness of the past would foster engagement in the present, thus maintaining a sense of both economic viability and tolerance within the community. By promoting the narrative of the oral history project, the WMAN Historical Awareness Committee sought to bring new like-minded people into the community and orient them toward intentional living, thereby carrying on that sense of stable diversity.

Epilogue

West Mount Airy and the Legacy of Integration

In 1975, Christie Balka graduated from Germantown Friends School and left her childhood home in Mount Airy to begin her freshman year at Colorado College in Colorado Springs, Colorado. When she arrived, the white, Jewish woman was appalled by the endemic racism that she encountered. "I was furious with my parents for giving me the impression that our society had overcome this," she recalled. The daughter of former WMAN president Jerry Balka, Christie had experienced racial difference throughout her life—when faculty laughed as she and her best friend, a black student, dressed as twins during the Henry School Halloween parade, when teachers disciplined her African American peers for skipping school as she went unpunished—but she felt unprepared for the level of intolerance that she witnessed when she left the protective bubble of Mount Airy. "My friends and I thought our values had been a wave that happened everywhere but Iowa and Mississippi," she said. "We were stunned at how unprepared we were to go into the 'real world.' "[1]

As West Mount Airy entered the new millennium, the neighborhood proudly brandished its reputation as one of the first and most successful models of economically stable racial integration in the United States. Local and national publications lauded the community's success as a symbol of tolerance and diversity. In 2004, Mount Airy was among the city's highest ranking neighborhoods in terms of community cohesion. "In a city of neighborhoods," the *Inquirer* reported, "West Mount Airy stands out in Philadelphia as one of diversity, artistic inclination, and, well, neighborliness."[2] Two years later, *O, the Oprah Magazine*, published a spread on the community. "Welcome to a neighborhood where people of just about every race, religion, class, belief system, and sexual orientation come together and play very nicely," wrote freelance journalist Lise Fundeberg. "In Mt. Airy, like almost nowhere else in the country, you can't generalize about the inhabitants' ethnicities, incomes, religions, sexual orientations, preferences in music, or even likelihood of shoveling when it snows." Fundeberg, the biracial product of a white mother and a black father, had moved to the neighborhood in 1996.[3] "Living in Mount Airy," she wrote, "is like having been dropped onto a stage set that matches my internal landscape. Living the inside out. It's not perfect, but it's alive and mostly well intentioned. And because of the effort people make, their willingness to partake in the process of becoming, their intentional wakefulness, this much is true: it is always a beautiful day in my neighborhood."[4] Once again, community efforts toward creative marketing had given way to a national reputation of the area as a vibrant, diverse neighborhood.

And indeed, in these early years of the twenty-first century, Mount Airy remains one of the most economically stable and diverse areas in Philadelphia. According to 2010 census data, the neighborhood is approximately 41 percent African American, 54 percent white, and 5 percent Asian or Latino, with roughly 3 percent of residents self-identifying as multiracial.[5] Between 2005–2009, the median household income in West Mount Airy was $84,593, nearly sixty percent higher than the national median for the same period, with more than a third of residents having earned graduate degrees, reflecting the neighborhood's reputation as a "PhD ghetto."[6] In March 2013, the Pew Charitable Trust named the 19119 zip code, which encompasses both East and West Mount Airy, the seventh-wealthiest zip code in Philadelphia.[7] The community also continues to serve as a haven for alternative families and progressive politics. Hybrid cars marked with bumper stickers proclaiming "Support Organic Farmers" and "Keep Abortion Legal" sit at the corner of Carpenter Lane and Green Street, the center of the original "integrated core," now marked by the Weaver's Way Food Cooperative, the Blue Marble Bookstore, and the High Point Cafe. Taken in aggregate, the picture evidences a thriving, open community.

A more nuanced evaluation of the region, though, reveals that racial isolation is increasing and that the class-based exclusivity so critical to the neighborhood's early success toward interracial living continues to pervade local housing patterns. In the last twenty years, the overall population of West Mount Airy has decreased from 17,434 in 1990 to 9,892 in 2010, with black residents accounting for 70 percent of that loss. In that same period, block-by-block integration saw a sharp decline. In 1990, the average black resident lived on a block comprised of approximately 75 percent of African Americans; by 2010, the same blocks had become almost entirely black. Further, whereas in 1990, African Americans were dispersed relatively evenly throughout the neighborhood, by 2000, they were disproportionately clustered in the southern and eastern regions of the community, adjacent to the poorer and blacker East Mount Airy and East Germantown. In 2009, in census tracts 234 and 236, which roughly approximate the neighborhood's "integrated core," the average household income was $128,491. Here, the population was approximately one-third black and two-thirds white.[8] It was in these pockets, in the late 1960s, where African American residents began to express discontent over the perceived isolation and alienation from West Mount Airy Neighbors' organizing efforts.[9] These numbers indicate a continuing and growing economic divide across the neighborhood, where true residential integration is predicated on a common fiscal and educational experience. In the twenty-first century, de facto economic restriction remains a key factor in predicting the success of residential integration and cultural diversity.

This demographic profile of West Mount Airy is set against a growing national critique of the goals of integration. In 1998, the left-leaning magazine, the *Nation*, published a special series examining the state of civil rights progress in the United States. The contributors, acclaimed scholars and journalists, sought to find meaning of the postwar efforts toward integration, and to apply that meaning to the current state of race relations at the turn of the century.[10] "Integration," wrote historian Eric Foner and legal scholar Randall Kennedy, "the ideal that once inspired an interracial mass movement to dream for a better America, has lately fallen into . . . disfavor. . . . Many leftists feel that as a political goal, integration fails to address deeply rooted economic inequalities. Many African Americans criticize it for implying the dismantling of a distinctive black culture and identity. Those who still favor the idea of integration often reduce it to a matter of 'color-blind' law and social practice."[11] According to Foner and Kennedy, the integrationist orientation was a flawed but well-intentioned movement for racial justice; it offered progress in the realm of American race relations, but it fell short of a full reorientation of the nation's racial hierarchy. As historian Judith Stein argued in the same series, racial integration was a postwar construction crafted by liberal elites seeking to heal American race relations. These efforts were rooted in Gunnar Myrdal's *An American Dilemma*, but where Myrdal's work focused on the reallocation of resources—according to Stein, "bringing rural blacks into the industrial economy and providing them with decent housing [and] . . . assum[ing] that a higher standard of living would then promote integration"—by placing the onus for racial progress on white Americans, the Swedish economist inadvertently established a class-blind ethos of racial justice.[12]

Throughout the 1950s and 1960s, integration became the mainstream rallying cry of the civil rights movement, a tangible goal in which middle-class white liberals and African Americans could ground their efforts. As Foner and Kennedy wrote, "The demand for integration proved a potent weapon for mobilizing Americans of all races to break down the walls of legalized segregation."[13] Activists made great strides in the larger struggle for racial justice, eroding barriers in employment, education, and even housing. But in subtle ways, the *Nation* collection suggests, each of these triumphs revealed the limits of integration. "During the post-war period," wrote scholar Robin D. G. Kelley, "the term [integration] was associated with liberals who conceived of integration as a means of creating racial harmony without a fundamental transformation of the social and economic order. In most white liberal circles . . . the goal was to produce fully assimilated black people devoted to the American dream. Sharing power was rarely part of the equation."[14] Integration, echoed Kennedy and Foner, "tended to encourage a view of race relations as a matter of interpersonal dynamics, and to identify the main problem facing African Americans as segregation—often understood as an abstraction—rather than emphasizing deprivations such as inadequate jobs, housing, and education."[15] The goal of integration, these scholars wrote, subverted efforts to reorient the material conditions of American society.

These larger critiques are manifested in the history of West Mount Airy itself. The neighborhood's integration efforts allowed long-standing residents to maintain the integrity of their region by welcoming in similarly situated African Americans. Together, they created a community grounded in the ideals of postwar racial liberalism, and they fought hard to maintain that ideal amid shifting economic and political pressures and evolving notions of racial justice. But the Mount Airy integration project never sought to be transformative; at its core, the neighborhood efforts were grounded in a desire to preserve their community, to retain its viability through celebrating interracial living.

For those who came of age in West Mount Airy in the decades following World War II, these efforts were at once empowering and dispiriting. "[The neighborhood] was full of people who in some cases broke with families and succeeded in creating something different," recalled Christie Balka. "That lesson of being able to make change because you believe it's right is really powerful. Mount Airy offered me a strong foundation. But it was an imperfect one. . . . None of us were prepared for the limits of this, to run into a brick wall [when we left the neighborhood]. . . . I didn't know racism. When that rug was pulled out from under me, I never wanted to come back." But even amid these limitations, the *process* of integration resonated loudly. "Something happened that was successful to a point," reflected Balka. "I grew up with a sense that if I didn't like something, I could succeed in changing it. That was, of course, both tinged by and reinforced by class, but all around me there were examples of people who saw things they didn't like and took steps to change them on a community level."[16]

The ethos of intentionality and activism in West Mount Airy—and the methods of organizing that community leaders developed—offered both residents and onlookers a framework for mobilizing in the decades following the Second World War. The neighborhood was able to effect sustainable change because it developed a sense of institutional accountability through meaningful partnerships, both within the community and outside of it. The creation of West Mount Airy Neighbors and the relationships between WMAN and governmental agencies throughout the city created a powerful structure for change-making within the neighborhood. "West Mount Airy succeeded . . . because of the public institutions it developed, organizations that made it their mission to be accountable to the neighborhood," reflected Balka, who made a career in community development and advocacy and ultimately returned to northwest Philadelphia, making a home in East Mount Airy with her partner, Rabbi Rebecca Alpert. "The lesson in West Mount Airy is that public institutions in a community can bring people together in sustained ways. . . . Not every neighborhood can support a Weaver's Way Co-op, but they can take these public institutions to scale to create sustainable change."[17]

Mount Airy's efforts toward intentional integration were a part of a small movement around the country to create stable interracial communities. These neighborhoods are not utopias, nor are they blueprints for achieved racial justice. But even if, as some scholars have noted, these integrated spaces serve as little more than a footnote in the larger narrative of racial struggle in the United States, they offer unique insight into the historic process of community-making in postwar American cities. As Balka suggests, throughout the latter half of the twentieth century community leaders in West Mount Airy developed and honed a model of neighborhood organizing that, when deployed effectively, fostered both racial tolerance and economic viability. The innovation of grassroots liberalism, the recognition of the bilateral need for structural accountability and individual action and responsibility, allowed residents to sustain a stable, open community in the midst of vast political, economic, and cultural change.

NOTES

Introduction

1. Keynote remarks of Eleanor Holmes Norton, June 20, 1975, WMAN, Urban Archives, Philadelphia, PA, Accession 737, Box 10, Folder 1.

2. See, e.g., Thomas J. Sugrue, *Origins of the Urban Crisis: Race and Inequality in Post-War Detroit* (Princeton, NJ: Princeton University Press, 1996); Arnold R. Hirsch, *Making the Second Ghetto: Race and Housing in Chicago, 1940–1960* (New York: Cambridge University Press, 1983); Stephen Grant Meyer, *As Long as They Don't Move Next Door: Segregation and Racial Conflict in American Neighborhoods* (Lanham, MD: Rowman and Littlefield, 2000); Jonathan Rieder, *Canarsie: The Jews and Italians of Brooklyn against Liberalism* (Cambridge: Harvard University Press, 1985); Kenneth T. Jackson, *Crabgrass Frontier: The Suburbanization of the United States* (New York: Oxford University Press, 1985); James Wolfinger, *Philadelphia Divided: Race and Politics in the City of Brotherly Love* (Raleigh: University of North Carolina Press, 2007). For an evaluation of white flight and its aftermath, see Rachael Woldoff, *White Flight/Black Flight: The Dynamics of Racial Change in an American Neighborhood* (Ithaca, NY: Cornell University Press, 2011).

3. For reference on efforts toward intentional integration, see, e.g., Barbara Ferman, Theresa Singleton, and Don DeMarco, "West Mount Airy, Philadelphia," *Cityscape: A*

Journal of Policy Development and Research 4, no. 2 (1998); Sheryll Cashin, *The Failures of Integration: How Race and Class Are Undermining the American Dream* (New York: PublicAffairs, 2005); Juliet Saltman, *A Fragile Movement: The Struggle for Neighborhood Stabilization* (New York: Greenwood Press, 1990); Juliet Saltman, *Open Housing: The Dynamics of a Social Movement* (New York: Praeger, 1978); William G. Grigsby and Chester Rapkin, *The Demand for Housing in Racially Mixed Areas: A Study of the Nature of Neighborhood Change* (Berkeley: University of California Press, 1960); Phyllis M. Palmer, *Living as Equals: How Three White Communities Struggled to Make Interracial Connections during the Civil Rights Era* (Nashville, TN: Vanderbilt University Press, 2008); Peter R. Eisenstadt, *Rochdale Village: Robert Moses, 6,000 Families, and New York's Greatest Experiment in Integrated Housing* (Ithaca, NY: Cornell University Press, 2010).

4. For additional works that discuss Mount Airy as an integrated community, see Ferman, Singleton, and DeMarco, "West Mount Airy, Philadelphia;" Cashin, *Failures of Integration*; Murray Friedman, ed., *Philadelphia Jewish Life, 1940–2000* (Philadelphia: Temple University Press, 2003); Jack M. Guttentag, "Racial Integration and Home Prices: The Case of West Mount Airy," *Wharton Quarterly* (Spring 1970); Leonard F. Heumann, "The Definition and Analysis of Stable Racial Integration: The Case of West Mount Airy, Philadelphia" (PhD diss., University of Pennsylvania, 1973); Saltman, *Fragile Movement*; Saltman, *Open Housing*; Juliet Anna Sternberg, "Can We Talk about Race? The Racial Discourse of Activists in a Racially 'Integrated' Neighborhood" (PhD diss., Rutgers University, 1996); Grigsby and Rapkin, *Demand for Housing*; Brian F. Leaf, "Breaking the Barrier: The Success of Racial Integration in the Philadelphia Community of Mount Airy, 1950–1975" (Senior honors thesis, University of Pennsylvania, 1995); Thomas J. Sugrue, *Sweet Land of Liberty: The Forgotten Struggle for Civil Rights in the North* (New York: Random House, 2008).

5. For reference, see, e.g., Sugrue, *Origins of the Urban Crisis*; Hirsch, *Making the Second Ghetto*; Meyer, *As Long as They Don't Move Next Door*; Rieder, *Canarsie*; Jackson, *Crabgrass Frontier*; Kevin Michael Kruse, *White Flight: Atlanta and the Making of Modern Conservatism* (Princeton, NJ: Princeton University Press, 2007); Matthew D. Lassiter, *The Silent Majority: Suburban Politics and the Sunbelt South* (Princeton, NJ: Princeton University Press, 2007); Robert O. Self, *American Babylon: Race and the Struggle for Post-War Oakland* (Princeton, NJ: Princeton University Press, 2003); Amanda I. Seligman, *Block by Block: Neighborhoods and Public Policy on Chicago's West Side* (Chicago: University of Chicago Press, 2005); Kevin Michael Kruse and Thomas J. Sugrue, eds., *The New Suburban History* (Chicago: University of Chicago Press, 2006); David M. P. Freund, *Colored Property: State Policy and White Racial Politics in Suburban America* (Chicago: University of Chicago Press, 2007); Jane Jacobs, *The Death and Life of Great American Cities* (New York: Random House, 1961).

6. Mario Luis Small, *Villa Victoria: The Transformation of Social Capital in a Boston Barrio* (Chicago: University of Chicago Press, 2004), vii.

7. Sugrue, *Sweet Land of Liberty*, 542.

8. The Urban Archives at Temple University in Philadelphia houses eighteen linear feet of material from the West Mount Airy Neighbors Association. Adding to this collection are several smaller archives that contribute to a historical understanding of West Mount Airy, including the Philadelphia City Archives, the University of Pennsylvania

Archives, the American Friends Service Committee Archives, the Germantown Historical Society, the Germantown Jewish Centre papers at the Philadelphia Jewish Archives, the Fairmount Park Commission archives, the George Schermer personal papers at the Amistad Archives in New Orleans, LA, the NAACP papers at the Library of Congress, the *Philadelphia Tribune* and the *Philadelphia Inquirer* archives, both digitized on Proquest Historical Newspapers, and the *Philadelphia Bulletin* clippings collection at the Urban Archives.

9. On liberalism in the twentieth century, see, e.g., Alan Brinkley, *The End of Reform: New Deal Liberalism in Recession and War* (New York: Alfred A. Knopf, 1995); Steve Fraser and Gary Gerstle, eds., *The Rise and Fall of the New Deal Order, 1930–1980* (Princeton, NJ: Princeton University Press, 1989); Alonzo L. Hamby, *Liberalism and Its Challengers: From FDR to Bush* (New York: Oxford University Press, 1985).

Chapter 1

1. Shelley v. Kraemer, 334 U.S. 1 (1948).

2. Peter H. Irons, *The Courage of Their Convictions: Sixteen Americans Who Fought Their Way to the Supreme Court* (New York: Free Press, 1988).

3. Shelley v. Kraemer, 334 U.S. 1 (1948).

4. Ibid.

5. Wendell E. Pritchett, "Shelley v. Kraemer: Racial Liberalism and the U.S. Supreme Court," in *Civil Rights Stories*, ed. Myriam E. Gilles and Risa L. Goluboff (New York: Foundation Press, 2008), 16.

6. See U.S. Constitution, article 4, section 3; U.S. Constitution, Third Amendment; U.S. Constitution, Fifth Amendment.

7. See, e.g., Mary Dudziak, *Cold War Civil Rights: Race and the Image of American Democracy* (Princeton, NJ: Princeton University Press, 2000); Thomas Borstelmann, *The Cold War and the Color Line: American Race Relations in the Global Arena* (Cambridge, MA: Harvard University Press, 2001); Kevin Michael Kruse and Stephen G. N. Tuck, eds., *Fog of War: The Second World War and the Civil Rights Movement* (New York: Oxford University Press, 2012).

8. For a discussion of residential segregation in postwar America, see, introduction, note 5.

9. Wolfinger, *Philadelphia Divided*; James N. Gregory, *The Southern Diaspora: How the Great Migrations of Black and White Southerners Transformed America* (Chapel Hill: University of North Carolina Press, 2005); Andrew Wiese, *Places of Their Own: African American Suburbanization in the Twentieth Century* (Chicago: University of Chicago Press, 2005).

10. Garrett Power, "Apartheid Baltimore Style: The Residential Segregation Ordinances of 1910–1913," *Maryland Law Review* 42, no. 289 (1983): 290.

11. Wolfinger, *Philadelphia Divided*, 12.

12. Heumann, "Definition and Analysis of Stable Racial Integration," 30; Julie Winch, *Philadelphia's Black Elite: Activism, Accommodation, and the Struggle for Autonomy, 1787–1848* (Philadelphia: Temple University Press, 1993).

13. Wolfinger, *Philadelphia Divided*, 12.

14. Power, "Apartheid Baltimore Style," 290.

15. Ibid., 299.

16. Ibid., 289.

17. Ibid., 303–304.

18. Buchanan v. Warley, 245 U.S. 60 (1917).

19. See, e.g., Angela P. Harris, "Equality Trouble: Sameness and Difference in 20th Century Race Law," *California Law Review* 88, no. 6 (December 2000).

20. Michael B. Katz and Thomas J. Sugrue, *W.E.B. DuBois, Race, and the City: "The Philadelphia Negro" and Its Legacy* (Philadelphia: University of Pennsylvania Press, 1998), 200.

21. Frederic Miller, "The Black Migration to Philadelphia: A 1924 Profile," *Pennsylvania Magazine of History and Biography* 108, no. 3 (July 1984): 315–16.

22. John F. Bauman, *Public Housing, Race, and Renewal: Urban Planning in Philadelphia, 1920–1974* (Philadelphia: Temple University Press, 1987), 36.

23. Ibid.

24. Ibid., 32.

25. Sadie Tanner Mossell, "The Standard of Living among One Hundred Negro Migrant Families in Philadelphia" (PhD diss., University of Pennsylvania, 1921), 177.

26. Wolfinger, *Philadelphia Divided*, 20.

27. Sugrue, *Sweet Land of Liberty*, 203.

28. These legal terms of art describe restrictions on the transfer and use of property. Defeasible fees create a conditional limitation on ownership, where property rights transfer once a particular event has taken place (for instance, the death of the current owner). A negative easement restricts the rights of one property owner from executing an otherwise lawful activity on their property (for instance, constructing a high wall), because of its impact on a second property owner. Finally, an equitable servitude is an interest in land held by a non-owning party (for instance, in a cooperative, condominium, or other common-interest community).

29. Ibid., 202.

30. Village of Euclid v. Ambler Realty Company, 272 U.S. 365 (1926).

31. Nectow v. City of Cambridge, et al., 277 U.S. 183 (1928).

32. Moore v. City of East Cleveland, 431 U.S. 494 (1977).

33. See, e.g., Freund, *Colored Property*; Meyer, *As Long as They Don't Live Next Door*; Kruse and Sugrue, *New Suburban History*; Sugrue, *Origins of the Urban Crisis*; Jackson, *Crabgrass Frontier*.

34. See, e.g., Freund, *Colored Property*, 113–14; Jackson, *Crabgrass Frontier*, 119–20; Meyer, *As Long as They Don't Live Next Door*, 53–54; Sugrue, *Origins of the Urban Crisis*, 44.

35. Freund, *Colored Property*, 113, citing Jackson, *Crabgrass Frontier*, 119–20. See also Amy Hillier, "Who Received Loans? Home Owners' Loan Corporation Lending and Discrimination in Philadelphia in the 1930s," *Journal of Planning History* 2, no. 1 (February 2003): 3–24, on the causal relationship between Home Owners' Loan Corporation maps and FHA racially restrictive policies.

36. Freund, *Colored Property*, 114.

37. FHA *Underwriter's Manual* cited in NAACP memo, October 20, 1944, NAACP Papers, Part 5, Group II, Box A–268, "FHA, General 194701948," Reel Five at 555, as cited in Meyer, *As Long as They Don't Live Next Door*, 53–54.

38. Leslie S. Perry, NAACP, Statement before the House Banking and Currency Committee, April 26, 1949, U.S. House of Representatives, Committee on Banking and Currency, *Housing Act of 1949: Hearings Before the Committee on Banking and Currency, House of Representatives, 81st Cong., 1st Sess. On H.R. 4009* (Washington, DC: Government Printing Office, 1949), 218–20, as cited in Meyer, *As Long as They Don't Live Next Door*, 53.

39. For reference, see, e.g., Gary Gerstle, "The Protean Character of American Liberalism," *American Historical Review* 99, no. 4 (October 1994); Neil R. McMillen, ed., *Remaking Dixie: The Impact of World War II on the American South* (Jackson: University Press of Mississippi, 1997); David W. Southern, *Gunnar Myrdal and Black-White Relations: The Use and Abuse of* An American Dilemma, *1944–1969* (Baton Rouge: Louisiana State University Press, 1987).

40. Sugrue, *Sweet Land of Liberty*, 63. See also Gunnar Myrdal, *An American Dilemma: The Negro Problem and Modern Democracy* (New York: Harper Publishing, 1944); William J. Barber, *Gunnar Myrdal: An Intellectual Biography* (New York: Palgrave Macmillan, 2008); Walter A. Jackson, *Gunnar Myrdal and America's Conscience: Social Engineering and Racial Liberalism, 1938–1987* (Chapel Hill: University of North Carolina Press, 1990).

41. *To Secure These Rights* (Washington, DC: Government Printing Office, 1947), 139–48, as cited in Dudziak, *Cold War Civil Rights*, 80.

42. Dudziak, *Cold War Civil Rights*, 7–13. See also Carol Anderson, *Eyes off the Prize: The United Nations and the African American Struggle for Human Rights, 1944–1955* (New York: Cambridge University Press, 2003).

43. Southern, *Gunnar Myrdal and Black-White Relations*, 108–110.

44. Ibid., 113.

45. Pritchett, "*Shelley v. Kraemer*," 19.

46. Ibid

47. Shelley v. Kraemer, 334 U.S. 1 (1948).

48. Press Release, May 3, 1948, NAACP, Part 5, Reel 2, as cited in Pritchett, "*Shelley v. Kraemer*," 21.

49. Lem Graves Jr., "Live Anywhere! High Court Rules," *Pittsburgh Courier*, May 8, 1948, as cited in Pritchett, "*Shelley v. Kraemer*," 21.

50. See, e.g., Myriam E. Gilles and Risa L. Goluboff, eds., *Civil Rights Stories* (New York: Foundation Press, 2008); Michael Klarman, *From Jim Crow to Civil Rights: The Supreme Court and the Struggle for Racial Equality* (New York: Oxford University Press, 2006).

51. See, e.g., Southern, *Gunnar Myrdal and Black-White Relations*; Dudziak, *Cold War Civil Rights*; Matthew Countryman, *Up South: Civil Rights and Black Power in Philadelphia* (Philadelphia: University of Pennsylvania Press, 2006).

52. Countryman, *Up South*, 59–61.

53. See, e.g., Gail F. Stern, *Traditions in Transition: Jewish Culture in Philadelphia, 1840–1940: An Exhibition in the Museum of the Balch Institute for Ethnic Studies* (Philadelphia:

Historical Society of Pennsylvania, 1989); Murray Friedman, ed., *Jewish Life in Philadelphia, 1830–1940* (Philadelphia: Institute for Human Issues, 1983); Friedman, *Philadelphia Jewish Life, 1940–2000*; Lance Jonathan Sussman, *Isaac Leeser and the Making of American Judaism* (Detroit, MI: Wayne State University Press, 1995); Robert Phillip Tabak, "The Transformation of Jewish Identity: The Philadelphia Jewish Experience, 1919–1945" (PhD diss., Temple University, 1990).

54. Friedman, *Philadelphia Jewish Life, 1940–2000*, xxv.

55. Countryman, *Up South*, 59–61.

56. George Schermer, interview by Civil Rights Documentation Project, November 4, 1967, written transcription, George Schermer Manuscript Collection, Amistad Archives, New Orleans, LA.

57. W. E. B. Dubois, as quoted in Wolfinger, *Philadelphia Divided*, 11.

58. Baumann, *Public Housing, Race, and Renewal*, 122.

59. See, e.g., Wolfinger, *Philadelphia Divided*; Sugrue, *Origins of the Urban Crisis*; Hirsch, *Making the Second Ghetto*; Rieder, *Canarsie*.

60. Countryman, *Up South*, 14.

61. Wolfinger, *Philadelphia Divided*, 87.

62. W. Benjamin Piggot, "The 'Problem' of the Black Middle Class: Morris Milgram's Concord Park and Residential Integration in Philadelphia's Postwar Suburbs," *Pennsylvania Magazine of History and Biography* 132, no. 2 (April 2008), citing "Housing Facts and Figures—Philadelphia, 1948," Philadelphia Housing Authority, July 1948, 1, accession 152.1, box A-622, Philadelphia City Archives.

63. For reference, see, e.g., Arnold R. Hirsch, "Massive Resistance in the Urban North: Trumbull Park, Chicago, 1953–1966," *Journal of American History* 82, no. 2 (September 1995): 522–50; Hirsch, *Making the Second Ghetto*; Sugrue, *Origins of the Urban Crisis*; Wolfinger, *Philadelphia Divided*.

64. For reference, see, e.g., Sugrue, *Origins of the Urban Crisis*; Rieder, *Canarsie*; Hirsch, *Making the Second Ghetto*.

65. Wolfinger, *Philadelphia Divided*, 85.

66. Sugrue, *Origins of the Urban Crisis*, 212–14.

67. Jackson, *Crabgrass Frontier*, 13–14.

68. See, e.g., Elaine Tyler May, *Homeward Bound: American Families in the Cold War Era* (New York: Basic Books, 1988); Lynn Spigel, *Make Room for TV: Television and the Family Ideal in Postwar America* (Chicago: University of Chicago Press, 1992); Lizabeth Cohen, *A Consumers' Republic: The Politics of Mass Consumption in Postwar America* (New York: Knopf, 2003).

69. Spigel, *Make Room for TV*, 32.

70. Thomas Sugrue, "The Unfinished History of Racial Segregation," in *The State of Fair Housing in America, presented by the National Commission on Fair Housing and Equal Opportunity*, July 15, 2008. Accessible at http://www.prrac.org/projects/fair_housing _commission/chicago/chicago_briefing.pdf.

71. May, *Homeward Bound*.

72. See, e.g., W. Edward Orser, *Blockbusting in Baltimore: The Edmondson Village Story* (Lexington: University Press of Kentucky, 1997); Meyer, *As Long As They Don't Move Next Door*.

73. For reference, see, e.g., Palmer, *Living as Equals*; Cashin, *Failures of Integration*; Saltman, *Fragile Movement*; Saltman, *Open Housing*.

74. Russell Frank Weigley, Nicholas B. Wainwright, and Edwin Wolf, *Philadelphia: A 300-Year History* (New York: W. W. Norton and Company, 1982), 64.

75. Ibid.

76. Weigley, *Philadelphia*, 64; Jackson, *Crabgrass Frontier*, 37; David R. Contosta, *Suburb in the City: Chestnut Hill, Philadelphia, 1850–1990* (Columbus: Ohio State University Press, 1992), 47–52.

77. Jackson, *Crabgrass Frontier*, 307.

78. Heumann, "Definition and Analysis of Stable Racial Integration," 20–22, 724.

79. Ibid., 29–31.

80. U.S. Bureau of the Census, *Census of the United States, Philadelphia SMSA* (Washington, DC: Government Printing Office, 1950).

81. U.S. Bureau of the Census, as cited by Leaf, "Breaking the Barrier," 10.

82. Memorandum, "History of Church Community Relations Council," undated, West Mount Airy Neighbors Paper, Manuscripts Collection, Accession 737, Box 20, Urban Archives, Philadelphia, PA; Meeting Report, Joint Meeting between the West Mount Airy Neighbors Association and the Church Community Relations Council, West Mount Airy Folder, American Friends Service Committee Archives, Philadelphia, PA, March 27, 1954.

83. Heumann, "Definition and Analysis of Stable Racial Integration," 22. Though Heumann's statistics come from a 1973 survey of the neighborhood, he points out that less than 10 percent of the housing stock resulted from postwar development. Only seven completely new blocks were built between 1951 and 1973, most of which were constructed as high quality one-of-a-kind projects prior to 1954 or after 1964. Thus, the overall physical landscape of the neighborhood changed little once integration began.

84. Heumann, "Definition and Analysis of Stable Racial Integration," 20; Mrs. Hiram MacIntosh, *An Incomplete History of West Mount Airy*, undated, WMAN, Urban Archives, Philadelphia, PA, Accession 274, Box 2, Folder 40.

85. Gladys Thompson Norton, interview by Vida Carson, 1993, audio recording, WMAN Oral History Project, Germantown Historical Society, Philadelphia, PA

86. Frank Harvey Jr., interview by Patricia Henning, 1993, audio recording, WMAN Oral History Project, Germantown Historical Society, Philadelphia, PA; Jim Foster, "Germantown 'Monopoly' Has a Parallel History," *Germantown Courier*, November 24, 2011.

87. Bernice Schermer, interview by Marjorie Kopeland, 1993, written transcription, WMAN Oral History Project, Germantown Historical Society, Philadelphia, PA.

88. Steve Sacks, interview by author, written transcription, Philadelphia, PA, February 17, 2011; Suzette Parmley, "The Day That Hollywood Glamour Came to West Mount Airy," *Philadelphia Inquirer*, May 16, 1998.

89. Shirley Melvin, interview by author, written transcription, Philadelphia, PA, November 28, 2006.

90. For a discussion of blue-collar anxiety toward integration, see, e.g., Rieder, *Canarsie*, 128.

91. For reference on movement toward intentional integration, see introduction, note 3.

Chapter 2

1. Jack Smyth, "Chestnut Hill Is Urged to Seek Integration Now," *Philadelphia Bulletin*, May 30, 1967.

2. For reference, see Myrdal, *American Dilemma*; Southern, *Gunnar Myrdal and Black-White Relations*; Barber, *Gunnar Myrdal: An Intellectual Biography*.

3. For more on educational integration, see chapter 5.

4. Real estate agents designate 1951 as the start of the interracial housing market in the neighborhood. Heumann, "Definition and Analysis of Stable Racial Integration," 28.

5. Ibid., 235–37.

6. Memorandum, "History of the Church Community Relations Council," undated, WMAN, Urban Archives, Philadelphia, PA, Accession 737, Box 20; Meeting Report, Joint meeting between the West Mount Airy Neighbors Association and the Church Community Relations Council, March 27, 1954, West Mount Airy Folder, American Friends Service Committee Archives, Philadelphia, PA.

7. For reference on the larger struggle over urban residential space, see introduction, note 2.

8. Memorandum, "History of the Church Community Relations Council," undated, WMAN, Urban Archives, Philadelphia, PA, Accession 737, Box 20.

9. Ibid.

10. Memorandum, "History of West Mount Airy Neighbors," undated, WMAN, Urban Archives, Philadelphia, PA, Accession 737, Box 20.

11. Meeting Minutes of West Mount Airy Group, March 4, 1954, West Mount Airy Folder, American Friends Service Committee Archives, Philadelphia, PA.

12. Memorandum, "History of West Mount Airy Neighbors," undated, WMAN, Urban Archives, Philadelphia, PA, Accession 737, Box 20; Meeting Minutes of West Mount Airy Group, March 4, 1954, West Mount Airy Folder, American Friends Service Committee Archives, Philadelphia, PA.

13. Memorandum, "History of the Church Community Relations Council," undated, WMAN, Urban Archives, Philadelphia, PA, Accession 737, Box 20.

14. Letter to George Schermer from Jane Reinheimer, February 19, 1954, West Mount Airy Folder, American Friends Service Committee Archives, Philadelphia, PA.

15. See, e.g., Jeff Woods, *Black Struggle, Red Scare: Segregation and Anti-Communism in the South, 1948–1968* (Baton Rouge: Louisiana State University Press, 2003); Stephen J. Whitfield, *The Culture of the Cold War, Second Edition* (Baltimore, MD: Johns Hopkins University Press, 1996).

16. Meeting Minutes of West Mount Airy Group, March 4, 1954, West Mount Airy Folder, American Friends Service Committee Archives, Philadelphia, PA.

17. Memorandum, "History of the Church Community Relations Council," undated, WMAN, Urban Archives, Philadelphia, PA, Accession 737, Box 20.

18. "This We Believe About Our Neighborhood: A Statement of Principle Adopted by the Church Community Relations Council, Pelham-Germantown," 1954, WMAN, Urban Archives, Philadelphia, PA, Accession 737, Box 1, Folder 16.

19. Ibid.

20. My conception of everyday performance was influenced by Erving Goffman, *The Presentation of Self in Everyday Life* (Garden City, NY: Doubleday Anchor Books, 1959). See also Bryant Simon, *Everything but the Coffee: Learning about America from Starbucks* (Berkeley: University of California Press, 2009).

21. "This We Believe About Our Neighborhood: A Statement of Principle Adopted by the Church Community Relations Council, Pelham-Germantown," 1954, WMAN, Urban Archives, Philadelphia, PA, Accession 737, Box 1, Folder 16.

22. Ibid.

23. For reference, see Saltman, *Fragile Movement*.

24. Ibid.; Cynthia Mills Richter, "Integrating the Suburban Dream: Shaker Heights, Ohio" (PhD diss., University of Minnesota, 1999).

25. Eunice S. Grier and George W. Grier, *Privately Developed Interracial Housing: An Analysis of Experience* (Berkeley: University of California Press, 1960), 8–12. During that same time period, there were ten million new housing units constructed across the country.

26. Thomas W. Ennis, "Suburb Breaks Racial Barrier," *New York Times*, March 10, 1957.

27. Piggot, "'Problem' of the Black Middle Class;" Sugrue, *Sweet Land of Liberty*, 232; Saltman, *Fragile Movement*, 23; Grier and Grier, *Privately Developed Interracial Housing*, as cited in Piggot, "'Problem of the Black Middle Class;" "Greenbelt Knoll National Register of Historic Places Registration Form" (Washington, DC: U.S. Department of the Interior, National Park Service, 2010); Lawrence Van Gelder, "Morris Milgram, 81: Built Interracial Housing," *New York Times*, June 26, 1997. Morris Milgram Papers, Collection 2176, Finding Aid, Historical Society of Pennsylvania.

28. George Schermer, interview by Judith Schermer, January 21, 1989, written transcription, WMAN Oral History Project, Germantown Historical Society, Philadelphia, PA.

29. "George Schermer, Biography," prepared by Gracia M. Hardacre, May 7, 1982, George Schermer Manuscripts Collection, Amistad Archives, New Orleans, LA.

30. Ibid.; George Schermer, interview by Civil Rights Documentation Project, November 4, 1967, written transcription, George Schermer Manuscript Collection, Amistad Archives, New Orleans, LA.

31. "George Schermer, Biography," prepared by Gracia M. Hardacre, May 7, 1982, George Schermer Manuscripts Collection, Amistad Archives, New Orleans, LA.

32. George Schermer, interview by Civil Rights Documentation Project, November 4, 1967, written transcription, George Schermer Manuscript Collection, Amistad Archives, New Orleans, LA; "George Schermer, Biography," prepared by Gracia M. Hardacre, May 7, 1982, George Schermer Manuscripts Collection, Amistad Archives, New Orleans, LA.

33. Bernice Schermer, interview by Marjorie Kopeland, 1993, written transcription, WMAN Oral History Project, Germantown Historical Society, Philadelphia, PA; "This

We Believe About Our Neighborhood: A Statement of Principle Adopted by the Church Community Relations Council, Pelham-Germantown," 1954, WMAN, Urban Archives, Philadelphia, PA, Accession 737, Box 1, Folder 16.

34. For more on the shifting notions of liberalism, see, e.g., Fraser and Gerstle, *Rise and Fall of the New Deal Order;* Brinkley, *End of Reform*, 268; Palmer, *Living as Equals*, 107.

35. George Schermer, interview by Judith Schermer, January 21, 1989, written transcription, WMAN Oral History Project, Germantown Historical Society, Philadelphia, PA.

36. "This We Believe About Our Neighborhood: A Statement of Principle Adopted by the Church Community Relations Council, Pelham-Germantown," 1954, WMAN, Urban Archives, Philadelphia, PA, Accession 737, Box 1, Folder 16.

37. Ibid.

38. For more on the relationship between religious affiliation and postwar residential patterns, see, e.g., Sugrue, *Origins of the Urban Crisis*; Rieder, *Canarsie*; Michael E. Staub, *Torn at the Roots: The Crisis of Jewish Liberalism in Postwar America* (New York: Columbia University Press, 2002); Gerald Gamm, *Urban Exodus: Why the Jews Left Boston and the Catholics Stayed* (Cambridge: Harvard University Press, 1999); John T. McGreevey, *Parish Boundaries: The Catholic Encounter with Race in the Twentieth-Century Urban North* (Chicago: University of Chicago Press, 1996).

39. David P. Varady, "Wynnefield: Story of a Changing Neighborhood," in Friedman, *Philadelphia Jewish Life 1940–2000*, 167.

40. Leo Dushoff, *From Dream to Reality: Story of the Germantown Jewish Centre* (Philadelphia: Germantown Jewish Centre, 1954).

41. Ibid.

42. Ibid.

43. Ibid.

44. "Set Formal Dedication of New Building of Germantown Jewish Centre," *Jewish Exponent*, May 21, 1954, Germantown Jewish Centre Papers, Philadelphia Jewish Archive Center, Accession 2040, Box 8, Folder 87.

45. Biographical Sketch, undated, Germantown Jewish Centre Papers, Philadelphia Jewish Archive Center, Accession 2040, Box 8, Folder 87.

46. New Member Correspondence, March 15, 1954, Germantown Jewish Centre Papers, Philadelphia Jewish Archive Center, Accession 2040, Box 2, Folder 58.

47. Personal Correspondence, undated, Germantown Jewish Centre Papers, Philadelphia Jewish Archive Center, Accession 2040, Box 4, Folder 7.

48. Personal Correspondence, August 28, 1951, Germantown Jewish Centre Papers, Philadelphia Jewish Archive Center, Accession 2040, Box 7, Folder 35.

49. Membership Correspondence, August 31, 1951, Germantown Jewish Centre Papers, Philadelphia Jewish Archive Center, Accession 2040, Box 7, Folder 35.

50. Integration Committee Meeting Announcement, October 19, 1955, Germantown Jewish Centre Papers, Philadelphia Jewish Archive Center, Accession 2040, Box 20, Folder 54.

51. E.g., editorial draft for The Family Tree for the Feldman Family, 1951, Germantown Jewish Centre Papers, Philadelphia Jewish Archive Center, Accession 2040, Box 7, Folder 10.

52. Marjorie Kopeland, interview by Patricia Henning, 1993, written transcription, WMAN Oral History Project, Germantown Historical Society, Philadelphia, PA; Shirley Melvin, interview by Patricia Henning, 1993, written transcription, WMAN Oral History Project, Germantown Historical Society, Philadelphia, PA.

53. Ibid.

54. Background, Fellowship Commission Papers, 1941–1986, Urban Archives, Philadelphia, PA, Accession 626; Marjorie Kopeland, interview by Patricia Henning, 1993, written transcription, WMAN Oral History Project, Germantown Historical Society, Philadelphia, PA; Bauman, 122.

55. Marjorie Kopeland, interview by Patricia Henning, 1993, written transcription, WMAN Oral History Project, Germantown Historical Society, Philadelphia, PA.

56. Ibid.

57. Ford Foundation Report, cited in Mie Augier and James G. March, *The Roots, Rituals, and Rhetorics of Change: North American Business Schools After the Second World War* (Palo Alto, CA: Stanford Business Books, 2011), 100; for reference, see Inderjeet Parmar, *Foundations of the American Century: The Ford, Carnegie, and Rockefeller Foundations in the Rise of American Power* (New York: Columbia University Press, 2012).

58. Augier and March, *The Roots, Rituals, and Rhetorics of Change*, 101.

59. Allens Lane Arts Center Lease, 1953, Manuscript Collection, Fairmount Park Commission, Philadelphia, PA; Shirley Melvin, interview by Patricia Henning, 1993, written transcription, WMAN Oral History Project, Germantown Historical Society, Philadelphia, PA.

60. Allens Lane Arts Center Lease, 1953, Manuscript Collection, Fairmount Park Commission, Philadelphia, PA.

61. Marjorie Kopeland, interview by Patricia Henning, 1993, written transcription, WMAN Oral History Project, Germantown Historical Society, Philadelphia, PA; Shirley Melvin, interview by Patricia Henning, 1993, written transcription, WMAN Oral History Project, Germantown Historical Society, Philadelphia, PA.

62. Bernice Schermer, interview by Marjorie Kopeland, 1993, written transcription, WMAN Oral History Project, Germantown Historical Society, Philadelphia, PA.

63. Ibid.; George Schermer, interview by Judith Schermer, January 21, 1989, written transcription, WMAN Oral History Project, Germantown Historical Society, Philadelphia, PA.

64. Bernice Schermer, interview by Marjorie Kopeland, 1993, written transcription, WMAN Oral History Project, Germantown Historical Society, Philadelphia, PA.

65. Marjorie Kopeland, interview by Pat Henning, 1993, written transcription, WMAN Oral History Project, Germantown Historical Society, Philadelphia, PA.

66. Shirley Melvin, interview by Patricia Henning, 1993, written transcription, WMAN Oral History Project, Germantown Historical Society, Philadelphia, PA.

67. Ibid.; Shirley Melvin, interview by Patricia Henning, 1993, written transcription, WMAN Oral History Project, Germantown Historical Society, Philadelphia, PA; Leaf, "Breaking the Barrier," 53.

68. Marjorie Kopeland, interview by Pat Henning, 1993, written transcription, WMAN Oral History Project, Germantown Historical Society, Philadelphia, PA.

69. Shirley Melvin, interview by Patricia Henning, 1993, written transcription, WMAN Oral History Project, Germantown Historical Society, Philadelphia, PA.

70. Shirley Melvin, interview by author, written transcription, Philadelphia, PA, November 28, 2006.

71. Heumann, "Definition and Analysis of Stable Racial Integration," 252.

72. Ibid., 119, 140–142, citing Hammer, Green, Siler Associates, *Regional Housing Planning: A Technical Guide* (Washington, DC: American Institute of Planners, 1972), 5; Grigsby and Rapkin, *Demand for Housing in Racially Mixed Areas;* Leaf, "Breaking the Barrier," 37.

73. Heumann, "Definition and Analysis of Stable Racial Integration," 48–49.

74. Ibid., 57–58.

75. George Schermer, interview by Civil Rights Documentation Project, November 4, 1967, written transcription, George Schermer Manuscript Collection, Amistad Archives, New Orleans, LA.

76. Ibid.; George Schermer, interview by Judith Schermer, January 21, 1989, written transcription, WMAN Oral History Project, Germantown Historical Society, Philadelphia, PA.

77. "The Neighbors' League of West Mount Airy," November 28, 1958, WMAN, Urban Archives, Philadelphia, PA, Accession 737, Box 20.

78. WMAN History, undated, WMAN, Urban Archives, Philadelphia, PA, Accession 737, Box 1, Folder 16.

79. Flier, "Are you interested in the future of your home and neighborhood?" January 13, 1959, WMAN, Urban Archives, Philadelphia, PA, Accession 737, Box 20.

80. By-laws of Incorporation, "West Mount Airy Neighbors," January 13, 1959, WMAN, Urban Archives, Philadelphia, PA, Accession 737, Box 20.

81. "What's On Your Mind?" 1959, WMAN, Urban Archives, Philadelphia, PA, Accession 737, Box 20.

82. Ibid.

83. Ibid.

84. Meeting Minutes, March 16, 1959, WMAN, Urban Archives, Philadelphia, PA, Accession 737, Box 20; Meeting Minutes, December 3, 1959, WMAN, Urban Archives, Philadelphia, PA, Accession 737, Box 20; Meeting Minutes, May 9, 1960, WMAN, Urban Archives, Philadelphia, PA, Accession 737, Box 20.

85. Heumann, "Definition and Analysis of Stable Racial Integration," 77.

86. Ibid., 74–80.

87. Memorandum, "History of West Mount Airy Neighbors," undated, WMAN, Urban Archives, Philadelphia, PA, Accession 737, Box 20.

88. Meeting Minutes, January 8, 1962, WMAN, Urban Archives, Philadelphia, PA, Accession 829, Box 1, Folder 4l; "Neighbors Lower Boom on Panic Sales Efforts," *Germantown Courier*, November 15, 1962.

89. "Neighbors Lower Boom on Panic Sales Efforts," *Germantown Courier*, November 15, 1962; Heumann, "Definition and Analysis of Stable Racial Integration," 59.

90. "Neighbors Lower Boom on Panic Sales Efforts," *Germantown Courier*, November 15, 1962.

91. Ibid.; Meeting Minutes, January 8, 1962, WMAN, Urban Archives, Philadelphia, PA, Accession 829, Box 1, Folder 4.

92. Meeting Minutes, January 8, 1962, WMAN, Urban Archives, Philadelphia, PA, Accession 829, Box 1, Folder 4.

93. Ibid.; Meeting Minutes, February 16, 1959, WMAN, Urban Archives, Philadelphia, PA, Accession 737, Box 3, Folder 2.

94. Real Estate Practice Committee Meeting Minutes, April 1959, WMAN, Urban Archives, Philadelphia, PA, Accession 274, Box 1, Folder 35.

95. Heumann, "Definition and Analysis of Stable Racial Integration," 62, citing Hamilton Savings and Loan, "West Mount Airy: Green Country Town in Philadelphia Welcomes You." Heumann notes in 1971 that the brochure was still in use in the neighborhood, but situates the campaign within WMAN's early efforts; its origins date to 1962. For a discussion of this brochure and the attendant advertising campaign, see chapter 3. Brochure, "West Mount Airy: Green Country Town in Philadelphia Welcomes You," 1962, WMAN, Urban Archives, Philadelphia, PA, Accession 737, Box 1, Folder 16.

96. Ibid., 57–59.

97. Leaf, "Breaking the Barrier," 38.

98. Church Community Relations Council, "Neighborhood Newsletter," 1959, WMAN, Urban Archives, Philadelphia, PA, Accession 737, Box 20.

99. Dennis Clark, "Mount Airy History," March 31, 1993, Mount Airy Historical Awareness Committee Address at Lovett Library, Philadelphia, PA.

100. Dorothy Anderson, "Germantown Group Assists Mother Mistreated by Neighbors," *Philadelphia Tribune*, September 24, 1957.

101. "Mount Airy, Philadelphia," *US News and World Report*, July 22, 1991.

102. "Quick Police Action Bags Gang Slayers of Korean Student, 27," *Philadelphia Tribune,* April 29, 1958.

103. Don Black, interview by Vida Carson, 1993, written transcription, WMAN Oral History Project, Germantown Historical Society, Philadelphia, PA.

104. "Housing Prices and Racial Integration in West Mount Airy: A Progress Report," April 9, 1969, WMAN, Urban Archives, Philadelphia, PA.

Chapter 3

1. "200 from 31 UN Countries Visit Mt. Airy to Get Close-Up of How Americans Live," *Philadelphia Evening Bulletin*, May 13, 1962.

2. Patricia Henning, "West Mount Airy Neighbors: An Overview of Origins and History," *West Mount Airy Neighbors* (Philadelphia: September 2006).

3. For information on other communities in which this white-centric notion of integration held strong, see, e.g., Palmer, *Living as Equals*, 100–106.

4. For more on this shift in the meaning of liberalism, see chapter 2, note 133.

5. For a discussion of African American conceptions of integration, see chapter 4.

6. See Palmer, *Living as Equals*, 93–94.

7. See, e.g., May, *Homeward Bound*; Cohen, *Consumer's Republic*.

8. David Ames, "Interpreting Post–World War II Suburban Landscapes as Historic Resources," in *Preserving the Recent Past*, ed. Deborah Slaton and Rebecca A. Shiffer (Washington, DC: Historic Preservation Education Foundation, 1995); Jackson, *Crabgrass Frontier*; Peter O. Muller, *Contemporary Suburban America* (Englewood Cliffs, NJ: Prentice-Hall, 1981), 51–52.

9. Herbert J. Gans, *The Levittowners: Ways of Life and Politics in a New Suburban Community* (New York: Pantheon Books, 1967), 36.

10. Jackson, *Crabgrass Frontier*, 236.

11. See Palmer, *Living as Equals*, 93–94.

12. Brochure, "West Mount Airy: Green Country Town in Philadelphia Welcomes You," 1962, WMAN, Urban Archives, Philadelphia, PA, Accession 737, Box 1, Folder 16.

13. Cited in Bauman, *Public Housing*, 3.

14. For a discussion of the perceived outdatedness of West Mount Airy, see Heumann, "Definition and Analysis of Stable Racial Integration," 252.

15. Kenneth G. Gehret, "Philadelphia's Mount Airy: Neighborhood Bucks Decline," *Christian Science Monitor*, April 14, 1962.

16. For more on the experience of African Americans in Mount Airy, see chapter 4.

17. *The Long Way Home*, DVD, directed by Lee R. Bobker (Ashville, NC: Dynamic Films Inc./Quality Information Publishers, 1957).

18. Ibid.

19. Integration Committee Meeting Announcement, October 19, 1955, Germantown Jewish Centre Papers, Philadelphia Jewish Archive Center, Accession 2040, Box 20, Folder 54.

20. Ellsworth Rosen, "When a Negro Moves Next Door," *Saturday Evening Post*, April 4, 1959.

21. See, e.g., Robin D. G. Kelley, "Integration: What's Left?" *Nation*, December 3, 1998; Michael T. Maly, *Beyond Segregation: Multiracial and Multiethnic Neighborhoods in the United States* (Philadelphia: Temple University Press, 2005); Preston H. Smith, II, "The Quest for Racial Democracy: Black Civic Ideology and Housing Interests in Postwar Chicago," *Journal of Urban History* 26, no. 2 (2000).

22. Marjorie Kopeland, interview by Patricia Henning, 1993, written transcription, WMAN Oral History Project, Germantown Historical Society, Philadelphia, PA.

23. Doris Polsky, interview by Patricia Henning, 1993, written transcription, WMAN Oral History Project, Germantown Historical Society, Philadelphia, PA.

24. See Press Release, "United Nations Delegates Weekend," April 1962, WMAN, Urban Archives, Philadelphia, PA, Accession 274, Box 2, Folder 12; Letter, Anita Schiff to Germantown Savings Bank, the Broad Street Trust, Liberty Real Estate Bank and Trust, First Pennsylvania Banking and Trust, and Girard Trust Corn Exchange, Re: UN Delegates Weekend Funding Request, April 11, 1961, WMAN, Urban Archives, Philadelphia, PA, Accession 274, Box 2, Folder 12; Letter, Dennis Clark to Marjorie Kopeland, April 26, 1961, WMAN, Urban Archives, Philadelphia, PA, Accession 274, Box 2, Folder 12.

25. For reference on Cold War efforts to bolster the nation's image abroad, see Dudziak, *Cold War Civil Rights*; Penny M. Von Eschen, *Satchmo Blows Up the World: Jazz Ambassadors Play the Cold War* (Cambridge: Harvard University Press, 2004); Laura A.

Belmonte, *Selling the American Way: U.S. Propaganda and the Cold War* (Philadelphia: University of Pennsylvania Press, 2008); Palmer, *Living as Equals,* 106.

26. Letter, Mrs. John (Elizabeth) Norton, Director, Private Entertainment for UN Delegation, Inc., to Dennis Clark, West Mount Airy Neighbors, April 26, 1961, WMAN, Urban Archives, Philadelphia, PA, Accession 274, Box 2, Folder 12.

27. Letter, Dennis Clark to Marjorie Kopeland, April 26, 1961, WMAN, Urban Archives, Philadelphia, PA, Accession 274, Box 2, Folder 12.

28. Letter, Mrs. John (Elizabeth) Norton, Director, Private Entertainment for UN Delegation, Inc., to Dennis Clark, West Mount Airy Neighbors, April 26, 1961, WMAN, Urban Archives, Philadelphia, PA, Accession 274, Box 2, Folder 12.

29. Ibid.

30. "The Best Kind of Diplomacy," *Philadelphia Sunday Bulletin*, May 13, 1962.

31. Press Release, "United Nations Delegates Weekend," April 1962, WMAN, Urban Archives, Philadelphia, PA, Accession 274, Box 2, Folder 12.

32. David W. Young, "The Battles of Germantown: Public History and Preservation in America's Most Historic Neighborhood during the Twentieth Century" (PhD diss., Ohio State University Press, 2009); Letter, Anita Schiff to Germantown Savings Bank, the Broad Street Trust, Liberty Real Estate Bank and Trust, First Pennsylvania Banking and Trust, and Girard Trust Corn Exchange, Re: UN Delegates Weekend Funding Request, April 11, 1961, WMAN, Urban Archives, Philadelphia, PA, Accession 274, Box 2, Folder 12.

33. Scholars have written at length about the gender dynamics of social movements. For reference, see, e.g., Gerda Lerner, "Neighborhood Women and Grassroots Human Rights," in *Women's America: Refocusing the Past*, by Linda K. Kerber, Jane Sherron De Hart, and Cornelia Hughes Dayton (New York: Oxford University Press, 2003); Palmer, *Living as Equals*, 117.

34. Isador Kranzel, interview by Betty Ann Fellner, 1993, written transcription, WMAN Oral History Project, Germantown Historical Society, Philadelphia, PA; Shirley Melvin, interview by Patricia Henning, 1993, written transcription, WMAN Oral History Project, Germantown Historical Society, Philadelphia, PA.

35. Press Release, "United Nations Delegates Weekend," April 1962, WMAN, Urban Archives, Philadelphia, PA, Accession 274, Box 2, Folder 12.

36. "UN Families Welcomed Saturday for Weekend," *Germantown Courier*, May 10, 1962.

37. "The Best Kind of Diplomacy," *Philadelphia Sunday Bulletin*, May 13, 1962.

38. "UN Families Welcomed Saturday for Weekend," *Germantown Courier*, May 10, 1962.

39. "Philadelphia Visit Set for 200 from UN," *New York Times*, April 29, 1962.

40. Kenneth G. Gehret, "Philadelphia's Mount Airy: Neighborhood Bucks Decline," *Christian Science Monitor*, April 14, 1962; Kenneth G. Gehret, "Community Pulls Up: Neighborly Philadelphia," *Christian Science Monitor*, April 24, 1962; Kenneth G. Gehret, "Delegates and Families at UN Weekend in Philadelphia Homes," *Christian Science Monitor*, August 22, 1962.

41. Kenneth G. Gehret, "Community Pulls Up: Neighborly Philadelphia," *Christian Science Monitor*, April 24, 1962.

42. Ibid.; Kenneth G. Gehret, "Delegates and Families at UN Weekend in Philadelphia Homes," *Christian Science Monitor*, August 22, 1962.

43. See, e.g., Elias Charry, "Integration without Disintegration: The Germantown Story," *Jewish Digest*, October 1966; Lois Mark Stalvey, "When Women Speak Their Minds about Prejudice," *Women's Day*, March 1968; Lois Mark Stalvey, "The Move We Almost Didn't Make," *McCall's*, February 1968; Evelyn S. Ringold, "Rearing Children of Good Will," *New York Times*, September 22, 1962.

44. Mabel Beverly Williams, interview by Szabi Zee and Vida Carson, 1993, written transcription, Germantown Historical Society, Philadelphia, PA.

Chapter 4

1. Gail Tomas, interview by author, written transcription, Philadelphia, PA, February 22, 2011.

2. Dorothy Anderson and Thomas Hanks, "Germantown an Integrated Community, Tribune Survey Says," *Philadelphia Tribune*, June 1, 1957.

3. "Mount Airy, Philadelphia," *U.S. News and World Report*, July 22, 1991; "Historic Marker in Mount Airy Honors Sadie Alexander," *Mount Airy Times Express*, May 26, 1993; "Mount Airy Hailed for Racial Stability," *Philadelphia Inquirer*, May 4, 1967; Joseph Coleman, interview by Szabi Zee, written transcription, Germantown Historical Society, Philadelphia, PA, 1993.

4. Dorothy Anderson and Thomas Hanks, "Germantown an Integrated Community, Tribune Survey Says," *Philadelphia Tribune*, June 1, 1957; Don Black, interview by Vida Carson, written transcription Germantown Historical Society, Philadelphia, PA, 1993.

5. For more on the class-based conceptions of integration among African Americans, see Smith, "Quest for Racial Democracy."

6. Ibid., 135.

7. For reference, see Preliminary Report, Pelham Centennial Oral History Project, undated, West Mount Airy Neighbors Oral History Collection, Germantown Historical Society, Philadelphia, PA.

8. Ed Henderson, interview by author, digital recording, Philadelphia, PA, March 22, 2007.

9. Ibid.

10. Eric Springer, "Civil Wrongs and Your Rights," *Pittsburgh Courier*, July 28, 1962.

11. For more on the rise of all-black suburban communities, see, e.g., Cashin, *Failure of Integration*; Mary Pattillo, *Black Picket Fences: Privilege and Peril among the Black Middle Class* (Chicago: University of Chicago Press, 1999); Wiese, *Places of Their Own*.

12. See, e.g., Pattillo, *Black Picket Fences*; Wiese, *Places of Their Own;* Karyn R. Lacy, *Blue-Chip Black: Race, Class, and Status in the New Black Middle Class* (Berkeley: University of California Press, 2007).

13. "Unitarian Church Points to Evil of Segregated Housing," *Pittsburgh Courier*, January 12, 1957. See also Beryl Satter, *Family Properties: Race, Real Estate, and the Exploitation of Black Urban America* (New York: Metropolitan Books, 2009).

14. Benjamin Mays, "Finance and Equality," *Pittsburgh Courier*, March 21, 1964. For more on the material benefits of integration, see "A Significant Study," *Pittsburgh Courier*, December 21, 1963. On the value of integrated education, see also Benjamin Mays, "Finance and Equality," *Pittsburgh Courier*, March 21, 1964; Richard Elmore, Bruce Fuller, and Gary Orfield, *Choice: The Cultural Logic of Families, the Political Rationality of Institution* (New York: Teachers College Press, 1995).

15. Dorothy Anderson, "Germantown Group Assists Mother Mistreated by Neighbors," *Philadelphia Tribune*, September 24, 1957.

16. Edward Henderson, interview by author, digital recording, Philadelphia, PA, March 27, 2007.

17. Ibid.

18. For more on class distinctions among African Americans, see, e.g., Weise, *Places of Their Own;* Lacy, *Blue-Chip Black*, 200; Pattillo, *Black Picket Fences*; Bettye Collier-Thomas and James Turner, "Race, Class, and Color: The African American Discourse on Identity," *Journal of American Ethnic History* 14, no. 1 (Fall 1994): 5–27.

19. 1960 Census Data, as cited by Ferman, Singleton, and DeMarco, "West Mount Airy, Philadelphia," 29–60.

20. See, e.g., Wiese, *Places of Their Own*, 131; Maly, *Beyond Segregation* 15; Dorothy Anderson and Thomas Hanks, "Germantown an Integrated Community, Tribune Survey Says," *Philadelphia Tribune*, June 1, 1957.

21. Ibid.

22. Dorothy Anderson, "Germantown an Integrated Community, Tribune Survey Shows," *Philadelphia Tribune*, June 1, 1957.

23. Ibid.

24. "Mount Airy, Philadelphia," *US News and World Report*, July 22, 1991.

25. Don Black, interview by Vida Carson, written transcription, Germantown Historical Society, Philadelphia, PA, 1993. The dates of the interview are unavailable.

26. Ibid.

27. "Mount Airy, Philadelphia," *US News and World Report*, July 22, 1991.

28. Don Black, interview by Vida Carson, written transcription, Germantown Historical Society, Philadelphia, PA, 1993.

29. Ed Henderson, interview by author, digital recording, Philadelphia, PA, March 22, 2007.

30. See, e.g., Arthur C. Willis, *Cecil's City: A History of Blacks in Philadelphia, 1638–1979* (New York: Carlton Press, 1990); Countryman, *Up South*; Gerald Early, *This Is Where I Came In: Black America in the 1960s* (Lincoln: University of Nebraska Press, 2003).

31. See, e.g., Countryman, *Up South*; Self, *American Babylon*; Peniel Joseph, *Waiting 'Til the Midnight Hour: A Narrative History of Black Power in America* (New York: Henry Holt and Co., 2006); Peniel Joseph, ed., *The Black Power Movement: Rethinking the Civil Rights–Black Power Era* (New York: Routledge, 2006).

32. See, e.g., Countryman, *Up South*; Willis, *Cecil's City*; Early, *This Is Where I Came In.*

33. Though scholars record Moore's date of birth as April 2, 1915, his daughters, Cecily Banks and Alexis Moore Bruton, believe that the actual year is up for debate.

See Cecily Banks and Alexis Moore Bruton, interview by author, written transcription, Philadelphia, PA: September 21, 2009; Paul Lermack, "Cecil Moore and the Philadelphia Branch of the National Association of Colored People: The Politics of Negro Pressure Group Organization," in *Black Politics in Philadelphia*, ed. Miriam Ershkowitz and Joseph Zikmund (New York: Basic Books, 1973), 146; Gerald L. Early, "Cecil B. Moore and the Rise of Black Philadelphia, 1964–1968," in *This Is Where I Came In*, 89.

34. Cecily Banks, interview by author, written transcription, Philadelphia, PA, September 21, 2009.

35. Ibid.; Mildred O'Neill, "Councilman Cecil Moore Dies," *Baltimore Afro-American*, February 24, 1979.

36. C. Stuart McGegee, "Bluefield State History," Bluefield State College Archive Collection, http://library.bluefieldstate.edu/archives/history.

37. Cecily Banks and Alexis Moore Bruton, interview by author, written transcription, Philadelphia, PA, September 21, 2009.

38. Ibid. As scholar Gerald L. Early writes, "Moore's entire history places him within W. E. B. Du Bois' 'talented tenth.' " Early, *This Is Where I Came In*, 89.

39. For more information on the Montford Point Marines, see, e.g., Melton Alonza McLaurin, *The Marines of Montford Point: America's First Black Marines* (Chapel Hill: University of North Carolina Press, 2007).

40. Cecily Banks and Alexis Moore Bruton, interview by author, written transcription, Philadelphia, PA, September 21, 2009.

41. See, e.g., Lawrence P. Scott and William M. Womack, *Double V: The Civil Rights Struggle and the Tuskegee Airmen* (East Lansing: Michigan State University Press, 1998); Eric Foner, *The Story of American Freedom* (New York: W. W. Norton, 1998).

42. Early, *This Is Where I Came In*, 91.

43. Samuel Alan Schrager, *A Trial Lawyer's Art* (Philadelphia: Temple University Press, 1999), 91.

44. Cecily Banks and Alexis Moore Bruton, interview by author, written transcription, Philadelphia, PA, September 21, 2009.

45. Ibid.

46. Early, *This Is Where I Came In*, 81; Willis, *Cecil's City*.

47. See Early, *This Is Where I Came In*, 82.

48. "Judge Alexander Denies Phila. 'A Racial Tinderbox,' Refutes Claims by Urban League Head That City is Headed for Explosion," *Philadelphia Tribune*, August 8, 1964.

49. Cecily Banks and Alexis Moore Bruton, interview by author, Philadelphia, PA, September 21, 2009; "Top Negroes Resided in North Philly," *Philadelphia Tribune*, June 20, 1965.

50. See, e.g., Countryman, *Up South*, 84–92; Manning Marable, *Race, Reform, and Rebellion: The Second Reconstruction of Black America, 1945–2006, Third Edition* (Jackson: University Press of Mississippi, 2007); Robin D. G. Kelly, *Race Rebels: Culture, Politics, and the Black Working Class* (New York: Free Press, 1996); Charles Flint Kellogg, *NAACP: A History of the National Association for the Advancement of Colored People* (Baltimore: Johns Hopkins University Press, 1967).

51. Press Release from Moore, August 10, 1964, NAACP Records, Part III: Branch Files, Philadelphia, 1956–65, Box C137, Folder 5, Library of Congress Archives, Washington, DC.

52. "Pennsylvania: The Goddam Boss," *Time Magazine*, September 11, 1964. As Countryman writes, "Moore rooted his claim to racial authenticity and identity with the majority of the city's blacks in his decision to keep his family in North Philadelphia." Countryman, *Up South,* 165.

53. "Pennsylvania: The Goddam Boss," *Time Magazine*, September 11, 1964.

54. Harold Cruse, *The Crisis of the Negro Intellectual* (New York: William Morrow, 1967), 548, 564.

55. "Pennsylvania: The Goddam Boss," *Time Magazine*, September 11, 1964; Cecily Banks and Alexis Moore Bruton, interview by author, written transcription, Philadelphia, PA, September 21, 2009.

56. See, e.g., Randall Kennedy, *Sellout: The Politics of Racial Betrayal* (New York: Pantheon Books, 2008); Joseph, *Black Power Movement*; Countryman, *Up South*, chapter 4.

57. Amy Jacques Garvey, *Garvey and Garveyism* (New York: Collier Books, 1970), 48–49.

58. *New York World*, August 11, 1920, as cited in C. W. E. Bigsby, *The Cambridge Companion to Modern American Culture* (New York: Cambridge University Press, 2006), 114.

59. "NAACP to War on Uncle Toms," *Philadelphia Tribune*, July 31, 1954.

60. "All Human Life Sacred," *Philadelphia Tribune*, July 20, 1954.

61. Ibid.

62. See, e.g., Randall, *Sellout.*

63. E. Franklin Frazier, *Black Bourgeoisie: The Rise of a New Middle-Class in the United States, Revised Edition* (Glencoe, IL: Free Press, 1962).

64. James E. Teele, *E. Franklin Frazier and the Black Bourgeoisie* (Columbia: University of Missouri Press, 2002).

65. "Muslims Call Ralph Bunche 'International Uncle Tom,' Dare Him to Speak at New York Mass Meeting," *Philadelphia Tribune*, July 21, 1961.

66. Cecily Banks and Alexis Moore Bruton, interview by author, written transcription, Philadelphia, PA, September 21, 2009.

67. C. Eric Lincoln, "The Negro Middle-Class Dream," *New York Times*, October 25, 1964.

68. Joseph Lelyveld, "Militant Ex-Marine Leads Philadelphia Negroes," *New York Times*, September 2, 1964.

69. Orrin Evans, "Moore Says His Three Critics Are 'Part-Time Negroes,'" *Philadelphia Bulletin*, April 20, 1967.

70. Countryman, *Up South*, 165; Chris Perry, "Negro Leaders Mum on Newest Cecil Moore Demands," *Philadelphia Tribune*, November 12, 1963; Letter from Raymond Pace Alexander to Mr. James Klash, WDAS, Raymond Pace Alexander Papers, University of Pennsylvania Archives, Philadelphia, PA, Accession 374, Box 89, Folder 19, June 18, 1963; Mark Lloyd, "Re: Raymond Pace Alexander (RPA) Papers," Personal e-mail, December 18, 2009.

71. Fred Bonaparte, "Big Crowd Jams Arena at NAACP 'Appreciation' Rally," *Philadelphia Tribune*, March 3, 1964.

72. Countryman, *Up South*, 167.

73. "Sadie Alexander, Austin Norris, Deny Moore's 'Part-Time Negro' Rap," *Philadelphia Tribune*, June 8, 1963.

74. Letter from Raymond Pace Alexander to Dr. Clifton H. Johnson, director, Amistad Research Center and Race Relations Department, Fisk University, 1969, Raymond Alexander Pace Papers, University of Pennsylvania Archives, Philadelphia, PA, Accession 374, Box 89, Folder 19.

75. "Sadie Alexander, Austin Norris, Deny Moore's 'Part-Time Negro' Rap," *Philadelphia Tribune*, June 8, 1963.

76. See, e.g., Curley Brown, "Readers Say: We Owe Great Debt to 'Uncle Toms' Who've Never Received Honors Due," *Philadelphia Tribune*, February 12, 1963; Louetta Seawell, "Readers Say: Dorothy Anderson Crude: Uncle Tom Not a Weakling but a Great, Good Man," *Philadelphia Tribune*, March 17, 1962; C. Eric Lincoln, "The Negro's Middle-Class Dream," *New York Times*, October 25, 1964.

77. Joseph Lelyveld, "Militant Ex-Marine Leads Philadelphia Negroes," *New York Times*, September 2, 1964.

78. Letter to Roy Wilkins from G.A. Wilson, with *Guardian* clippings, June 10, 1963, NAACP Records, Part III: Branch Files, Philadelphia, 1956–65, Box C137, Folder 3, Library of Congress Archives, Washington, DC.

79. Ibid.

80. G.A. Wilson, "Other Look at Him: Cecil Moore Takes a Look at 'His City,'" *Pennsylvania Guardian*, June 7, 1963.

81. Letter from Herman Price to Roy Wilkins, June 10, 1963, NAACP Records, Part III: Branch Files, Philadelphia, 1956–65, Box C137, Folder 3, Library of Congress Archives, Washington, DC.

82. Letter from Burton Caine to Roy Wilkins, June 10, 1963, NAACP Records, Part III: Branch Files, Philadelphia, 1956–65, Box C137, Folder 3, Library of Congress Archives, Washington, DC.

83. Complaint against Cecil B. Moore, filed to the National Board from Viola Allen, Alphonso Deal, Dolores Tucker, Ethel Barnett, Senora Gratton, and James Smith, June 10, 1963, NAACP Records, Part III: Branch Files, Philadelphia, 1956–65, Box C137, Folder 5, Library of Congress Archives, Washington, DC.

84. "NAACP Tries Its Own," *Philadelphia Evening Bulletin*, December 5, 1964.

85. Owen Evans, "NAACP Votes to Fight Split: Moore Supporters Say They'll Resist National Policy," *Philadelphia Bulletin*, December 5, 1965.

Chapter 5

1. Bernard Watson, Keynote Speech at Thirteenth Annual WMAN Meeting, April 26, 1971, WMAN, Urban Archives, Philadelphia, PA, Accession 274, Box 1, Folder 38.

2. Ibid.

3. For reference on education in post–World War II cities, see, e.g., John L. Rury, "Race and Politics of Chicago's Public Schools: Benjamin Willis and the Tragedy of Urban Education," in *Urban Education in the United States: A Historical Reader*, ed. John L. Rury (New York: Palgrave Macmillan, 2005); John L. Rury, *Education and Social Change: Contours in the History of American Schooling* (New York: Routledge, 2009); Anne Ellen Phillips, "The Struggle for School Desegregation in Philadelphia, 1945–1967" (PhD diss., University of Pennsylvania, 2000); Countryman, *Up South*, 223–257; Palmer, *Living as Equals*, 137–69.

4. Peter A. Janssen, "Education and You: Public School Sets Exciting Example," *Philadelphia Inquirer*, July 18, 1965.

5. Phillips, "Struggle for School Desegregation in Philadelphia."

6. For more on the Emlen School, see Vincent Paul Franklin, *Education of Black Philadelphia: The Social and Educational History of a Minority Community, 1900–1950* (Philadelphia: University of Pennsylvania Press, 1979).

7. Statistics appeared in WMAN reports, as well as in the *Philadelphia Bulletin*. Report on the Data Subcommittee to the WMAN Schools Committee, July 1961, WMAN, Urban Archives, Philadelphia, PA, Accession 274, Box 1, Folder 38; Report, "Elementary School Enrollment in Northwest Philadelphia: A study of enrollment trends in terms of school capacity and racial composition, 1955–1960," undated, WMAN, Urban Archives, Philadelphia, PA, Accession 274, Box 1, Folder 39; Peter Binzen, "City Schools Accused of Segregation Laxity," *Philadelphia Bulletin*, January 15, 1961. Houston, in contrast, dropped from 99 percent white in 1955 to 86 percent white in 1960.

8. Marjorie Kopeland, interview by Patricia Henning, 1993, written transcription, WMAN Oral History Project, Germantown Historical Society, Philadelphia, PA.

9. Report, "Elementary School Enrollment in Northwest Philadelphia: A study of enrollment trends in terms of school capacity and racial composition, 1955–1960," undated, WMAN, Urban Archives, Philadelphia, PA, Accession 274, Box 1, Folder 39.

10. Ibid.

11. WMAN Meeting Minutes, November 9, 1959, WMAN, Urban Archives, Philadelphia, PA, Accession 274, Box 2, Folder 33.

12. WMAN Meeting Minutes, April 11, 1960, WMAN, Urban Archives, Philadelphia, PA, Accession 274, Box 2, Folder 33.

13. Ibid.

14. Ibid.

15. Ibid.

16. See Heumann, "Definition and Analysis of Stable Racial Integration"; Saltman, *Fragile Movement*; Cashin, *Failures of Integration*.

17. WMAN Meeting Minutes, May 6, 1960, WMAN, Urban Archives, Philadelphia, PA, Accession 274, Box 2, Folder 33.

18. Report, "Elementary School Enrollment in Northwest Philadelphia: A study of enrollment trends in terms of school capacity and racial composition, 1955–1960," undated, WMAN, Urban Archives, Philadelphia, PA, Accession 274, Box 1, Folder 39.

19. Report of the Data Subcommittee to the WMAN Schools Committee, July 1961, WMAN, Urban Archives, Philadelphia, PA, Accession 274, Box 1, Folder 38.

20. Ibid.

21. Franklin, *Education of Black Philadelphia*, 200.

22. Leon J. Obermayer, "For Every Child: The Story of Integration in the Philadelphia Public Schools," *Report by the Philadelphia Board of Public Education*, October 1960.

23. Report of the Data Subcommittee to the WMAN Schools Committee, July 1961, WMAN, Urban Archives, Philadelphia, PA, Accession 274, Box 1, Folder 38.

24. For reference, see, e.g., Bernice Schermer, interview by Marjorie Kopeland, 1993, written transcription, WMAN Oral History Project, Germantown Historical Society, Philadelphia, PA; Marjorie Kopeland, interview by Patricia Henning, 1993, written transcription, WMAN Oral History Project, Germantown Historical Society, Philadelphia, PA; Don Black, interview by Vida Carson, 1993, written transcription, WMAN Oral History Project, Germantown Historical Society, Philadelphia, PA.

25. Marjorie Kopeland, interview by Patricia Henning, 1993, written transcription, WMAN Oral History Project, Germantown Historical Society, Philadelphia, PA.

26. Don Black, interview by Vida Carson, 1993, written transcription, WMAN Oral History Project, Germantown Historical Society, Philadelphia, PA.

27. Palmer, *Living as Equals*, 123.

28. Bernice Schermer, interview by Marjorie Kopeland, 1993, written transcription, WMAN Oral History Project, Germantown Historical Society, Philadelphia, PA; Peter A. Janssen, "Public School Sets Exciting Example," *Philadelphia Inquirer*, July 18, 1965.

29. Peter A. Janssen, "Public School Sets Exciting Example," *Philadelphia Inquirer*, July 18, 1965.

30. Lois Mark Stalvey, *Getting Ready: The Education of a White Family in Inner-City Schools* (New York: William Morrow and Company, 1975), 68.

31. Ibid., 21–23.

32. Ibid., 30.

33. Eve Oshtry, interview by Marjorie Kopeland, 1993, written transcription, WMAN Oral History Project, Germantown Historical Society, Philadelphia, PA; Stalvey, *Getting Ready;* Lois Mark Stalvey, The *Education of a WASP* (New York: William Morrow and Company, 1970).

34. Minutes of Open Meeting of WMAN Schools Committee, *Schools Report*, 1961, WMAN, Urban Archives, Philadelphia, PA, Accession 274, Box 1, Folder 38.

35. Heumann, "Definition and Analysis of Stable Racial Integration," 74.

36. WMAN Proposal on the expansion of the Charles W. Henry School, December 22,1964, WMAN, Urban Archives, Philadelphia, PA, Accession 274, Box 1, Folder 40; Letter from Dr. Robert Rutman to Dr. C. Taylor Whittier, Superintendent, October 9, 1964, WMAN, Urban Archives, Philadelphia, PA, Accession 274, Box 1, Folder 40.

37. Minutes of Open Meeting of WMAN Schools Committee, *Schools Report*, 1961, WMAN, Urban Archives, Philadelphia, PA, Accession 274, Box 1, Folder 38.

38. WMAN Proposal on the expansion of the Charles W. Henry School, December 22, 1964, WMAN, Urban Archives, Philadelphia, PA, Accession 274, Box 1, Folder 40; Letter from Dr. Robert Rutman to Dr. C. Taylor Whittier, Superintendent, October 9, 1964, WMAN, Urban Archives, Philadelphia, PA, Accession 274, Box 1, Folder 40.

39. Stalvey, *Getting Ready*, 167; WMAN Meeting Minutes, March 8, 1965, WMAN, Urban Archives, Philadelphia, PA, Accession 274, Box 2, Folder 36.

40. Letter from Dr. Robert Rutman to Dr. C. Taylor Whittier, Superintendent, October 9, 1964, WMAN, Urban Archives, Philadelphia, PA, Accession 274, Box 1, Folder 40.

41. Ibid.

42. "West Mount Airy Unit Requests Addition to Henry School," *Philadelphia Bulletin*, April 25, 1965.

43. Letter from Dr. Robert Rutman to Dr. C. Taylor Whittier, Superintendent, October 9, 1964, WMAN, Urban Archives, Philadelphia, PA, Accession 274, Box 1, Folder 40; Stalvey, *Getting Ready*, 180; Eve Oshtry, interview by Marjorie Kopeland, 1993, written transcription, WMAN Oral History Project, Germantown Historical Society, Philadelphia, PA.

44. WMAN Proposal on the expansion of the Charles W. Henry School, December 22, 1964, WMAN, Urban Archives, Philadelphia, PA, Accession 274, Box 1, Folder 40.

45. "West Mount Airy Unit Requests Addition to Henry School," *Philadelphia Bulletin*, April 25, 1965.

46. "WMAN Statement of the Schools Committee on the 1963 Operating Budget of the Philadelphia Board of Public Education," 1963, WMAN, Urban Archives, Philadelphia, PA, Accession 274, Box 1, Folder 3.

47. See, e.g., Phillips, "Struggle for School Desegregation in Philadelphia;" Jon S. Birger, "Race, Reaction, and Reform: The Three Rs of Philadelphia School Politics, 1965–1971," *Pennsylvania Magazine of History and Biography* 120, no. 3, (July 2006): 177–78.

48. WMAN Meeting Minutes, March 8, 1965, WMAN, Urban Archives, Philadelphia, PA, Accession 274, Box 2, Folder 36.

49. Letter from Louis Levy to Dr. C. Taylor Whittier, Superintendent, March 11, 1965, WMAN, Urban Archives, Philadelphia, PA, Accession 274, Box 1, Folder 40.

50. Letter from Dr. Robert J. Rutman to Dr. C. Taylor Whittier, Superintendent, October 9, 1964, WMAN, Urban Archives, Philadelphia, PA, Accession 274, Box 1, Folder 40.

51. Birger, "Race, Reaction, and Reform," 177–78.

52. J. Donald Porter, "Dr. Whittier, Departing School Head, Didn't Get Fair Chance, Says Nicholas," *Philadelphia Tribune*, December 3, 1966.

53. Burr Van Atta, "Mark R. Shedd Dies; Rebuilt School System," *Philadelphia Inquirer*, November 18, 1986.

54. J. Donald Porter, "Dr. Whittier, Departing School Head, Didn't Get Fair Chance, Says Nicholas," *Philadelphia Tribune*, December 3, 1966.

55. Henry S. Resnik, *Turning on the System: War in the Philadelphia Public Schools* (New York: Pantheon Books, 1970), as cited in Ronald Gross, "The Revolution That Failed, And Yet . . . : Turning on the System," *New York Times*, May 24, 1970.

56. "Dr. Mark Shedd Answers Charge of School Conformity," *Philadelphia Tribune*, July 29, 1967.

57. By-laws of Incorporation, "West Mount Airy Neighbors," January 13, 1959, WMAN, Urban Archives, Philadelphia, PA, Manuscripts Collection, Accession 737, Box 20.

58. Robert Allan Sedler, "The Profound Impact of *Milliken v. Bradley,*" 33 *Wayne Law Review,* no. 5 (1987).

59. Petition to the Philadelphia Board of Public Education, July 6, 1966, WMAN, Urban Archives, Philadelphia, PA, Accession 274, Box 1, Folder 40.

60. Phillips, "Struggle for School Desegregation in Philadelphia," 185–86.

61. Ibid.

62. Petition to the Philadelphia Board of Public Education, July 6, 1966, WMAN, Urban Archives, Philadelphia, PA, Accession 274, Box 1, Folder 40.

63. Ibid.

64. Stalvey, *Getting Ready;* WMAN Schools Committee Meeting Minutes, May 7, 1968, WMAN, Urban Archives, Philadelphia, PA, Accession 274, Box 1, Folder 42.

65. Northwest Philadelphia is home to a number of private schools, including Germantown Friends School, Chestnut Hill Academy, Springside School, Greene Street Friends, and the William Penn Charter School. Many of these schools have long-standing Quaker roots. Until 1960, Germantown Academy was also located in northwest Philadelphia; that year, however, the school relocated to a tract of land in the western suburb of Fort Washington (the land was first offered to the Germantown Friends School, who declined in favor of remaining committed to the Germantown community). The region also had several parochial schools, including Norwood Academy, the Cecilian Academy by the Sisters of St. Joseph, Holy Cross Parochial School; Little Flower Parochial School; and Saint Madeleine Sophie Parochial School. Mount Airy Guide, 1956, Mount Airy Collection, Germantown Historical Society, Box B; Heumann, 26, 306–7.

66. These numbers were gathered through a content analysis of school directories, housed in the Germantown Friends School archives. It should be noted that the 19119 zip code encompasses both East and West Mount Airy; however, the overall trends evidence a marked increase in new student movement from neighborhood public schools to area private schools.

67. Information gathered from a content analysis of school directories housed at the Chestnut Hill Academy archives.

68. Joan Cannady Countryman, telephone interview by author, Philadelphia, PA, April 2, 2010.

69. Ibid.

70. Mark Dixon, "Price of Change: Money was the Motivation when a Local School Accepted its First Black Student," *Main Line Today,* August 14, 2007; Joan Cannady Countryman, telephone interview by author, Philadelphia, PA, April 2, 2010.

71. Joan Cannady Countryman, telephone interview by author, Philadelphia, PA, April 2, 2010.

72. This information was gathered through a rather crude content analysis of high school yearbooks at Germantown Friends School, as well as of other area private schools including Chestnut Hill Academy, the William Penn Charter School, and Norwood Academy. Because enrollment statistics in the 1960s were not available, I used the method of counting faces to get a sense of the number of students of color at the schools; while problematic, this was the closest approximation that I could get for a general picture of the student body.

73. Ibid.

74. WMAN Meeting Minutes, May 8, 1968, WMAN, Urban Archives, Philadelphia, PA, Accession 274, Box 2, Folder 38.

75. Stalvey, *Getting Ready*, 34–36.

76. Ibid., 60–61.

77. WMAN Schools Committee Meeting Minutes, May 7, 1968, WMAN, Urban Archives, Philadelphia, PA, Accession 274.

78. Stalvey, *Getting Ready*, 34–36, 101–2, 111.

79. *Loving v. Virginia*, 388 U.S. 1 (1967).

80. On the history of miscegenation and interracial relationships, see, e.g., Delores P. Aldridge, "The Changing Nature of Interracial Marriage in Georgia: A Research Note," *Journal of Marriage and the Family* 35, no. 4 (November 1973): 641–42; Phyl Newbeck, *Virginia Hasn't Always Been for Lovers: Interracial Marriage Bans and the Case of Richard and Mildred Loving* (Carbondale: Southern Illinois University Press, 2008); Peggy Pascoe, *What Comes Naturally: Miscegenation and the Making of Race in America* (New York: Oxford University Press, 2010); Peggy Pascoe, "Miscegenation Law, Court Cases, and the Ideologies of 'Race' in Twentieth Century America," in *Sex, Love, Race: Crossing Boundaries in North American History*, ed. Martha Elizabeth Hodes (New York: New York University Press, 1999); Renee Christine Romano, *Race Mixing: Black-White Marriage in Postwar America* (Cambridge: Harvard University Press, 2003); Peter Wallenstein, *Tell the Court I Love My Wife: Race, Marriage, and the Law—An American History* (New York: Palgrave Macmillan, 2004). On the culture of dating in post–World War II America more broadly, see Beth L. Bailey, *From Front Porch to Back Seat: Courtship in Twentieth Century America* (Baltimore: Johns Hopkins University Press, 1989).

81. Simeon Booker, "A Challenge for the Guy Smiths: Peggy Rusk, Negro Husband Face Their Future with Smile," *Ebony*, December 1967.

82. *Time Magazine*, September 29, 1967.

83. "Races: A Marriage of Enlightenment," *Time Magazine*, September 29, 1967, as cited in Mark Harris, *Pictures at a Revolution: Five Movies and the Birth of the New Hollywood* (New York: Penguin Press, 2008), 371–73.

84. "Guess Who's Coming to Dinner," *Internet Movie Database,* http://www.imdb.com/title/tt0061735/; Harris, *Pictures at a Revolution*, 418.

85. Stalvey, *Getting Ready*, 111.

86. For a sophisticated analysis of the long history of black power in Philadelphia and a detailed account of the demonstrations of 1967, see Countryman, *Up South*.

87. Countryman, 225; Henry S. Resnik, "The Shedd Revolution: A Philadelphia Story," *Urban Review* 3, no. 3 (January 1969): 22. See also Resnik, *Turning on the System*.

88. Matthew Countryman, "'From Protest to Politics': Community Control and Black Independent Politics in Philadelphia, 1965–1984," *Journal of Urban History* 32, no. 6 (September 2006): 826.

89. Ron Whitehorne, "1967: African American Students Strike, Survive Police Riot to Force Change," *Philadelphia Public School Notebook* 10, no. 1 (Fall 2002).

90. See, e.g., Stalvey *Getting Ready*; Len Lear, "Demand Student Shooting Probe: 2 Students Shot, Probe Is Demanded," *Philadelphia Tribune*, October 21, 1967; Len Lear, "Parents of G'tn High 'Exiles' Called Bigots," *Philadelphia Tribune*, January 13, 1968;

Jeff Zimmerman, interview by author, written transcription, Huntingdon Valley, PA, March 8, 2011.

91. Bruce Ticker, "Samson Freedman Did Not Want Mount Airy to Die," *Philadelphia Tribune*, August 22, 1972.

92. Jeff Zimmerman, interview by author, written transcription, Huntingdon Valley, PA, March 8, 2011.

93. Stalvey, *Getting Ready*, 184.

94. William Mandel and Clemson Page Jr., "Parents of Leeds Pupils Demand Better Security," *Philadelphia Bulletin*, April 14, 1970.

95. Stalvey, *Getting Ready*, 184.

96. Laurence Geller, "Jews Aiding Blacks Picketed by Others," *Philadelphia Tribune*, October 31, 1970; "Olney Teacher Is Suspended in School Row," *Philadelphia Bulletin*, June 20, 1970.

97. Stalvey, *Getting Ready*, 184; "Olney Teacher Is Suspended in School Row," *Philadelphia Bulletin*, June 20, 1970.

98. William Mandel and Clemson Page Jr., "Parents of Leeds Pupils Demand Better Security," *Philadelphia Bulletin*, April 14, 1970.

99. Stalvey, *Getting Ready*, 132.

100. Dennis Clark, "Mount Airy History," Mount Airy Historical Awareness Committee Address at Lovett Library, Philadelphia PA, March 31, 1993.

101. Palmer, *Living as Equals*, 150–51.

102. Heumann, "Definition and Analysis of Stable Racial Integration," 306.

103. David J. Merkowitz, "The Segregating City: Philadelphia's Jews and the Urban Crisis, 1964–1984" (PhD diss., University of Cincinnati, 2010).

104. Charles Montgomery, "Teacher Is Slain, Schools to Come," *Philadelphia Tribune*, February 2, 1971.

105. Margaret Halsey, "Youth Sent to Leeds after Father Showed Gun, Principal Says," *Philadelphia Bulletin*, February 5, 1971.

106. Charles Montgomery, "Teacher Is Slain, Schools to Come," *Philadelphia Tribune*, February 2, 1971.

107. "Wanted to 'Scare' Teacher, Not Shoot Him, Youth Says," *Philadelphia Bulletin*, March 23, 1972.

108. "Public Schools Closed in Teacher's Memory," *Philadelphia Bulletin*, February 3, 1971.

109. Ibid.

110. Roy Poorman, "Again and Again," *Philadelphia Tribune*, February 13, 1971.

111. "Huge, Impersonal School Buildings Factor In Leeds 'Double Tragedy,' Group Declares," *Philadelphia Tribune*, February 27, 1971.

112. "Saddened," *Philadelphia Tribune*, February 13, 1971.

113. Stalvey, *Getting Ready*, 220.

114. Margaret Halsey, "Slain Teacher Wanted Guards at Leeds School," *Philadelphia Bulletin*, February 4, 1971; See also Stalvey, *Getting Ready*, 220.

115. Margaret Halsey, "Slain Teacher Wanted Guards at Leeds School," *Philadelphia Bulletin*, February 4, 1971.

116. *Report from the School District of Philadelphia*, "Facts and Figures," 1976, WMAN, Urban Archives, Philadelphia, PA, Accession 737, Box 2, Folder 10.

117. See note 65.

118. Howard S. Shapiro, "Happy Birthday: Civic Group Celebrates Unique Urban Life-style," *Philadelphia Inquirer*, July 7, 1979.

Chapter 6

1. Emily Starr, "West Mount Airy: Period of Change?" *Chestnut Hill Local*, June 19, 1975.

2. Jerome Balka, Esq., WMAN Newsletter, April 1967, WMAN, Urban Archives, Philadelphia, PA, Accession 737, Box 12, Folder 12.

3. WMAN Newsletter, vol. 9, no. 4, Summer 1967, WMAN, Urban Archives, Philadelphia, PA, Accession 737, Box 12, Folder 12.

4. WMAN Executive Board Meeting Minutes, November 24, 1969, WMAN, Urban Archives, Philadelphia, PA, Accession 274, Box 2, Folder 39.

5. Don Black, interview by Vida Carson, 1993, written transcription, WMAN Oral History Project, Germantown Historical Society, Philadelphia, PA.

6. Mabel Beverly Williams, interview by Szabi Zee and Vida Carson, 1993, written transcription, WMAN Oral History Project, Germantown Historical Society, Philadelphia, PA.

7. WMAN Meeting Minutes, June 8, 1968, WMAN, Urban Archives, Philadelphia, PA, Accession 274, Box 2, Folder 38.

8. Ibid.

9. Wellspring Brochure, citing an October 25, 1966 *Philadelphia Bulletin* article, undated, WMAN, Urban Archives, Philadelphia, PA, Accession 274, Box 5, Folder 5.

10. Wellspring Brochure, undated, WMAN, Urban Archives, Philadelphia, PA, Accession 274, Box 5, Folder 5.

11. Program from the Junior League of Philadelphia Black-White Confrontation, undated, WMAN, Urban Archives, Philadelphia, PA, Accession 274, Box 5, Folder 5.

12. WMAN Meeting Minutes, September 9, 1968, WMAN, Urban Archives, Philadelphia, PA, Accession 274, Box 2, Folder 38.

13. Ibid.; "Confrontation in Black and White," Face to Face News Release, October 29, 1968, WMAN, Urban Archives, Philadelphia, PA, Accession 274, Box 5, Folder 5.

14. Face to Face Letter to West Mount Airy Residents, undated, WMAN, Urban Archives, Philadelphia, PA, Accession 274, Box 5, Folder 5.

15. "Confrontation in Black and White," Face to Face News Release, October 29, 1968, WMAN, Urban Archives, Philadelphia, PA, Accession 274, Box 5, Folder 5.

16. Lillian Williams, Letter to West Mount Airy Neighbors, November 1, 1968, WMAN, Urban Archives, Philadelphia, PA, Accession 274, Box 5, Folder 5.

17. Sybil E. Watson, Letter to West Mount Airy Neighbors, October 20, 1968, WMAN, Urban Archives, Philadelphia, PA, Accession 274, Box 5, Folder 5.

18. Helen Worfman, Letter to Face to Face, undated WMAN, Urban Archives, Philadelphia, PA, Accession 274, Box 5, Folder 5.

19. Anonymous Letter to West Mount Airy Neighbors, October 26, 1968, WMAN, Urban Archives, Philadelphia, PA, Accession 274, Box 5, Folder 5.

20. Unsigned Letter to West Mount Airy Neighbors, October 22, 1968, WMAN, Urban Archives, Philadelphia, PA, Accession 274, Box 5, Folder 5.

21. WMAN Meeting Minutes, undated, WMAN, Urban Archives, Philadelphia, PA, Accession 274, Box 5, Folder 5.

22. Face to Face Brochure, undated, WMAN, Urban Archives, Philadelphia, PA, Accession 274, Box 5, Folder 5.

23. "Confrontation in Black and White," Face to Face News Release, October 29, 1968, WMAN, Urban Archives, Philadelphia, PA, Accession 274, Box 5, Folder 5.

24. Matthew Bullock, Letter to Jerry Balka, December 9, 1968, WMAN, Urban Archives, Philadelphia, PA, Accession 274, Box 5, Folder 6.

25. WMAN Board Minutes, January 13, 1969, WMAN, Urban Archives, Philadelphia, PA, Accession 274, Box 2, Folder 39.

26. Ibid.

27. Ibid.

28. For reference, see, e.g., Sugrue, *Origins of the Urban Crisis*; Jefferson Cowie, *Capital Moves: RCA's Seventy-Year Quest for Cheap Labor* (New York: New Press, 2001); Suleiman Osman, *The Invention of Brownstone Brooklyn: Gentrification and the Search for Authenticity in Postwar New York* (New York: Oxford University Press, 2011).

29. Suleiman Osman, "The Decade of the Neighborhood," in *Rightward Bound: Making America Conservative in the 1970s*, ed. Bruce J. Schulman and Julian E. Zelizer (Cambridge: Harvard University Press, 2008).

30. According to the 1970 census, 37.6 percent of the nation was living in suburbs, an increase of 8 percent. In contrast, 31.4 percent were living in cities, a 1 percent drop. In Philadelphia, the shift had taken place a decade earlier; 1960 census data indicated that, for the first time, more people lived in the seven outlying counties of Pennsylvania and New Jersey than within the city's municipal borders. S. A. Paolantonio, *Frank Rizzo: The Last Big Man in Big City America* (Philadelphia: Camino Books, 1993), 71.

31. Osman, "Decade of the Neighborhood," 110.

32. West Mount Airy Action Mission Statement, 1974, WMAN, Urban Archives, Philadelphia, PA, Accession 7373, Box 10, Folder 23.

33. Ellen V.P. Wells, "'Know Your Neighbor' is the Best Defense, Mount Airyites Say," *Chestnut Hill Local*, January 13, 1972.

34. Leaf, "Breaking the Barrier," 14–15.

35. "West Mount Airy in Deep Trouble at This Time, WMAN Leader Warns," *Philadelphia Tribune*, November 30, 1971.

36. See, e.g., Craig Cox, *Storefront Revolution: Food Co-ops and the Counterculture* (New Brunswick, NJ: Rutgers University Press, 1994); John Curl, *For All the People: Uncovering the Hidden History of Cooperation, Cooperative Movements, and Communalism in America* (Oakland, CA: PM Press, 2009).

37. Area Leader-Board member: Job Description, 1969, WMAN, Urban Archives, Philadelphia, PA, Accession 274, Box 1, Folder 21.

38. Heumann, "Definition and Analysis of Stable Racial Integration," 67. See also Palmer, *Living as Equals*, 139.

39. WMAN Newsletter, vol. 11, no. 5, September 1969, WMAN, Urban Archives, Philadelphia, PA, Accession 274, Box 1, Folder 21; WMAN Board Minutes, September 1970, WMAN, Urban Archives, Philadelphia, PA, Accession 274, Box 1, Folder 21.

40. WMAN, "Statement of Crisis," November 8, 1969, WMAN, Urban Archives, Philadelphia, PA, Accession 274, Box 1, Folder 19.

41. WMAN Board Meeting, September 8, 1969, WMAN, Urban Archives, Philadelphia, PA, Accession 274, Box 1, Folder 21.

42. West Mount Airy Action Statement, 1974, WMAN, Urban Archives, Philadelphia, PA, Accession 737, Box 10, Folder 23. Crime data specific to West Mount Airy is unavailable.

43. Memo, November 24, 1970, WMAN, Urban Archives, Philadelphia, PA, Accession 274, Box 1, Folder 37.

44. *Philadelphia Bulletin*, April 22, 1944, as cited in Paolantonio, *Frank Rizzo*, 39.

45. Peter Binzen and Joseph R. Daughen, *The Cop Who Would Be King: The Honorable Frank Rizzo* (New York: Little, Brown, and Company, 1977), 69–70.

46. "Mag. Harris, Rizzo Settle Differences," *Philadelphia Tribune*, March 14, 1953.

47. Senate Permanent Subcommittee on Investigation, 1962 Transcript, as cited in Paolantonio, *Frank Rizzo*, 70.

48. Paolantonio, *Frank Rizzo*, 63.

49. Ibid.

50. See Countryman, *Up South*, 133–34.

51. Richard D. Siegel, "Rights Expert to Move to Washington," *Philadelphia Inquirer*, July 4, 1965.

52. "George Schermer Resigns," *Detroit News*, June 6, 1963.

53. Letter to George Schermer, from C. W. Henry School Home and School Association, June 4, 1963, George Schermer Collection, Amistad Archives, New Orleans, LA, Box 3, Folder 9.

54. ACLU Press Release, June 4, 1963, George Schermer Collection, Amistad Archives, New Orleans, LA, Box 3, Folder 9.

55. Paolantonio, *Frank Rizzo*, 92.

56. Countryman, "From Protest to Politics," 826–27.

57. Bernard McCormick, "The War of the Cops," *New York Times*, October 18, 1970.

58. Report to WMAN Board on West Mount Airy Action, Inc., May 12, 1975, WMAN, Urban Archives, Philadelphia, PA, Accession 737, Box 10, Folder 23.

59. WMAN Meeting Minutes, June 30, 1969, WMAN, Urban Archives, Philadelphia, PA, Accession 274, Box 2, Folder 39.

60. Report to WMAN Board on West Mount Airy Action, Inc., May 12, 1975, WMAN, Urban Archives, Philadelphia, PA, Accession 737, Box 10, Folder 23.

61. Emily Starr, "West Mount Airy: Period of Change?" *Chestnut Hill Local,* June 19, 1975. For more on the response of African Americans to increased crime rates in the 1970s, see James Forman Jr., "Racial Critiques of Mass Incarceration: Beyond the New Jim Crow," *New York University Law Review* 87, no. 21 (2012).

62. See Forman, "Racial Critiques of Mass Incarceration."

63. "Curricular Approach to Integration Urged," *Philadelphia Bulletin*, July 7, 1969.

64. "Chief Troubleshooter Works to End School Disruption," *Philadelphia Bulletin*, September 28, 1970.

65. West Mount Airy Action Mission Statement, 1974, WMAN, Urban Archives, Philadelphia, PA, Accession 737, Box 10, Folder 23.

66. Ibid.

67. Public Letter from Doug Gaston, WMAN President, November 7, 1974, WMAN, Urban Archives, Philadelphia, PA, Accession 737, Box 10, Folder 23.

68. "Don't be a Victim," WMAA Flyer, April 27, 1975, WMAN, Urban Archives, Philadelphia, PA, Accession 737, Box 10, Folder 23.

69. "Don't be a Victim, of Scare Tactics," WMAN Flyer, April 1975, WMAN, Urban Archives, Philadelphia, PA, Accession 737, Box 10, Folder 23.

70. Ruth Steele: A Perspective, April 27, 1975, WMAN, Urban Archives, Philadelphia, PA, Accession 737, Box 10, Folder 23; Flora Wolf, interview by author, written transcription, Philadelphia, PA, February 24, 2012,.

71. Letter to the WMAN Board, from Flora Wolf, April 8, 1975, WMAN, Urban Archives, Philadelphia, PA, Accession 737, Box 10, Folder 23.

72. Emily Starr, "West Mount Airy: Period of Change?" *Chestnut Hill Local,* June 19, 1975.

73. "Crime Prevention Funding Approved," WMAN Newsletter, June 1975, WMAN, Urban Archives, Philadelphia, PA, Accession 737, Box 10, Folder 23.

74. "Opposition to Funding of WMAA," WMAN Newsletter, June 1975, WMAN, Urban Archives, Philadelphia, PA, Accession 737, Box 10, Folder 23.

75. Ashley Halsey, III, "Crime Program Funding Approved," *Germantown Courier*, May 15, 1975.

76. Ibid.

77. For more on this connection between race, power, and fear, see, e.g., William L. Van Deburg, *New Day in Babylon: The Black Power Movement and American Culture, 1965–1975* (Chicago: University of Chicago Press, 1992); Self, *American Babylon*; Joseph, *Black Power Movement*.

78. Editorial, "Reunite Mount Airy," *Germantown Courier*, May 22, 1975.

79. Bonnie Cook and Ashley Halsey III, "Mount Airy Funding Request Dropped: Disputed Anti-Crime Program Abandoned?" *Germantown Courier*, May 29, 1975.

80. Oliver Lancaster, Open Letter to the Board of WMAN, May 23, 1975, WMAN, Urban Archives, Philadelphia, PA, Accession 737, Box 10, Folder 23.

81. See, e.g., Cashin, *Failures of Integration*; Palmer, *Living as Equals*; Saltman, *Fragile Movement*.

82. Saltman, *Fragile Movement*; Cashin, *Failures of Integration*; Wiese, *Places of Their Own*; Lacy, *Blue-Chip Black*.

83. Chris Van de Velde, interview by author, written transcription, Philadelphia, PA, September 30, 2011.

84. Ruth R. Russell, "Former Lindsay Aide Heads WMAN," *Chestnut Hill Local*, September 18, 1975; Chris Van de Velde, interview by author, written transcription, Philadelphia, PA, September 30, 2011.

85. Ruth R. Russell, "Former Lindsay Aide Heads WMAN," *Chestnut Hill Local*, September 18, 1975.

86. "Mend the Wounds," *Germantown Courier*, June 19, 1975.

87. Chris Van de Velde, interview by author, written transcription, Philadelphia, PA, September 30, 2011.

88. Ibid.; Chris Van de Velde, 1975–76 Annual Report, undated, WMAN, Urban Archives, Philadelphia, PA, Accession 737, Box 4, Folder 43.

89. Chris Van de Velde, interview by author, written transcription, Philadelphia, PA, September 30, 2011.

90. Howard S. Shapiro, "Happy Birthday: Civic Organization Celebrates Unique Urban Life-style," *Philadelphia Inquirer*, July 7, 1979.

Chapter 7

1. Obituary, Patrician Henning, *Philadelphia Inquirer*, June 11, 2005; Alan Heavens, "A Diverse Enclave Celebrates a Century," *Philadelphia Inquirer*, January 17, 2003; "Forty Good Neighbors: Pat Henning," *West Mount Airy Neighbors*, available from http://www.wman.net/40-good-neighbors/henning-pat.

2. Laura Siena, "Pat Henning," Keynote address at the Germantown Historical Society Hall of Fame Induction, May 20, 2005; available from http://www.wman.net/pdfs/pathenning.pdf.

3. For reference on the shift away from integration, see, e.g., Judith Stein, "History of an Idea," *Nation* (December 14, 1998); Eric Foner and Randall Kennedy, "Reclaiming Integration," *Nation*, December 4, 1998; Robin D. G. Kelley, "Integration: What's Left?" *Nation*, December 3, 1998; Matthew Johnson, "The Origins of Diversity: Managing Race at the University of Michigan, 1963–2006" (PhD diss., Temple University, 2011); Bruce J. Schulman, *The Seventies: The Great Shift in American Culture, Society, and Politics* (Boston: De Capo Press, 2002).

4. Marilyn Nolen, letter to the editor, *Philadelphia Bulletin*, October 20 1978.

5. Johnson, "Origins of Diversity." See also Frank Dobbin, *Inventing Equal Opportunity* (Princeton: Princeton University Press, 2009); Nancy MacLean, *Freedom Is not Enough: The Opening of the American Workplace* (Cambridge: Harvard University Press, 2008); Jennifer Delton, *Racial Integration in Corporate America, 1940–1990* (New York: Cambridge University Press, 2009); Ellen Berrey, "Why Diversity Became Orthodox in Higher Education, and How It Changed the Meaning of Race on Campus," *Critical Sociology* 37, no. 5 (2011): 1–24; Marcia Graham Synnott, "The Evolving Diversity Rationale in University Admissions from *Regents v. Bakke* to the University of Michigan Cases," *Cornell Law Review* 90, no. 2 (January 2005): 463–504; Erin Kelly and Frank Dobbin, "How Affirmative Action Became Diversity Management," in *Color Lines: Affirmative Action, Immigration, and the Civil Rights Options for America*, ed. John David Skrentny (Chicago: University of Chicago Press, 2001.); Schulman, *Seventies*; Beth L. Bailey and David R. Farber, *America in the Seventies* (Lawrence: University Press of Kansas, 2004), 50–74.

6. Phrase invoked by Howard Shapiro in "Happy Birthday: Civic Group Celebrates Unique Urban Life-style," *Philadelphia Inquirer*, July 7, 1979.

7. Ellen Tichenor, interview by author, written transcription, Philadelphia, PA, July 26, 2012.

8. Ibid.

9. Mark Stein, *City of Sisterly and Brotherly Loves: Lesbian and Gay Philadelphia, 1945–1972* (Philadelphia: Temple University Press, 2004), 44.

10. Ellen Tichenor, interview by author, written transcription, Philadelphia, PA, July 26, 2012.

11. Ibid., 45.

12. Marc Killinger, "As Gay and Lesbians Come Out, 'Gay Neighborhoods' Flourish," *Philadelphia Gay News*, May 13, 1983.

13. Ibid.; Ellen Tichenor, interview by author, written transcription, Philadelphia, PA, July 26, 2012.

14. Ibid.

15. Ewart Rouse, "Food Buyers of the World, Unite!" *Philadelphia Inquirer*, November 12, 1981. For more on the cooperative movement of the 1960s and 1970s, see Cox, *Storefront Revolution*.

16. Ellen Tichenor, interview by author, written transcription, Philadelphia, PA, July 26, 2012.

17. Linda Holtzman, interview by author, written transcription, Philadelphia, PA, October 3, 2012.

18. Richard Hirsh, "The Founding of the Reconstructionist Rabbinical College: A Retrospective from the Pages of the *Reconstructionist*," *Reconstructionist* 63, no. 1 (Fall 1998): 101. For more on the institutional history of Reconstructionism, see Deborah Waxman, "Faith and Ethnicity in American Judaism: Reconstructionism as Ideology and Institution, 1935–1959" (PhD diss., Temple University, 2010); Ira Eisenstein, "From School of Thought to Movement." *Reconstructionist* 41, no. 1 (February 1975): 5.

19. Rebecca Alpert, interview by author, written transcription, Philadelphia, PA, June 13, 2012.

20. Ibid.

21. See Mark Oppenheimer, *Knocking on Heaven's Door: American Religion in the Age of Counterculture* (New Haven, CT: Yale University Press, 2003), 95–129; Riv-Ellen Prell, *Prayer and Community: The Havurah in American Judaism* (Detroit, MI: Wayne State University Press, 1989).

22. Jonathan D. Sarna, *American Judaism: A History* (New Haven: Yale University Press, 2005), 319.

23. Julia Cass, "A Jewish Rebirth in Mount Airy," *Philadelphia Inquirer*, April 15, 1987.

24. Ibid.

25. Sarna, *American Judaism*, 323.

26. Rebecca Alpert, interview by author, written transcription, Philadelphia, PA, June 13, 2012; David Teutsch, interview by author, written transcription, Philadelphia, PA, July 23, 2012.

27. Sarna, *American Judaism,* 323; David Teutsch, interview by author, written transcription, Philadelphia, PA, July 23, 2012; Rebecca Alpert, interview by author, written transcription, Philadelphia, PA, June 13, 2012.

28. David Teutsch, interview by author, written transcription, Philadelphia, PA, July 23, 2012.

29. Rebecca Alpert, interview by author, written transcription, Philadelphia, PA, June 13, 2012.

30. David Teutsch, interview by author, written transcription, Philadelphia, PA, July 23, 2012.

31. Rebecca Alpert, interview by author, written transcription, Philadelphia, PA, June 13, 2012.

32. David Teutsch, interview by author, written transcription, Philadelphia, PA, July 23, 2012.

33. Julia Cass, "A Jewish Rebirth in Mount Airy," *Philadelphia Inquirer*, April 15, 1987.

34. David Teutsch, interview by author, written transcription, Philadelphia, PA, July 23, 2012.

35. WMAN Newsletter, "Gray Panther Maggie Kuhn to Speak at Summit Church," March 1981, WMAN, Urban Archives, Philadelphia, PA, Accession 829, Box 4, Folder 44.

36. WMAN Newsletter, May 1981, WMAN, Urban Archives, Philadelphia, PA, Accession 829, Box 4, Folder 44.

37. Mount Airy Times Express Annual Report, 1982, WMAN, Urban Archives, Philadelphia, PA, Accession 737, Box 1, Folder 8.

38. Annual Report, 1983–1984, WMAN, Urban Archives, Philadelphia, PA, Accession 737, Box 1, Folder 9.

39. Beth Gillin, "Co-op Troubled by Doing So Well as It Does Good," *Philadelphia Inquirer*, July 25, 1985.

40. Beth Gillin, "A Learning Tree Takes Root in Mount Airy," *Philadelphia Inquirer*, March 27, 1986.

41. Vernon Loeb, "Selling Desegregation—One School's Struggle for the Hearts and Minds," *Philadelphia Inquirer*, February 6, 1984.

42. Ibid.

43. Dale Mezzacappa and Aletta Emeno, "Grassroots Integration—Parents in an Integrated Neighborhood Struggle to Keep a School Racially Balanced," *Philadelphia Inquirer*, May 17, 2004.

44. Vernon Loeb, "Selling Desegregation—One School's Struggle for the Hearts and Minds," *Philadelphia Inquirer*, February 6, 1984.

45. Michael Ruane, "A Boom Is Testing Mount Airy," *Philadelphia Inquirer*, February 25, 1987.

46. Ibid.

47. For more on liberalism and Ronal Reagan, see Gil Troy and Vincent J. Cannato, eds., *Living in the Eighties* (New York: Oxford University Press, 2009); Gil Troy, *Morning in America: How Ronald Reagan Invented the 1980s* (Princeton, NJ: Princeton University Press, 2007); Robert M. Collins, *Transforming America: Politics and Culture during the Reagan Years* (New York: Columbia University Press, 2007); Daniel Rogers, *Age of Fracture* (Cambridge: Belknap Press of Harvard University Press, 2012).

48. David Greenberg, "The Reorientation of Liberalism in the 1980s," in Troy and Cannato, *Living in the Eighties*, 54.

49. For a discussion on the legacy of deindustrialization, see, e.g., Jefferson Cowie and Joseph Heathcott, eds., *Beyond the Ruins: The Meaning of Deindustrialization* (Ithaca, NY: ILR Press, 2003); Jefferson Cowie, *Stayin' Alive: The 1970s and the Last Days of the Working Class* (New York: New Press, 2012); Judith Stein, *Pivotal Decade: How the United States Traded Factories for Finance in the Seventies* (New Haven, CT: Yale University Press, 2011); Rogers, *Age of Fracture*.

50. Michelle Alexander, *The New Jim Crow: Mass Incarceration in the Age of Colorblindness* (New York: New Press, 2012), 51.

51. See, e.g., Alexander, *New Jim Crow;* Troy and Cannato, *Living in the Eighties*, 33–34.

52. Thomas Gibbins and Mark Wagenveld, "Bystander Hit in Drug Shootout," *Philadelphia Inquirer*, March 16, 1989; Jack McGuire and Leon Taylor, "Shootout Wounds Teen, Two Arrested," *Philadelphia Inquirer*, March 16, 1989; Ginny Weigand, "On Besieged Street, a Blessed Peace Follows Shootout," *Philadelphia Inquirer*, March 17, 1989.

53. Beth Gillin and Robert Terry, "Police Think Drugs Figured in Mount Airy Killings," *Philadelphia Inquirer*, May 10, 1989; Beth Gillin, "A Neighborhood's Fear of Drugs Is Tie That Binds—and Terrifies," *Philadelphia Inquirer*, May 14, 1989.

54. Terence Samuel, "AIDS Center Opens Doors in Mount Airy," *Philadelphia Inquirer*, October 7, 1991.

55. Terence Samuel, "Unease over Home for Youths: Mount Airy Residents Near the Planned Home Fear for Their Children's Safety," *Philadelphia Inquirer*, November 29, 1992.

56. Dale Mezzacappa and Aletta Emeno, "Grassroots Integration," *Philadelphia Inquirer*, May 17, 2004.

57. Dale Mezzacappa, "A Struggle with Crowded Schools: High Schools, Especially, Are Brimming, Enrollment Rose by 2,300," *Philadelphia Inquirer*, November 11, 1992.

58. Martha Woodall, "Private School Costs Up, Top Tuition Nearing $10,000," *Philadelphia Inquirer*, February 24, 1991.

59. On the links between oral history and historical memory, see, e.g., Lynn Abrams, *Oral History Theory* (New York: Routledge, 2010); Michael H. Frisch, *A Shared Authority: Essays on the Craft and Meaning of Oral and Public History* (Albany: State University of New York Press, 1990); Leslie Roy Ballard, Thomas L. Charlton, Lois E. Myers, Rebecca Sharpless, Ronald J. Grele, Mary A. Larson, Linda Shopes, Charles T. Morrissey, James E. Fogerty, and Elinor A. Maze, *History of Oral History: Foundations and Methodology* (Lanham, MD: AltaMira Press, 2007); Paula Hamilton and Linda Shopes, eds., *Oral History and Public Memories* (Philadelphia: Temple University Press, 2008); Luisa Passerini, *Fascism in Popular Memory: The Cultural Experience of the Turin Working Class* (New York: Cambridge University Press, 1987); Alessandro Portelli, *The Death of Luigi Trastulli and Other Stories: Form and Meaning in Oral History* (Albany: State University of New York Press, 1991).

60. Patricia Henning, Mount Airy Historical Awareness Committee Statement, May 1993, WMAN Oral History Project, Germantown Historical Society, Philadelphia, PA.

61. Project Report, November 28, 1993, WMAN Oral History Project, Germantown Historical Society, Philadelphia, PA.

62. Grant Application, Undated, WMAN Oral History Project, Germantown Historical Society, Philadelphia, PA.

63. Ibid.

64. Ibid.

65. Patricia Henning, Mount Airy Historical Awareness Committee Statement, May 1993, WMAN Oral History Project, Germantown Historical Society, Philadelphia, PA.

66. *Mount Airy Times Express*, December 9, 1992, 26.

67. Project Report, November 28, 1993, WMAN Oral History Project, Germantown Historical Society, Philadelphia, PA.

68. Wright is the father of Pastor Jeremiah Wright Jr., of Trinity United Church of Christ, President Barack Obama's former church. The junior Wright grew up a product of the integrationist West Mount Airy.

69. Joseph Coleman, interview by Szabi Zee, 1993, written transcription, WMAN Oral History Project, Germantown Historical Society, Philadelphia, PA; Marjorie Kopeland, interview by Patricia Henning, 1993, written transcription, WMAN Oral History Project, Germantown Historical Society, Philadelphia, PA; Shirley Melvin, interview by Patricia Henning, 1993, written transcription, WMAN Oral History Project, Germantown Historical Society, Philadelphia, PA; Doris Polsky, interview by Patricia Henning, 1993, written transcription, WMAN Oral History Project, Germantown Historical Society, Philadelphia, PA; Jeremiah Wright Sr., interview by Vida Carson, 1993, written transcription, WMAN Oral History Project, Germantown Historical Society, Philadelphia, PA; George Schermer, interview by Judith Schermer, 1989, written transcription, WMAN Oral History Project, Germantown Historical Society, Philadelphia, PA.

70. Frank Harvey, interview by Patricia Henning, 1993, audio recording, WMAN Oral History Project, Germantown Historical Society, Philadelphia, PA.

71. Gladys Thompson Norris, interview by Vida Carson, 1993, audio recording, WMAN Oral History Project, Germantown Historical Society, Philadelphia, PA.

72. For a discussion of the relationship between oral history and history "from above," see Kevin Blackburn, "History from Above," in Hamilton and Shopes, *Oral History and Public Memories*, 31–32.

73. Project Report, November 28, 1993, WMAN Oral History Project, Germantown Historical Society, Philadelphia, PA.

74. Ibid.

75. This conception of mediation comes from Hamilton and Shopes, *Oral History and Public Memories*, introduction.

76. Project Report, November 28, 1993, WMAN Oral History Project, Germantown Historical Society, Philadelphia, PA.

77. Alan Heavens, "A Diverse Enclave Celebrates a Century," *Philadelphia Inquirer*, January 17, 1993.

78. Roxanne Jones, "City Community Prides Itself on its Diversity, Country Beauty," *Philadelphia Inquirer*, March 13, 1994.

79. See, e.g., Vernon Loeb, "Selling Desegregation—One School's Struggle for Hearts and Minds," *Philadelphia Inquirer*, February 6, 1984; Beth Gillin, "A Learning

Tree Takes Root in Mount Airy," *Philadelphia Inquirer*, March 27, 1986; Michael Ruane, "A Boom Is Testing Mount Airy," *Philadelphia Inquirer*, February 25, 1987.

80. Ferman, Singleton, and DeMarco. "West Mount Airy."

81. The article contains thirty-five footnotes; notes 9, 16, 26–31, and 33 cite either the Oral History Project or these newspaper articles. The Oral History Project is also cited as a general reference of the research.

82. Ferman, Singleton, and DeMarco, "West Mount Airy," 44.

Epilogue

1. Christie Balka, interview by author, written transcription, Philadelphia, PA., September 20, 2012.

2. "Healthy Places: A Study of 45 Philadelphia Neighborhoods Shows a Connection between Social Bonds and Personal Wellness," *Philadelphia Inquirer*, March 1, 2004; Sheila Dyan, "Architecture Worthy of a Notable Neighborhood—Greene Manor, West Mount Airy, Philadelphia," *Philadelphia Inquirer*, April 9, 2004.

3. Lise Funderberg, "Our Town," *O, the Oprah Magazine*, April 2006; Lise Funderberg, "Bloodlines," *Breathe Magazine*, March–April 2005.

4. Lise Funderberg, "Our Town," *O, the Oprah Magazine*, April 2006.

5. Sugrue, *Sweet Land of Liberty*, 542; Rory Kramer, "What Is on the Other Side of the Tracks?: A Spatial Examination of Neighborhood Boundaries and Segregation (PhD diss., University of Pennsylvania, 2012). Kramer notes that between 2000 and 2010, the neighborhood shifted from majority-black (52 percent) to majority-white (54 percent). Additional data reported by sociologist Sarah Johnson. Special thanks to Johnson for sharing with me an unpublished ethnographic study on the community.

6. U.S. Census Data from the American Community Survey, cited by John Duchneskie and Dylan Purcell, "Average Household Income in Philadelphia," *Philly.com*, available at http://www.philly.com/philly/news/2010_Census_Philly.html?c=r; Ferman, Singleton, and DeMarco, "West Mount Airy," 44. National median household income for 2005–2009 was $50,221.

7. "The Ten Richest Zip Codes in Philadelphia," *Philly.com PhillyLists*, March 29, 2013, available at http://www.philly.com/philly/blogs/phillylists/The-10-richest-zip-codes-in-Philadelphia.html.

8. Kramer, "What Is on the Other Side of the Tracks?" chapter 6. According to Kramer, the decrease in population in West Mount Airy is reflective of broader population depletion in Philadelphia; the city lost 200,000 white residents between 1990 and 2000. During that same period, the black population rose by close to 40,000, the Latino population by 60,000, and the Asian population by 30,000. See also Sugrue, *Sweet Land of Liberty*, 542–43; Johnson, ethnographic study, 2012. Johnson notes the limitations of using "mean household income," rather than "median;" however, median data was not available at the tract level.

9. See chapter 6.

10. *Nation*, December 1998.

11. Eric Foner and Randall Kennedy, "Reclaiming Integration," *Nation*, December 4, 1998.

12. Judith Stein, "History of an Idea," *Nation,* December 14, 1998.

13. Foner and Kennedy, "Reclaiming Integration."

14. Robin D. G. Kelley, "Integration: What's Left?," *Nation*, December 3, 1998.

15. Foner and Kennedy, "Reclaiming Integration."

16. Christie Balka, interview by author, written transcription, Philadelphia, PA, September 20, 2012.

17. Ibid.

Bibliography

Abrams, Lynn. *Oral History Theory*. New York: Routledge, 2010.

Aldridge, Delores P. "The Changing Nature of Interracial Marriage in Georgia: A Research Note." *Journal of Marriage and the Family* 35, no. 4 (November 1973).

Alexander, Jeffrey C. *The Civil Sphere*. New York: Oxford University Press, 2006.

Alexander, Michelle. *The New Jim Crow: Mass Incarceration in the Age of Colorblindness*. New York: New Press, 2012.

Anderson, Carol. *Eyes off the Prize: The United Nations and the African American Struggle for Human Rights, 1944–1955*. New York: Cambridge University Press, 2003.

Anderson, Elijah. "Being Here and Being There: Fieldwork Encounters and Ethnographic Discoveries." Annals of the American Academy of Political and Social Science 595, no. 1 (2004).

———. *Streetwise: Race, Class, and Change in an Urban Community*. Chicago: University of Chicago Press, 1992.

Anderson, Elijah, and Douglas Massey. *Problem of the Century: Racial Stratification in the United States*. New York: Russell Sage Foundation, 2004.

Augier, Mie, and James G. March. *The Roots, Rituals, and Rhetorics of Change: North American Business Schools After the Second World War*. Palo Alto, CA: Stanford Business Books, 2011.

Bailey, Beth L. *From Front Porch to Back Seat: Courtship in Twentieth Century America.* Baltimore, MD: Johns Hopkins University Press, 1989.

Bailey, Beth L., and David R. Farber, eds. *America in the Seventies.* Lawrence: University Press of Kansas, 2004.

Ballard, Leslie Roy, Thomas L. Charlton, Lois E. Myers, Rebecca Sharpless, Ronald J. Grele, Mary A. Larson, Linda Shopes, Charles T. Morrissey, James E. Fogerty, and Elinor A. Maze. *History of Oral History: Foundations and Methodology.* Lanham, MD: AltaMira Press, 2007.

Banner-Haley, Charles P. T. *The Fruits of Integration: Black Middle-Class Ideology and Culture, 1960–1990.* Jackson: University Press of Mississippi, 1994.

Barber, William J. *Gunnar Myrdal: An Intellectual Biography.* New York: Palgrave Macmillan, 2008.

Bauman, John F. *Public Housing, Race, and Renewal: Urban Planning in Philadelphia, 1920–1974.* Philadelphia: Temple University Press, 1987.

Belmonte, Laura A. *Selling the American Way: U.S. Propaganda and the Cold War.* Philadelphia: University of Pennsylvania Press, 2008.

Berman, William C. *The Politics of Civil Rights in the Truman Administration.* Columbus: Ohio State University Press, 1970.

Berrey, Ellen. "Why Diversity Became Orthodox in Higher Education, and How It Changed the Meaning of Race on Campus." *Critical Sociology* 37, no. 5 (2011).

Bigsby, C. W. E. *The Cambridge Companion to Modern American Culture.* New York: Cambridge University Press, 2006.

Binzen, Peter, and Joseph R. Daughen. *The Cop Who Would Be King: The Honorable Frank Rizzo.* New York: Little, Brown and Company, 1977.

Biondi, Martha. *To Stand and Fight: The Struggle for Civil Rights in Postwar New York City.* Cambridge: Harvard University Press, 2003.

Birger, Jon S. "Race, Reaction, and Reform: The Three Rs of Philadelphia School Politics, 1965–1971." *Pennsylvania Magazine of History and Biography* 120, no. 3 (July 2006).

Blight, David W. *Race and Reunion: The Civil War in American Memory.* New York: Belknap Press of Harvard University Press, 2001.

Borstelmann, Thomas. *The Cold War and the Color Line: American Race Relations in the Global Arena.* Cambridge: Harvard University Press, 2001.

Brinkley, Alan. *The End of Reform: New Deal Liberalism in Recession and War.* New York: Knopf, 1995.

Brodkin, Karen. *How Jews Became White Folks, and What That Says about Race in America.* New Brunswick, NJ: Rutgers University Press, 1998.

Brooks, Roy L. *Integration or Separation? A Strategy for Racial Equality.* Cambridge: Harvard University Press, 1999.

Brown, Samuel R. "Community Attachment in a Racially Integrated Neighborhood." PhD diss., University of Pennsylvania, 1990.

Cashin, Sheryll. *The Failures of Integration: How Race and Class Are Undermining the American Dream.* New York: PublicAffairs, 2005.

Cohen, Felix S. "Dialogue on Private Property." *Rutgers Law Review* 9, no. 357 (1954).

Cohen, Lizabeth. *A Consumers' Republic: The Politics of Mass Consumption in Postwar America*. New York: Knopf, 2003.

Cohen, Morris R. "Property and Sovereignty." *Cornell Law Quarterly* 13, no. 8 (1927).

Collier-Thomas, Bettye, and James Turner. "Race, Class, and Color: The African American Discourse on Identity." *Journal of American Ethnic History* 14, no. 1 (Fall 1994).

Collins, Robert M. *Transforming America: Politics and Culture during the Reagan Years*. New York: Columbia University Press, 2007.

Contosta, David R. *Suburb in the City: Chestnut Hill, Philadelphia, 1850–1990*. Columbus: Ohio State University Press, 1992.

Countryman, Matthew. "'From Protest to Politics': Community Control and Black Independent Politics in Philadelphia, 1965–1984." *Journal of Urban History* 32, no. 6 (September 2006).

———. *Up South: Civil Rights and Black Power in Philadelphia*. Philadelphia: University of Pennsylvania Press, 2006.

Cowie, Jefferson. *Capital Moves: RCA's Seventy-Year Quest for Cheap Labor*. New York: New Press, 2001.

———. *Stayin' Alive: The 1970s and the Last Days of the Working Class*. New York: New Press, 2012.

Cowie, Jefferson, and Joseph Heathcott, eds. *Beyond the Ruins: The Meanings of Deindustrialization*. Ithaca, NY: ILR Press, 2003.

Cox, Craig. *Storefront Revolution: Food Co-ops and the Counterculture*. New Brunswick, NJ: Rutgers University Press, 1994.

Cruse, Harold. *The Crisis of the Negro Intellectual*. New York: William Morrow and Company, 1967.

Curl, John. *For All the People: Uncovering the Hidden History of Cooperation, Cooperative Movements, and Communalism in America*. Oakland, CA: PM Press, 2009.

Cutler, William W., and Howard Gillette, eds. *The Divided Metropolis: Social and Spatial Dimensions of Philadelphia, 1800–1975*. Westport, CT: Greenwood Press, 1980.

Delany, Frank X. "Germantown and Its Civic Organizations, 1946–1981: A Community in Search of Effective Form." *Germantown Crier* 52, no. 1 (Spring 2002).

Delton, Jennifer. *Racial Integration in Corporate America, 1940–1990*. New York: Cambridge University Press, 2009.

Dobbin, Frank. *Inventing Equal Opportunity*. Princeton, NJ: Princeton University Press, 2009.

Duany, Andres, Elizabeth Plater-Zyberk, and Jeff Speck. *Suburban Nation: The Rise of Sprawl and the Decline of the American Dream*. New York: North Point Press, 2001.

Dudziak, Mary. *Cold War Civil Rights: Race and the Image of American Democracy*. Princeton, NJ: Princeton University Press, 2000.

Early, Gerald L. *This Is Where I Came In: Black America in the 1960s*. Lincoln: University of Nebraska Press, 2003.

Eisenstadt, Peter R. *Rochdale Village: Robert Moses, 6,000 Families, and New York's Greatest Experiment in Integrated Housing*. Ithaca, NY: Cornell University Press, 2010.

Eisenstein, Ira. "From School of Thought to Movement." *Reconstructionist* 41, no. 1 (February 1975).

Ellen, Ingrid Gould. *Sharing America's Neighborhoods: The Prospects for Stable Racial Integration*. Cambridge: Harvard University Press, 2000.

Elmore, Richard, Bruce Fuller, and Gary Orfield, eds. *Choice: The Cultural Logic of Families, the Political Rationality of Institutions*. New York: Teachers College Press, 1995.

Fainstein, Susan S., and Scott Campbell. *Readings in Urban Theory*. 2nd ed. Hoboken, NJ: Wiley-Blackwell, 1996.

Farber, David R., and Eric Foner. *The Age of Great Dreams: America in the 1960s*. New York: Hill and Wang, 1994.

Feagin, Joe R., and Melvin P. Sikes. *Living with Racism: The Black Middle-Class Experience*. Boston: Beacon Press, 1994.

Ferman, Barbara, and Patrick Kaylor. "Building the Spatial Community: A Case Study of Neighborhood Institutions." *Policy Studies Review* 18, no. 4 (2001).

Ferman, Barbara, Theresa Singleton, and Don DeMarco. "West Mount Airy, Philadelphia." *Cityscape: A Journal of Policy Development and Research* 4, no. 2 (1998).

Fishman, Robert. *Bourgeois Utopias: The Rise and Fall of Suburbia*. New York: Basic Books, 1987.

Foner, Eric. *The Story of American Freedom*. New York: W. W. Norton, 1998.

Forman, James Jr. "Racial Critiques of Mass Incarceration: Beyond the New Jim Crow," *New York University Law Review* 87 (2012).

Franklin, Vincent Paul. *Education of Black Philadelphia: The Social and Educational History of a Minority Community, 1900–1950*. Philadelphia: University of Pennsylvania Press, 1979.

Fraser, Steve, and Gary Gerstle, eds. *The Rise and Fall of the New Deal Order, 1930–1980*. Princeton, NJ: Princeton University Press, 1989.

Frazier, E. Franklin. *Black Bourgeoisie: The Rise of a New Middle-Class in the United States*. rev. ed. Glencoe, IL: Free Press, 1962.

Freund, David M. P. *Colored Property: State Policy and White Racial Politics in Suburban America*. Chicago: University of Chicago Press, 2007.

Friedman, Lawrence M. *American Law in the Twentieth Century*. New Haven, CT: Yale University Press, 2002.

Friedman, Murray, ed. *Philadelphia Jewish Life, 1830–1940*. Philadelphia: Institute for the Study of Human Issues, 1983.

———. *Philadelphia Jewish Life, 1940–2000*. Philadelphia: Temple University Press, 2003.

Frisch, Michael H. *A Shared Authority: Essays on the Craft and Meaning of Oral and Public History*. Albany: State University of New York Press, 1990.

Gamm, Gerald. *Urban Exodus: Why the Jews Left Boston and the Catholics Stayed*. Cambridge: Harvard University Press, 1999.

Gans, Herbert J. *The Levittowners: Ways of Life and Politics in a New Suburban Community*. New York: Pantheon Books, 1967.

Garvey, Amy Jacques. *Garvey and Garveyism*. New York: Collier Books, 1970.

Gerstle, Gary. "The Protean Character of American Liberalism." *American Historical Review* 99, no. 4. (1994).

Gilles, Myriam E., and Risa L. Goluboff, eds. *Civil Rights Stories*. New York: Foundation Press, 2008.

Goffman, Erving. *The Presentation of Self in Everyday Life*. Garden City, NY: Doubleday Anchor Press, 1959.

Gordon, Milton M. "The Girard College Case: Desegregation and a Municipal Trust." *Annals of the American Academy of Political and Social Science* 304 (March 1956).

Graglia, Lino A. "State Action: Constitutional Phoenix." *Washington University Law Quarterly* 67, no. 77 (1989).

Grazian, David. *Blue Chicago: The Search for Authenticity in Urban Blues Clubs*. Chicago: University of Chicago Press, 2005.

Green, Adam. *Selling the Race: Culture, Community, and Black Chicago, 1940–1955*. Chicago: University of Chicago Press, 2007.

Greenberg, Cheryl Lynn. *Troubling the Waters: Black-Jewish Relations in the American Century*. Princeton, NJ: Princeton University Press, 2006.

Greenberg, Jack. *Crusaders in the Courts: How a Dedicated Band of Lawyers Fought for the Civil Rights Revolution*. New York: Basic Books, 1994.

Gregory, James N. *Southern Diaspora: How the Great Migrations of Black and White Southerners Transformed America*. Chapel Hill: University of North Carolina Press, 2005.

Grier, Eunice S., and George W. Grier. *Privately Developed Interracial Housing: An Analysis of Experience*. Berkeley: University of California Press, 1960.

Grigsby, William G., and Chester Rapkin. *The Demand for Housing in Racially Mixed Areas: A Study of the Nature of Neighborhood Change*. Berkeley: University of California Press, 1960.

Guttenberg, Jack M. "Racial Integration and Home Prices: The Case of West Mount Airy." *Wharton Quarterly* (Spring 1970).

Hamby, Alonzo L. *Liberalism and Its Challengers: From FDR to Bush*. New York: Oxford University Press, 1985.

Hamilton, Paula, and Linda Shopes, eds. *Oral History and Public Memories*. Philadelphia: Temple University Press, 2008.

Haney-Lopez, Ian F. *White by Law: The Legal Construction of Race*. New York: New York University Press, 1996.

Harper, Philip Brian. *Are We Not Men? Masculine Anxiety and the Problem of African American Identity*. New York: Oxford University Press, 1996.

Harris, Angela P. "Equality Trouble: Sameness and Difference in 20th Century Race Law." *California Law Review* 88, no. 6 (December 2000).

Harris, Mark. *Pictures at a Revolution: Five Movies and the Birth of the New Hollywood*. New York: Penguin Press, 2008.

Henkin, Louis. "Shelley v. Kraemer: Notes for a Revised Opinion." *University of Pennsylvania Law Review* 110, no. 4 (February 1962).

Heumann, Leonard F. "The Definition and Analysis of Stable Racial Integration: The Case of West Mount Airy, Philadelphia." PhD diss., University of Pennsylvania, 1973.

Higley, Stephen Richard. *Privilege, Power, and Place: The Geography of the American Upper Class*. Lanham, MD: Rowman and Littlefield, 1995.

Hillier, Amy. "Who Received Loans? Home Owners' Loan Corporation Lending and Discrimination in Philadelphia in the 1930s." *Journal of Planning History* 2, no. 1 (2003).

Hirsch, Arnold R. *Making the Second Ghetto: Race and Housing in Chicago, 1940–1960*. New York: Cambridge University Press, 1983.

———. "Massive Resistance in the Urban North: Trumbull Park, Chicago, 1953–1966." *Journal of American History* 82, no. 2 (September 1995).

Hirsh, Richard. "The Founding of the Reconstructionist Rabbinical College: A Retrospective from the Pages of the *Reconstructionist*." *Reconstructionist* 63, no. 1 (Fall 1998).

Hodes, Martha Elizabeth, ed. *Sex, Love, Race: Crossing Boundaries in North American History*. New York: New York University Press, 1999.

Hornstein, Jeffrey M. *A Nation of Realtors: A Cultural History of the Twentieth-Century American Middle Class*. Durham, NC: Duke University Press, 2005.

Horowitz, Morton J. *The Transformation of American Law, 1887–1960: The Crisis of Legal Orthodoxy*. New York: Oxford University Press, 1992.

Hughes, Langston. *Fight for Freedom: The Story of the NAACP*. New York: W. W. Norton, 1962.

Hula, Richard C., and Cynthia Jackson-Elmoore. *Nonprofits in Urban America*. Westport, CT: Quorum Books, 2000.

Irons, Peter H. *The Courage of Their Convictions: Sixteen Americans Who Fought Their Way to the Supreme Court*. New York: Free Press, 1988.

Jackson, Kenneth T. *Crabgrass Frontier: The Suburbanization of the United States*. New York: Oxford University Press, 1985.

Jackson, Ronald L. *Scripting the Black Masculine Body: Identity, Discourse, and Racial Politics in Popular Media*. Albany: State University of New York Press, 2006.

Jackson, Walter A. *Gunnar Myrdal and America's Conscience: Social Engineering and Racial Liberalism, 1938–1987*. Chapel Hill: University of North Carolina Press, 1990.

Jacobs, Jane. *The Death and Life of Great American Cities*. New York: Random House, 1961.

Jacoby, Tamar. *Someone Else's House: America's Unfinished Struggle for Integration*. New York: Free Press, 1998.

Johnson, Matthew. "The Origins of Diversity: Managing Race at the University of Michigan, 1963–2006." PhD diss., Temple University, 2011.

Jonas, Gilbert. *Freedom's Sword: The NAACP and the Struggle against Racism in America, 1909–1969*. New York: Routledge, 2005.

Jones, Patrick D. *The Selma of the North: Civil Rights Insurgency in Milwaukee*. Cambridge: Harvard University Press, 2009.

Joseph, Peniel, ed. *The Black Power Movement: Rethinking the Civil Rights–Black Power Era*. New York: Routledge, 2006.

———. *Waiting 'Til the Midnight Hour: A Narrative History of Black Power in America*. New York: Henry Holt and Company, 2006.

Jost, Timothy. "The Defeasible Fee and the Birth of the Modern Residential Subdivision." *Missouri Law Review* 49, no. 695 (1984).

Kahen, Harold I. "The Validity of Anti-Negro Restrictive Covenants: A Reconsideration of the Problem." *University of Chicago Law Review* 12, no. 2 (February 1945).

Katz, Michael B., and Thomas J. Sugrue. *W. E. B. DuBois, Race, and the City: "The Philadelphia Negro" and Its Legacy.* Philadelphia: University of Pennsylvania Press, 1998.

Katz, Stanley N. "Thomas Jefferson and the Right to Property in Revolutionary America." *Journal of Law and Economics* 19, no. 3 (1976).

Katzman, David M. *Before the Ghetto: Black Detroit in the Nineteenth Century.* Urbana: University of Illinois Press, 1973.

Kellogg, Charles Flint. *NAACP: A History of the National Association for the Advancement of Colored People.* Baltimore, MD: Johns Hopkins University Press, 1967.

Kelly, Robin D. G. *Race Rebels: Culture, Politics, and the Black Working Class.* New York: Free Press, 1996.

Kennedy, Randall. *Sellout: The Politics of Racial Betrayal.* New York: Pantheon Books, 2008.

Kerber, Linda K., Jane Sherron De Hart, and Cornelia Hughes Dayton. *Women's America: Refocusing the Past.* New York: Oxford University Press, 2003.

King, Richard H. *Civil Rights and the Idea of Freedom.* New York: Oxford University Press, 1992.

Klarman, Michael J. *From Jim Crow to Civil Rights: The Supreme Court and the Struggle for Racial Equality.* New York: Oxford University Press, 2006.

Kramer, Rory. "What Is on the Other Side of the Tracks? A Spatial Examination of Neighborhood Boundaries and Segregation." PhD diss., University of Pennsylvania, 2012.

Kruse, Kevin Michael. *White Flight: Atlanta and the Making of Modern Conservatism.* Princeton, NJ: Princeton University Press, 2007.

Kruse, Kevin Michael, and Thomas J. Sugrue, eds. *The New Suburban History.* Chicago: University of Chicago Press, 2006.

Kruse, Kevin Michael, and Steven G. N. Tuck, eds. *Fog of War: The Second World War and the Civil Rights Movement.* New York: Oxford University Press, 2012.

Lacy, Karyn R. *Blue-Chip Black: Race, Class, and Status in the New Black Middle Class.* Berkeley: University of California Press, 2007.

Landry, Bart. *The New Black Middle Class.* Berkeley: University of California Press, 1987.

Lassiter, Matthew D. *The Silent Majority: Suburban Politics and the Sunbelt South.* Princeton, NJ: Princeton University Press, 2007.

Leaf, Brian F. "Breaking the Barrier: The Success of Racial Integration in the Philadelphia Community of Mount Airy, 1950–1975." Senior honors thesis, University of Pennsylvania, March 1995.

Lermack, Paul. "Cecil Moore and the Philadelphia Branch of the National Association of Colored People: The Politics of Negro Pressure Group Organization." In *Black Politics in Philadelphia*, eds. Miriam Ershkowitz and Joseph Zikmund. New York: Basic Books, 1973.

Levy, Peter B. *Civil War on Race Street: The Civil Rights Movement in Cambridge, Maryland.* Gainesville: University Press of Florida, 2003.

Lukas, J. Anthony. *Common Ground: A Turbulent Decade in the Lives of Three American Families.* New York: Vintage Books, 1986.

MacLean, Nancy. *Freedom Is Not Enough: The Opening of the American Workplace.* Cambridge: Harvard University Press, 2008.

Maly, Michael T. *Beyond Segregation: Multiracial and Multiethnic Neighborhoods in the United States.* Philadelphia: Temple University Press, 2005.

Marable, Manning. *Race, Reform, and Rebellion: The Second Reconstruction in Black America, 1945–2006.* 3rd ed. Jackson: University Press of Mississippi, 2007.

Massey, Douglas S., and Nancy A. Denton. *American Apartheid: Segregation and the Making of the Underclass.* Cambridge: Harvard University Press, 1993.

May, Elaine Tyler. *Homeward Bound: American Families in the Cold War Era.* New York: Basic Books, 1988.

McGirr, Lisa. *Suburban Warriors: The Origins of the New American Right.* Princeton, NJ: Princeton University Press, 2001.

McGreevy, John T. *Parish Boundaries: The Catholic Encounter with Race in the Twentieth-Century Urban North.* Chicago: University of Chicago Press, 1996.

McLaurin, Melton Alonza. *The Marines of Montford Point: America's First Black Marines.* Chapel Hill: University of North Carolina Press, 2007.

McMillen, Neil R., ed. *Remaking Dixie: The Impact of World War II on the American South.* Jackson: University Press of Mississippi, 1997.

Meek, Sylvia. "Integration and Egalitarian Education." Master's thesis, University of Pennsylvania, 1966.

Meier, August, and Elliott M. Rudwick. *CORE: A Study in the Civil Rights Movement, 1942–1968.* New York: Oxford University Press, 1973.

Merkowitz, David J. "The Segregating City: Philadelphia Jews and the Urban Crisis, 1964–1984." PhD diss., University of Cincinnati, 2010.

Meyer, Stephen Grant. *As Long as They Don't Move Next Door: Segregation and Racial Conflict in American Neighborhoods.* Lanham, MD: Rowman and Littlefield, 2000.

Miller, Frederic. "The Black Migration to Philadelphia: A 1924 Profile." *Pennsylvania Magazine of History and Biography* 108, no. 3 (July 1984).

Moore, Jesse Thomas. *A Search for Equality: The National Urban League, 1910–1961.* University Park: Pennsylvania State University Press, 1981.

Mossell, Sadie Tanner. "The Standard of Living among One Hundred Negro Migrant Families in Philadelphia." PhD diss., University of Pennsylvania, 1921.

Muller, Peter O. *Contemporary Suburban America.* Englewood Cliffs, NJ: Prentice-Hall, 1981.

Myrdal, Gunnar. *An American Dilemma: The Negro Problem and Modern Democracy.* New York: Harper Publishing, 1944.

Newbeck, Phyl. *Virginia Hasn't Always Been for Lovers: Interracial Marriage Bans and the Case of Richard and Mildred Loving.* Carbondale: Southern Illinois State University Press, 2008.

Nyden, Philip, Michael Maly, and John Lukehart. "The Emergence of Stable Racially and Ethnically Diverse Urban Communities: A Case Study of Nine U.S. Cities." *Housing Policy Debate* 8, no. 2 (1997).

Ogbar, Jeffrey Ogbonna Green. *Black Power: Radical Politics and African American Identity*. Baltimore, MD: Johns Hopkins University Press, 2004.

Oppenheimer, Mark. *Knocking on Heaven's Door: American Religion in the Age of Counterculture*. New Haven, CT: Yale University Press, 2003.

Orser, W. Edward. *Blockbusting in Baltimore: The Edmondson Village Story*. Lexington: University Press of Kentucky, 1997.

Osman, Suleiman. *The Invention of Brownstone Brooklyn: Gentrification and the Search for Authenticity in Postwar New York*. New York: Oxford University Press, 2011.

Palmer, Phyllis M. *Living as Equals: How Three White Communities Struggled to Make Interracial Connections During the Civil Rights Era*. Nashville, TN: Vanderbilt University Press, 2008.

Paolantonio, S. A. *Frank Rizzo: The Last Big Man in Big City America*. Philadelphia: Camino Books, 1993.

Parmar, Inderjeet. *Foundations of the American Century: The Ford, Carnegie, and Rockefeller Foundations in the Rise of American Power*. New York: Columbia University Press, 2012.

Pascoe, Peggy. *What Comes Naturally: Miscegenation and the Making of Race in America*. New York: Oxford University Press, 2010.

Passerini, Luisa. *Fascism in Popular Memory: The Cultural Experience of the Turin Working Class*. New York: Cambridge University Press, 1987.

Pattillo, Mary E. *Black on the Block: The Politics of Race in the City*. Chicago: University of Chicago Press, 2007.

———. *Black Picket Fences: Privilege and Peril among the Black Middle Class*. Chicago: University of Chicago Press, 1999.

Phillips, Anne Ellen. "The Struggle for School Desegregation in Philadelphia, 1945–1967." PhD diss., University of Pennsylvania, 2000.

Piggot, W. Benjamin. "The 'Problem' of the Black Middle Class: Morris Milgram's Concord Park and Residential Integration in Philadelphia's Postwar Suburbs." *Pennsylvania Magazine of History and Biography* 132, no. 2 (April 2008).

Portelli, Alessandro. *The Death of Luigi Trastulli and Other Stories: Form and Meaning in Oral History*. Albany: State University of New York Press, 1991.

Power, Garrett. "Apartheid Baltimore Style: The Residential Segregation Ordinances of 1910–1913." *Maryland Law Review* 42, no. 289 (1983).

Prell, Riv-Ellen. *Prayer and Community: The Havurah in American Judaism*. Detroit, MI: Wayne State University Press, 1989.

Pritchett, Wendell E. "Shelley v. Kraemer: Racial Liberalism and the U.S. Supreme Court," In *Civil Rights Stories*, eds. Myriam E. Gilles and Risa L. Goluboff. New York: Foundation Press, 2008.

Reed, Merl Elwyn. *Seedtime for the Modern Civil Rights Movement: The President's Committee on Fair Employment Practice, 1941–1946*. Baton Rouge: Louisiana State University Press, 1991.

Resnik, Henry S. "The Shedd Revolution: A Philadelphia Story," *Urban Review* 3, no. 3 (January 1969).

———. *Turning on the System: War in the Philadelphia Public Schools*. New York: Pantheon Books, 1970.

Richter, Cynthia Mills, "Integrating the Suburban Dream: Shaker Heights, Ohio." PhD diss., University of Minnesota, 1999.

Rieder, Jonathan. *Canarsie: The Jews and Italians of Brooklyn against Liberalism*. Cambridge: Harvard University Press, 1985.

Rogers, Daniel T. *The Age of Fracture*. Cambridge: Belknap Press of Harvard University Press, 2012.

Romano, Renee Christine. *Race Mixing: Black-White Marriage in Postwar America*. Cambridge: Harvard University Press, 2003.

Romano, Renee Christine, and Leigh Raiford, eds. *The Civil Rights Movement in American Memory*. Athens: University of Georgia Press, 2006.

Rome, Adam Ward. *The Bulldozer in the Countryside: Suburban Sprawl and the Rise of American Environmentalism*. New York: Cambridge University Press, 2001.

Rose, Carol M. *Property and Persuasion: Essays on the History, Theory, and Rhetoric of Ownership*. New York: Westview Press, 1994.

Rosen, Mark D. "Was *Shelley v. Kraemer* Incorrectly Decided? Some New Answer." *California Law Review* 95, no. 2 (April 2007).

Rury, John L. *Education and Social Change: Contours in the History of American Schooling*. New York: Routledge, 2009.

———. *Urban Education in the United States: A Historical Reader*. New York: Palgrave Macmillan, 2005.

Saltman, Juliet. *A Fragile Movement: The Struggle for Neighborhood Stabilization*. New York: Greenwood Press, 1990.

———. "Maintaining Racially Diverse Neighborhoods." *Urban Affairs Quarterly* 26, no. 3 (March 1991).

———. *Open Housing: The Dynamics of a Social Movement*. New York: Praeger, 1978.

Sarna, Jonathan D. *American Judaism: A History*. New Haven, CT: Yale University Press, 2005.

Satter, Beryl. *Family Properties: Race, Real Estate, and the Exploitation of Black Urban America*. New York: Metropolitan Books, 2009.

Schrager, Samuel Alan. *A Trial Lawyer's Art*. Philadelphia: Temple University Press, 1999.

Schulman, Bruce J. *The Seventies: The Great Shift in American Culture, Society, and Politics*. Boston: De Capo Press, 2002.

Schulman, Bruce J., and Julian E. Zelizer. *Rightward Bound: Making America Conservative in the 1970s*. Cambridge: Harvard University Press, 2008.

Scott, Lawrence P., and William M. Womack. *Double V: The Civil Rights Struggle and the Tuskegee Airmen*. East Lansing: Michigan State University Press, 1998.

Sedler, Robert Allan. "The Profound Impact of *Milliken v. Bradley*." *Wayne Law Review* 33, no. 5 (1987).

Seitles, Marc. "The Perpetuation of Residential Racial Segregation in America: Historical Discrimination, Modern Forms of Exclusion, and Inclusionary Remedies." *Journal of Land Use and Environmental Law* 14, no. 1 (Fall 1998).

Self, Robert O. *American Babylon: Race and the Struggle for Post-War Oakland*. Princeton, NJ: Princeton University Press, 2003.

Seligman, Amanda I. *Block by Block: Neighborhoods and Public Policy on Chicago's West Side*. Chicago: University of Chicago Press, 2005.

Simon, Bryant. *Everything but the Coffee: Learning about America from Starbucks.* Berkeley: University of California Press, 2009.

Singer, Joseph William. *Entitlement: The Paradoxes of Property.* New Haven, CT: Yale University Press, 2000.

———. *Property Law: Rules, Policies, and Practices.* 4th ed. New York: Aspen Publishing Group, 2006.

Skrentny, John David, ed. *Color Lines: Affirmative Action, Immigration, and Civil Rights Options for America.* Chicago: University of Chicago Press, 2001.

Slaton, Deborah, and Rebecca A. Shiffer, eds. *Preserving the Recent Past.* Washington, DC: Historic Preservation Education Foundation, 1995.

Small, Mario Luis. *Villa Victoria: The Transformation of Social Capital in a Boston Barrio.* Chicago: University of Chicago Press, 2004.

Smith, Preston H., II. "The Quest for Racial Democracy: Black Civic Ideology and Housing Interests in Postwar Chicago." *Journal of Urban History* 26, no. 2 (2000).

Southern, David W. *Gunnar Myrdal and Black-White Relations: The Use and Abuse of An American Dilemma, 1944–1969.* Baton Rouge: Louisiana State University Press, 1987.

Spigel, Lynn. *Make Room for TV: Television and the Family Ideal in Postwar America.* Chicago: University of Chicago Press, 1992.

Stalvey, Lois Mark. *The Education of a WASP.* New York: William Morrow and Company, 1970.

———. *Getting Ready: The Education of a White Family in Inner-City Schools.* New York: William Morrow and Company, 1975.

Staub, Michael E. *Torn at the Roots: The Crisis of Jewish Liberalism in Postwar America.* New York: Columbia University Press, 2002.

Stein, Judith. *Pivotal Decade: How the United States Traded Factories for Finance in the Seventies.* New Haven, CT: Yale University Press, 2011.

Stein, Marc. *City of Sisterly and Brotherly Loves: Lesbian and Gay Philadelphia, 1945–1972.* Philadelphia: Temple University Press, 2004.

Steinfeld, Robert J. "Property and Suffrage in the Early American Republic." *Stanford Law Review* 41, no. 2 (1989).

Stern, Gail F. *Traditions in Transition: Jewish Culture in Philadelphia, 1840–1940: An Exhibition in the Museum of the Balch Institute for Ethnic Studies.* Philadelphia: Historical Society of Pennsylvania, 1989.

Sternberg, Juliet Anna. "Can We Talk about Race? The Racial Discourse of Activists in a Racially 'Integrated' Neighborhood." PhD diss., Rutgers University, 1996.

Sugrue, Thomas J. *Origins of the Urban Crisis: Race and Inequality in Postwar Detroit.* Princeton, NJ: Princeton University Press, 1996.

———. *Sweet Land of Liberty: The Forgotten Struggle for Civil Rights in the North.* New York: Random House, 2008.

———. "The Unfinished History of Racial Segregation." In *The State of Fair Housing in America, presented by the National Commission on Fair Housing and Equal Opportunity*, July 15, 2008. Accessible at http://www.prrac.org/projects/fair_housing_commission /chicago/chicago_briefing.pdf.

Sullivan, Patricia. *Days of Hope: Race and Democracy in the New Deal Era.* Chapel Hill: University of North Carolina Press, 1996.

Sussman, Lance Jonathan. *Isaac Leeser and the Making of American Judaism.* Detroit: Wayne State University Press, 1995.

Synnott, Marcia Graham. "The Evolving Diversity Rationale in University Admissions from *Regents v. Bakke* to the University of Michigan Cases." *Cornell Law Review* 90, no. 2 (January 2005).

Tabak, Robert Phillip. "The Transformation of Jewish Identity: The Philadelphia Jewish Experience, 1919–1945." PhD diss., Temple University, 1990.

Teaford, Jon C. *The Rough Road to Renaissance: Urban Revitalization in American, 1940–1985.* Baltimore, MD: Johns Hopkins University Press, 1990.

Teele, James E. *E. Franklin Frazier and the Black Bourgeoisie.* Columbia: University of Missouri Press, 2002.

Theoharis, Jeanne, and Komozi Woodard. *Freedom North: Black Freedom Struggles outside the South, 1940–1980.* New York: Macmillan, 2003.

Theoharis, Jeanne, and Komozi Woodard, eds. *Groundwork: Local Black Freedom Movements in America.* New York: New York University Press, 2005.

Thompson, Heather Ann. "Why Mass Incarceration Matters: Rethinking Crisis, Decline, and Transformation in Postwar American History." *Journal of American History* 97, no. 3 (December 2010).

Troy, Gil. *Morning in America: How Ronald Reagan Invented the 1980s.* Princeton, NJ: Princeton University Press, 2007.

Troy, Gil, and Vincent J. Cannato, eds. *Living in the Eighties.* New York: Oxford University Press, 2009.

Tushnet, Mark. "Shelley v. Kraemer and Theories of Equality." *New York Law School Law Review* 33, no. 383 (1988).

Van Deburg, William L. *New Day in Babylon: The Black Power Movement and American Culture, 1965–1975.* Chicago: University of Chicago Press, 1992.

Varady, David P. "Wynnefield: Story of a Changing Neighborhood," In *Philadelphia Jewish Life, 1940–2000,* ed. Murray Friedman. Philadelphia: Temple University Press, 2003.

Von Eschen, Penny M. *Satchmo Blows Up the World: Jazz Ambassadors Play the Cold War.* Cambridge: Harvard University Press, 2004.

Vose, Clement E. *Caucasians Only: The Supreme Court, the NAACP and the Restrictive Covenant Cases.* Berkeley: University of California Press, 1959.

Wallenstein, Peter. *Tell the Court I Love My Wife: Race, Marriage, and the Law–An American History.* New York: Palgrave Macmillan, 2004.

Waxman, Deborah. "Faith and Ethnicity in American Judaism: Reconstructionism as Ideology and Institution, 1935–1959." PhD diss., Temple University, 2010.

Weigley, Russell Frank, Nicholas B. Wainwright, and Edwin Wolf. *Philadelphia: A 300-Year History.* New York: W. W. Norton and Company, 1982.

Whitfield, Stephen J. *The Culture of the Cold War.* 2nd ed. Baltimore, MD: Johns Hopkins University Press, 1996.

Wiese, Andrew. *Places of Their Own: African American Suburbanization in the Twentieth Century.* Chicago: University of Chicago Press, 2005.

Williams, Yuhuru. *Black Politics/White Power: Civil Rights, Black Power, and the Black Panthers in New Haven.* New York: Wiley Blackwell, 2000.

Willis, Arthur C. *Cecil's City: A History of Blacks in Philadelphia, 1638–1979.* New York: Carlton Press, 1990.

Winch, Julie. *Philadelphia's Black Elite: Activism, Accommodation, and the Struggle for Autonomy, 1787–1848.* Philadelphia: Temple University Press, 1993.

Woldoff, Rachael. *White Flight/Black Flight: The Dynamics of Racial Change in an American Neighborhood.* Ithaca, NY: Cornell University Press, 2011.

Wolfinger, James. *Philadelphia Divided: Race and Politics in the City of Brotherly Love.* Raleigh: University of North Carolina Press, 2007.

Woods, Jeff. *Black Struggle, Red Scare: Segregation and Anti-Communism in the South, 1948–1968.* Baton Rouge: Louisiana State University Press, 2003.

Young, David W. "The Battles of Germantown: Public History and Preservation in America's Most Historic Neighborhood during the Twentieth Century." PhD diss., Ohio State University Press, 2009.

Index